BECOMING MACHINES
400 Years of Combat
Between Man and Machine

Denis Collin

BECOMING MACHINES
400 Years of Combat
Between Man and Machine

Max Milo

Introduction

In March 2023, we learn that a website dedicated to computer technology is laying off twelve journalists, who will be replaced by a "conversational agent", the famous "chat-GPT" capable of answering all questions, writing articles or producing the code for a computer program. After the manual workers, the skilled laborers who have been replaced by robots more skilled than themselves, the "great replacement" continues apace, a great replacement that is not that of Europeans by immigrants (as Renaud Camus repeats), but that of men by machines, including those men who had dedicated themselves to intellectual work, thus giving a new example of that "obsolescence of man" to which Günther Anders has devoted many writings. In the same month of March 2023, the magazine *Pour la Science* devoted a lengthy article to the development of "autonomous lethal weapons", i.e. the applications of artificial intelligence and robotization to the art of killing human beings. As we witness the devastation of a world dominated by machines, we are forced to question the techno-scientific destiny of modernity anew. Do we need a Morpheus to awaken the Neo in us, as in the famous *Matrix* film, where the hero has to give up the images injected into him by machines in order to discover the real world? Our relationship with the machine is not a social or technical question, but an ontological one. There is something of a "becoming machine" of man, a becoming that takes on several dimensions: the invasion of the world of life by machines, the "machinic" conception of the living being and the mind, the transformation of social life into a megamachine and, finally, the reification of man, produced as we produce machines.

I had originally planned to write a critique of neuroscientific reason, with the aim of challenging the foundations of the neuroscientific project, i.e. the project to understand and modify—for the better, it goes without saying—human thought. I saw in this the return of La Mettrie's "man-machine". I also saw the link with everything that is happening around "artificial intelligence", which is based on "cognitive science" and in turn supports these same "sciences". Along the way, this return of the man-machine revealed itself not as a deviation or a scientific or epistemological error, but as a much more global trend of our times, the march towards man becoming a machine. Günther Anders (see the two volumes of his *Obsolescence of Man*) addressed these issues some time ago, notably through the idea of "Promethean shame"—the shame that ordinary man feels, or should feel, in the face of machine perfection. It couldn't be clearer. In my own way, I'd like to follow in the footsteps of Günther Anders, by showing how the triumph of technoscience is leading to the devastation of the world-of-life, to use an expression from phenomenology.

Technoscience is the triumph of rational activity by finality: its value lies in the ability to implement the means to achieve any end. Max Weber foresaw the creation of a "steel cage" that would imprison modern man, entirely subject to the bureaucratic norms of a society in which all human activities would be rationally conceived as means to an end that would be totally beyond individual control. We are now prisoners of this steel cage. It encircles all our actions and gradually shapes our ways of thinking. In a previous book, *À dire vrai* (published by Armand Colin, 2013), I highlighted the "progress" (dare we say it) of the proceduralization of thought and the development of a one-dimensional language of standards and "quality questionnaires".

But what has been thought out in the theoretical or philosophical sphere is nothing other than the expression of the radical transformations taking place in the "world of life". First of all, it was the mode of production that was subjected to rationalization and systematic control: these were the heyday of the scientific organization of work (SOW) and methods offices. But today, life as a whole, including that part of our lives when we think we're escaping the imperatives and norms of production, leisure time or love, is in turn entering the realm of "scientific" organization. When I enter a museum, I'm asked for my department's zip code, which is entered into the museum's computer system for statistical purposes. I've paid with my credit card, and this payment will tell us a great deal about me, including whether I was at the museum's ticket office at a particular time on a particular day. But this information can be enriched by searching for the various places where my phone has landed during the day. If I've activated geolocation, it's easy to track my movements. All my personal details are stored in dozens of servers: employers, insurance companies, health insurers, the government, companies I've bought something from—and not just through e-commerce—all have a trace of me. Even walking down the street, I'm filmed by CCTV cameras, and all it takes is facial recognition software to detect "anti-social" behavior and propose automatic fines or penalties. You're exaggerating," I'm told, "this isn't China. Yes, we are! In fact, the Chinese started out by copying the West, and are now showing the way in those countries where they still pride themselves on "our values", "freedom" and so on. Speed cameras "flash" speeding drivers or those who run amber lights, and the driver's photo is taken. The police have become anonymous and purely mechanical. There's no stopping a machine that's off to a good start: we're already testing artificial intelligence computer systems that could "help" magistrates to judge... Why not a continuous chain: the offence is spotted by the various means of electronic surveillance (speed cameras, cameras and facial recognition), processed by machines and the punishment is triggered automatically, exactly on the model of traffic offences. We're also working on "predictive policing" to determine which subjects are most likely to be delinquents. It's no longer clear where the boundary lies between today's reality and the famous dystopias of the last century (such as Philip K. Dick's *Minority Report*). Perhaps it's not a steel cage that's being built, but an "electronic cage", a cage of copper wires, optical fibers and semiconductors.

All networks are increasingly interconnected, and those that aren't can be interconnected at very low cost. The techno-science that promised us wonders is now posing a terrible threat. But the reality is perhaps even more worrying. It's not just our behaviors that are enslaved to the techno-scientific system, but life itself that is incorporated into this system, losing everything that makes it special, as individuals' own bodies are reduced to nothing more than a mass of meat—a particular manifestation of what Pierre Legendre calls the "butcher conception of humanity". It's no longer our appearance or behavior that's the object of identification and tracking, it's our bodies. We leave "DNA traces" everywhere. And with these DNA traces, we can easily be found. But that's not all. DNA makes it possible to verify actual kinship. The civil status and mother's word that used to establish filiation are giving way to the "biological truth" proven by DNA tests, which are now almost within everyone's reach. It's an old story: some men found it difficult to adhere to the Civil Code, which states that the father is the husband of the woman giving birth. Paternity suits are now finding a practical and inexpensive way to liquidate this wise Civil Code. It's time to replace civil status with a herd-book, as with selected horses and cattle. Speaking of selection, DNA tests provide information on the ethnic groups—we no longer call them racial, the word has been banned—from which we come. The Nazis, with their methods of studying skulls to determine who was Jewish or not, are outdated. Now, technoscience gives us the "truth" about the blood that runs through your veins.

But it's not just the classification of humans that has entered the realm of technoscience; it's also their production. The baby factory is starting to run at full speed. PMA, initially conceived to remedy couples' infertility problems, also makes it possible to select embryos according to sex, and eventually according to whatever criteria one chooses. For better or for worse. The introduction of technical procedures into human reproduction is turning genealogical order upside down. It is claimed that two women can have a child together, and that the same applies to two men if they find a surrogate mother in one of the countries where GPA is legally practiced. DIY can go even further. Transgender practices allow for all kinds of combinations: a "man" with a full beard and all the outward features of a man can find himself "pregnant" if he has taken the precaution of not having his female genitalia removed. Gender indifferentiation is gradually spreading, while technoscience plays an increasingly important role in the processes that ensure human reproduction. In early 2023, we learned that a Norwegian researcher was proposing to use the bodies of brain-dead women to carry out GPA. It was also the first time that a human embryo had been produced from stem cells, i.e. without male and female gametes.

It's like stepping straight into a horror film. The truth is, what is being accomplished before our very eyes, in small steps, and most often for the "good" or to cure "ill-being", is quite simply the program of transhumanism: the increasing technicization of the human being and reification, i.e. the transformation of the human body into an experimentable thing.

Today, neuroscience is regarded as the science that explains everything, the all-encompassing science that encompasses everything that can fall into a human mind. Knowledge of the brain—the subject of a branch of biology—is supposed to provide a comprehensive understanding of all things human: psychology, social and economic behavior, learning and pedagogy, and even knowledge of scientific knowledge itself. Neuroscience is the science of everything, including itself. We'd say—if we weren't in the 21st CENTURY—that they're "divine sciences". Exaggeration? Not at all. Just browse the catalogs of publishers of books on science, management techniques, pedagogy, personal development, etc., and you'll see why. It's also enough to read or listen to neuroscience researchers to understand that they have found the "philosopher's stone" in neuroscience. This is obviously not the case. In the field of theology, nothing can disturb the peace of mind of believers, who always have proof of God's existence to provide. The same applies to neuroscience, where proofs are abundantly provided in which the conclusion was contained in the premises, proofs accompanied, more often than not, by polemical twists of contempt towards those who do not adhere to the new faith. What is at issue is the claim to make biology, under the name of neuroscience, an explanatory science of "mental life". Claude Bernard, a great scientist and master of the epistemology of the life sciences, admitted that he had never found the soul under his scalpel. But in the same way, no neurobiologist has ever observed a thought with his functional magnetic resonance imaging (fMRI) machine, for example. We can observe what happens in the brain when the subject thinks about the first chapters of the *Critique of Pure Reason*, or when he has an orgasm, but nobody is capable of observing transcendental aesthetics or knowing what the subject feels when he has an orgasm! We can certainly admit that depression is "linked" (how, is another matter) to serotonin reuptake in synaptic connections, but an individual who is depressed because he has lost his job and his wife has left him will never invoke serotonin reuptake as the cause of his depressive state, and rightly so! Because the real cause of depression is not biochemical, but social and psychological. We could always say that we're being fooled by ordinary psychology and that science is showing us this hidden reality that we, poor ordinary mortals, cannot perceive! But this sort of poor man's Platonism, which serves as the epistemology and ontology of too many scientists today, cannot convince us. Behind our world, the "world of life", there isn't another world, the "true world" of science, of which our world is just an illusory veil. The "world of science" is not a world, and it's not "real", any more than a $1:^{25},000$-scale map is the mountain slope I hike through while sweating. The green of the meadow where cows graze peacefully is not radiation between 577 and 492 nm. A born blind man can understand 577 and 492 nm, but he can't know what green is! As you can see, the discussion about the validity and scope of neuroscience takes us a long way towards redefining the value and scope of the natural sciences, those "sciences of fact" referred to by Husserl. The neuroscientific project is reductionist: it aims to reduce man to a perfected machine. It is accompanied by a destitution of the subject, reified and turned into a predictable being. This type of project was analyzed long ago by Herbert Marcuse *in One-Dimensional Man*. It has nothing to do with the medical objectives of neurobiology, a science that can help to heal, and must above all not seek to use technical procedures to secure control over the sick… or the healthy. The aim of medicine is not to create a superman! But neuroscience is proposing nothing less and nothing more than such a superman.

Neuroscience is closely linked to research into artificial intelligence (AI). AI, which is as old as computer science and even a little older (see Leibniz), claims to build a machine that is the functional equivalent of the human brain, a machine capable of thinking. In fact, the first computers in France were dubbed "electronic brains". It was Hobbes who formulated the sentence: "To think is to calculate", taken up in another form by Leibniz, who sought a language of symbols equivalent to that of mathematics, but capable of covering the entire field of knowledge, in order to replace all the inextricable difficulties of morality and law by a "calculon" supposed to provide univocal and absolutely certain answers. It was in this extraordinary seventeenth century that the AI project took shape, whose "exploits" are sung daily by the mainstream media. It's not just a question of these machines simulating thought, but of producing new knowledge, and above all of producing results that are more accurate and faster than the humble human can do. Properly trained AI machines are said to be far better than the best oncologists at detecting cancer. An AI machine has succeeded in deciphering a particularly damaged 2,000-year-old manuscript. Not just in place of man, but better than him! It's not just craftsmen and workers who will have to feel ashamed before the perfection of machines, but doctors, lawyers, engineers and paleographers…

The machinic corset that encircles us modifies behavior. The whole of life must follow procedures. Public and private administrations alike operate according to procedure. Quality standards impose ways of doing things and documents to be filled in to comply with the procedure. The most extravagant standards are dictated for construction and interior installations, but also for the production of training courses. Many professions are protesting against the suffocating growth of bureaucracy. Computers have made it possible to multiply administrative documents at an apparent zero cost, since no paper is consumed. We are constantly learning how to become more agile as we move through the labyrinth. We're like laboratory rats, whose behavior a scientist observes and looks for ways to reinforce what they've learned. Gradually, individuals become prostheses of the machine…

All these trends are absolutely obvious, as soon as you try to step back a little. But it's hard to take a step back, because procedures don't just complicate our lives, they make it easier by reassuring us: the steps to follow are given, and those who don't follow them quickly learn the cost. No longer waiting, getting an immediate response, no longer cluttering up your memory or rummaging through your papers, having the world at your fingertips, being able to buy and give free rein to your desires without leaving your desk or bedroom—it's a sensation, an intoxication of power that takes hold of us. The more the individual is integrated into the system, the more he becomes an example of the average man, and the more he feels master of the world, a world that apparently revolves around him. The spectacle of the world replaces the lived world. Illusions become truer than life.

For a long time, "progressives" (including the author of these lines) consoled themselves by asserting the neutrality of technoscience, whose misuse alone was to be condemned. After all, with a good knife you can prepare your food or kill your neighbor, and it's not the knife that should be blamed, they say. But this apparent common sense intoxicates us. Following in Jacques Ellul's footsteps, we must denounce these illusions and expose what he calls "the technological bluff". Technology is not neutral, and neither is science! Bernard Charbonneau defended the idea that the totalitarian system is the fulfillment of all the possibilities of technology, an idea that overlaps in various respects with the theses of Herbert Marcuse in *One-Dimensional Man*: the industrial and technical civilization of the "consumer society" is indeed, in its essence, totalitarian, and in this development, it is essential to question our relationship to science, insofar as it claims to know the world objectively, but also our relationship to technology insofar as it sums up all our relationships with the outside world. I have already addressed these questions in a short book published in 2022, *Malaise dans la science* (Nouvelle Librairie). Here, I take them up again in greater depth, placing them in a broader perspective.

In the pages that follow, I'd like to show that all these trends, which are undermining our civilization at its core, are the fruit of the expansion of the capitalist mode of production over the last six centuries, and not of unfortunate drifts that could be contained with reforms and two ladles of humanism on top! The machinery is the body of capital, and its soul is the fetish par excellence, money. The dynamic of capital is the triumph of the inert over the living. In this sense, it is impossible to undertake a serious critique of techno-scientific totalitarianism without going back to Marx's brilliant analyses. Those who refuse to do so belong to that category of human beings of whom, according to Bossuet, God laughs [because they] deplore the effects of which they cherish the causes.

Secondly, I will show that it is life itself that is being expelled from the human world. The vital process, having been enslaved to commodity production, is now purely and simply dismantled. Biotechnology is the starting point for the "technologies of death". This situation, dramatic in many ways, stems from the way in which Galilean science took over the living and transformed them into chemical machines. In the background, there is a purely deterministic vision of nature, which may have its practical, technical efficacy, but cannot claim to be the sole mode of access to truth. Fundamentally, it's a question of questioning the quasi-fusion between science and technology that has been taking place since the beginning of modern times, and which today leads to the swallowing up of knowledge by technology.

Thirdly, we will see that humanity's ultimate refuge, thought as a property of consciousness, must be dislodged in favor of the physico-chemical sciences and mechanistic conceptions that are the common thread running through mainstream neuroscience and research into artificial intelligence technologies. This is not to deny the contributions of neurobiology, which can be very useful in medicine, but to refute the philosophical and epistemic relevance of a whole called "neurosciences", which has at its center the "cognitive neurosciences" supposed to decode human thought and designed to improve man, to make him more "efficient", according to the demands of the "profitability principle". I will show the close and necessary connections between neuroscience and AI, and demonstrate that this is partly a scientific deception, partly an ideology suited to the age of "absolute capitalism", and partly the development of techniques for formatting thoughts and colonizing consciousness.

Fourthly, I will show that all this is part of an attempt to eliminate subjectivity outright, to reduce the individual to a specimen of mass production, and to strip the human being of all depth. I will show its philosophical origins and the terrifying consequences that are already crystallizing. De-subjectification" is the common thread running through all the new forms of techno-scientific barbarism. It was already central to the Stalinist and Nazi systems, but the undertaking was carried out with frustrating means that could only hasten the downfall of these systems. Today, this de-subjectification is carried out with the most refined means, and is all the more dangerous for it—all the more dangerous for anyone who continues to believe in the eminent dignity of the individual, which sometimes seems to be no more than an idea on the verge of extinction...

Let me conclude with the extraordinary paradox that lies at the heart of modernity. On the one hand, it presented itself as an exaltation of man's power—you can read the real program in Pico della Mirandola's beautiful text, *On the Dignity of Man*, or that other program-text, the sixth part of Descartes' *Discourse on Method*. On the other hand, it projected a total enslavement of the human being, the likes of which no previous political regime had ever dreamed of. Modernity has highlighted the determinisms of nature, so as to be able to act and control it better, but it has transformed human beings into predictable, determined beings, for whom the word freedom no longer has any meaning. We have thus reached the ultimate stage of reification.

What we need to think about here is the very possibility of human freedom, in all its meanings, and to draw the necessary political and moral consequences if we are not to resign ourselves to living and thinking like machines, i.e., becoming the living dead. The question is to know in what forms and to what extent we can still "unplug" from the machine, to get out of the matrix. In his novel, *Le successeur de Pierre*, Jean-Michel Truong calls "*no plugs*" individuals who have decided to remain free and not be locked up in the wired pyramids where the last humans live. Can we be "*no plug*", "unplugged" from the megamachine made up of all networked machines? We have reason to hope. Freud, in *Malaise in Civilization*, said: "It does not appear that man can be induced by any means whatsoever to exchange his nature for that of a termite; he will always be inclined to defend his right to individual freedom against the will of the mass. Passions are ineliminable, and no more so than passions, the anguish of death, which the most advanced technoscience cannot soothe. Paradoxically, it is on this most archaic soil of the human species that we can found some hope of resisting the total reification of man.

Chapter I: Dead Capital and the Machine

Since the 17th century, to put it somewhat arbitrarily, our world has been shaped by the capitalist mode of production, even if its beginnings go back much further. The expansion of trade and the prodromes of the capitalist mode of production can sometimes be traced back to antiquity, and developed rapidly with the birth or rebirth of cities. By the end of the Middle Ages, Europe was ripe for this new mode of production. But navigation and what came to be known as the "Great Discoveries" transformed the situation. The world had become global, you might say, and was open to limitless exploitation. The Earth's surface has been so radically transformed that many authors characterize our era as a new geological epoch, the Anthropocene. Nature has been pushed out of the human world. The world we live in is made up of concrete, glass and metal constructions, machines for working, moving, writing, listening to music and seeing images. Even thought, the impregnable domain of mankind, is now subject to the rhythm of machines and their instructions for use—which, to put it scientifically, are called algorithms. Worldwide, the productivity of human labor has become enormous, surpassing anything we could have imagined. As Marx marveled,

The bourgeoisie revealed how the brutal manifestation of force in the Middle Ages, so admired by reaction, found its natural complement in the crassest laziness. The bourgeoisie was the first to show what human activity is capable of. It created wonders other than the Egyptian pyramids, Roman aqueducts and Gothic cathedrals; it led expeditions other than invasions and crusades.

Communist Party Manifesto, 1848

The development and conquest of the world by machinery is the work of capitalism. There used to be war machines and trades, but these tools were merely extensions of the warrior's or worker's hand. With capitalism, quantity has become quality! Jean-Marc Jancovici has a habit of counting the work done with a machine and by a machine in terms of the number of slaves: a man can develop a power of around 100 W and, therefore, if each human has an average of 30,000 kWh of energy per year, then he deduces that everything happens as if we had at our disposal a few hundred slaves working for us 24 hours a day, 365 days a year. These calculations should not be taken at face value, but they do give an idea of the extraordinary increase in labor productivity made possible by machinismo, which is no longer based on the use of human mechanical power, but on the consumption of energy derived from nature (wood, fossil fuels, hydraulic or wind power, atomic energy). But all this is not the implementation of a good philanthropic intention that would alleviate man's suffering—in the *Discourse on Method*, Part Six, Descartes announces that the new science will enable us to know the forces of nature "as distinctly as we know the various trades of our craftsmen" and thus "we could employ them in the same way for all the uses to which they are suited" allowing, among other things, "the invention of an infinite number of artifices, which would enable us to enjoy the fruits of the Earth and all the conveniences found therein without any difficulty". In reality, this was both the result and the means of the development of the capitalist mode of production, which, until the beginning of modern times, existed in its infancy only in the interstices of old society, and from then on progressively occupied all available space, including the space of our brains!

The Body of Capital

Machinism and capital are thus consubstantial. In its early forms—usury capital, land rent and even manufacturing—capital is indifferent to the means of labor. But capital is not yet truly itself. Capital, in flesh and blood, appears with large-scale industry and is embodied in machines, which if possible operate day and night all year round. In *Das Kapital*, Marx uses the term *Maschinerie*. Machinery is not a collection of machines, but a functioning system. The real living thing of capital is this machinery: a factory at a standstill is immobilized capital, capital that produces nothing, and therefore dead capital. On the other hand, capital is money, money spent to buy means of labor and labor power, and which emerges from the production cycle swollen and embellished with surplus value. For the capitalist investor, money seems a pure phantom, and its material existence has nothing to do with its real content and power: whether money is used to buy machines or to employ workers, the investor doesn't care; what counts is the ROI, the return on investment. Machinismo and capital seem to have nothing to do with each other, just as soul and body, while substantially united, have no necessary relation to each other in Cartesian metaphysics. Yet capital only really became itself with the advent of machinismo and large-scale industry, which brought science into the production process. In the *Grundrisse* (manuscripts of 1857-1858), Marx writes:

> The science that compels the lifeless members of the machine, by virtue of their construction, to act in the desired way, like an automaton, does not exist in the consciousness of the worker, but acts

upon him through the machine as a foreign force, as a force of the machine itself.

Grundrisse, II, p. 185

Man does not become "master and possessor" of nature through the science that enables him to build machines. Exactly the opposite will happen: science incorporated into the machine will become man's master.

Machinism would have remained marginal without the development of the capitalist mode of production. It's therefore a good idea to say that capital and machinism or machinery (to follow Jean-Pierre Lefebvre's translation of *Capital*) are indeed the same thing under "two different attributes", and if they are "the same thing", it's easy to understand that the very categories of thought are formed on this model. Machinery invades our lives, subdues our every gesture and behavior, regulates our activities, but, in the process, ends up becoming the paradigm dominating all our thoughts. Rational thought is a set of cogs that fit together to produce a new thought, just as a good machine "grinds" all kinds of ingredients to make a finished product. In cartoons, Chicago's slaughterhouses were depicted as cows entering a large factory alive, with cans *of corned beef* at the exit. In fact, the first real modern factory was Heinz's tomato sauce factory (1888)… In any case, our thinking must follow this model: there is input data, a "process" and, at the output, results that must conform to specifications.

The work of capital could be summed up as follows: to transform life into machinery, i.e. to transform the living labor of living individuals, as practical sentient beings, into objectified labor, capital in machine form being nothing other than gelled labor, "coagulated" labor. To begin with, let's recall an essential thesis of Marx's: capital is nothing other than the process that transforms living labor into dead labor. In this sense, capital is mortifying, or the bearer of death! When Marx shows the long-term trend in the growth of constant capital relative to variable capital, he's saying nothing else. The famous law of the tendency of the rate of profit to fall is the mathematical formulation of this process. This tendency expresses the "progressive" character of the capitalist mode of production: "the increasing volume of the means of production expresses, compared with the labor power incorporated in it, the increasing productivity of labor" (*Capital*, I). In other words, the increasing productivity of labor is expressed in the accumulation of machines… which don't work, but merely wear out. Of course, the capitalist doesn't buy machines for pleasure: as long as he can do without them and benefit from cheap labor, he does. As long as the child in Kivu costs less than the excavator used to extract cobalt, he might as well use the child. But labor power can run out, it can't be consumed 24 hours a day, and competitors can use mechanization to increase their profits by capturing a larger share of global surplus value. We are witnessing a tangle of trends and counter-trends. However, this whole process highlights the obvious contradiction: living labor alone produces value, but the dynamic of "value valorization" is that of the substitution of dead labor for living labor. When capitalists fight to save *labor*, they are in fact, paradoxically, fighting to lower the value of their products! This can't go on forever! "The dead seize the living".

Duality of Work

So we need to return first to work in general, and then to work in the capitalist mode of production. In itself, work is ambivalent: it is both a "punishment inflicted on man", according to the biblical curse. But, on the other hand, it is the production of life and the means by which man asserts his power. Work is the suffering of the mother who is about to give birth, but it is also the condition of childbirth. We might want to be "liberated from work", but perhaps we'd be liberated from life at the same time! In short, work can only be grasped dialectically; it is a "contradiction on trial".

This duality of work, expounded by Hegel, Marx and others, has also been judiciously analyzed by psychoanalysis with its own categories. Indeed, there is a constraint to work that is necessary to the pursuit of human life. Constraint, because work opposes the pleasure principle and thus expresses the reality principle. Working does not mean renouncing pleasure, but deferring its satisfaction. All human societies organize this contradictory requirement in their own way. But how is it possible for the subject to defer satisfaction? Freud was to demonstrate the ambivalent nature of satisfaction—another dialectical trick! Life is a balancing act between excitation, which we can seek, and satisfaction, which brings excitation down to its lowest level. Extending Freud's reflections, we can say that life is always affected by the death drive, which aims to return us to an inert state, or at least to the lowest level of vital excitation. It's not for nothing that we speak of "little death" to designate the state that immediately follows orgasm. But this pattern is not limited to sexual life. Eros and Thanatos are the two great poles of life. From this point of view, by transforming nature into things that satisfy our needs, work is indeed on the side of "creative destruction". It destroys the spontaneous order of nature, levelling hills, building bridges over rivers, transforming rock into metal and waste... It is indeed on the side of Thanatos in reducing the living to the inert. But like Eros, work, insofar as it builds civilization, also builds larger entities: human societies are gigantic organisms, bodies composed of many, many bodies. It gives rise to new forms and fights against the natural tendency towards levelling and the growth of disorder. In the face of growing entropy, work is negentropy. We can thus consider that, through work, civilization turns aggressive and destructive impulses in its favor, and also, indirectly, in favor of Eros. Civilization uses destructive impulses, which can be vital (in work, in combat rituals such as sport, or in religious manifestations) to its advantage, and transforms them into means of safeguarding the possibility of new aggregations. The work of artistic creation would be the prototype of work that offers strong libidinal satisfaction: it's about destroying the alien being of things, of matter, to transform them into works in which the spirit recognizes and contemplates itself. In *Malaise in Civilization* (or *Malaise in Culture,* depending on the translation), Freud shows that the primary aim of civilization is to force man to work, but that this constraint can only be endured in the long term if man derives narcissistic satisfaction from it. This is the process of "sublimation". It has often been reduced to artistic creation, but narcissistic pleasure is to be found in the sense of satisfaction derived from a job well done, "beautiful work". Great works of art (bridges, towers, etc.) often provide this kind of satisfaction for the workers involved in their construction. It's also what Bernard Lavilliers sings about, when he says he'd like to "work some more" to "forge red steel with [his] golden hands".

For Herbert Marcuse, the meaning of the word "sublimation" can therefore be modified: sublimation is not just impulsive repression; there could be a "non-repressive sublimation" in artistic production, and more generally in what Marx called free production or free creation. But such work is very rare in today's society. Indeed, it may well be even rarer in a "socialist society", as the labor necessary to sustain life is not often the object of aesthetic satisfaction... The "sadistic" character of alienated labor remains dominant. Labor, especially in the production process of modern industrial society, appears to be a sublimated destructiveness, an extroverted destruction (the hill is destroyed to make a quarry, the trees to make wood for carpentry, etc.):

However, extrovert destruction remains destruction: in most cases, its objects are actually and violently assaulted, and they are only rebuilt after partial destruction; units are divided by force and components assembled in other ways by force. Nature is literally "violated". Only in certain categories of sublimated aggression (such as surgical practice) does such a violation directly reinforce the life of its object. Destructiveness seems more directly satisfied in breadth and depth, in civilization, than libido.

Marcuse, Eros and Civilization, 1955

Destructive impulses are also sources of intense pleasure. A couple in crisis breaks dishes. Children love to destroy, and teenagers and post-adolescents who burn cars, bus shelters and garbage cans, before setting fire to stores and schools, are intoxicated. The noise of fireworks, the astonishing fascination of fighter jets taking off, the spectacle of explosions, etc., are all phenomena that attest to the power of this destructive impulse, a manifestation of the destructiveness analyzed at length by Eric Fromm.

In ordinary times, the life drive and the death drive are linked or intertwined. One always goes with the other. But they can also disintegrate. The unbinding of the life drive and the death drive, and thus the absolute triumph of Thanatos, is what societies dominated by the capitalist mode of production gave us the terrible spectacle of during the last century, and which is flourishing today, even if the forms may change. We have seen how the highest creations of the human mind have been put at the service of the destruction of human civilization.

Eros and Thanatos or Dr. Jekill and Mr. Hyde: this ambivalence of work, in general, is a fundamental philosophical problem, even if it's impossible to deal with it here, which would take us too far from our subject. Suffice it to say that we are never content with what we have, and always want new constructions, new productions for our comfort or pleasure, and that, deep down, many of us like to work to see what comes out of our own being: the amateur gardener or the Sunday tinkerer are significant examples of this thirst for work. But at the same time, we're looking to reduce working hours, to replace human labor with machines, and we're raving about the wonders of human ingenuity. All things that can't be explained by the appetite to get rich. Reducing work to torture, following the dubious etymology of *tripalium*, the instrument used to punish slaves who tried to escape, is a dead end. Not all work is forced labor. After a day's work or a lifetime's work, rest is welcome, but we also occupy our leisure time by working, cultivating our garden or tinkering. Work is pain and pleasure, indissolubly, and in this it expresses human life—work is the essence of man, as Marx would say.

A society dominated by the capitalist mode of production pushes the contradictions of work to the limit. No society has exalted work so much, but none has made it such a living hell. As a result, it's hard to understand what work is, independently of the mode of production in which it takes place.

The Concept of Dead Work

We now need to understand labor in a specific form, and return to the fundamental points of Marx's analysis. Indeed, any serious reflection on labor must, at one point or another, tackle the present form in which labor appears on a massive scale, i.e., the capital-labor relation or, to put it more concisely, capital itself, since capital is not a thing, but a social relation.

Let's approach this problem from a very specific angle, starting with the concept of "dead labor". The concept of dead labor clearly plays a very important role in Marx's thought. It is the necessary flip-side of living labor, and in the opposition between living and dead labor undoubtedly lies the crux of the "critique of political economy", as Marx called his undertaking, which was indeed intended to be in some way scientific, but which never aimed at the construction of a "science of economics". Marx wrote lapidary:

Capital is dead labor, which only comes alive by sucking like a vampire on living labor, and which is all the more alive the more it sucks.

Capital, I, 1875

It's important to understand what Marx means by this. From a certain point of view, any product, in any form of society, is "objectified" labor: the carpenter's subjective power, intelligence and energy are reflected in the piece of furniture. But in the capitalist mode of production, something else happens: the worker has sold his labor power, and it has thus become part of capital, which uses it as it pleases, just as any consumer can use the things he has acquired. Labor no longer appears as a finalized activity, but as an element in the capitalist production process.

The domination of the capitalist mode of production thus produces a veritable inversion of the real: it confers magical power on inert things and relegates human power to the rank of things. An arm or a leg are organs in the same way as a machine tool or a welding robot. The analysis of the commodity, the very cell of bourgeois society, makes this clear. Human labor "naturally" produces things useful to human life. This is its most essential object, and in so doing, says Marx, it produces human life itself. In its most immediate form, this work presents no mystery: the producer plants potatoes or weaves wool for use by himself, his family or the social group to which he belongs. Roles are often divided: some people hunt, others cultivate yams. Then, the products of the work are divided up, first according to need—it's important to ensure that the children can grow up—or according to custom. As soon as the work product exceeds immediate needs, the surplus is first used for ornamentation and sacrifices, to ingratiate oneself with the gods, but also for gifts to ensure the giver's social status—see the *potlach* ritual. Things began to change when commercial exchange was instituted. All this took a long time to come about, requiring major social and political transformations (the birth of states and administrations) and the appearance of money. The commodity only takes on its developed form with the capitalist mode of production, which generalizes the commodity form (the wealth of societies dominated by capital appears as an immense accumulation of commodities, as *Capital* begins).

The commodity is not a thing, but a form that expresses a social relationship between men as a relationship between things. This is called "commodity fetishism"—fetishism being understood in the sense of fetishist religions. The mystery is this: how can we exchange commodities, i.e. consider that "x commodity A = y commodity B"? These two commodities are things of qualitatively different utility, of different form and material, and so on. Taken in themselves, as things belonging to the sensible world, they are incommensurable: there is no common measure between 15 meters of cloth, a quintal of wheat, or an electric battery. The only quality they have in common is that they are products of human labor, human labor now coagulated, gelled (all these words are Marx's). Each commodity is produced because it corresponds to something useful for the potential buyer, something that is subjectively determined: some have spiritual needs and will buy a Bible, others have needs for spirits and will acquire a bottle of cognac! These needs have no quantitative relationship. Similarly, the printer's business and the winegrower's business are qualitatively different and require different, incomparable subjective investments. But by the time they reach the market, goods have lost their flavor, their smell, their shape, they've become exchange values, things bearing a label, their price. The shimmering world of living human reality gives way to the cold world of calculation. Commodities are the realm of abstraction. Relationships between men, between butcher and carpenter, between printer and winemaker, are now presented as relationships between things, themselves reduced, according to the precepts of modern science, to mathematical formulations. We have left the real world to enter the world of economists, a

Chapter I – Dead Capital and the Machine

world that will present itself as "the real world", when in fact it is only a fantasy, a hallucinated projection, since what is dead—money, machines, etc.—seems to be endowed with life, while the living, human labor power, disappears in the capitalist furnace. Paraphrasing Marx, Guy Debord begins *The Society of the Spectacle* (1967) as follows:

> The whole life of societies in which modern conditions of production prevail is shaping up as an immense accumulation of *spectacles*. Everything that used to be directly experienced has been distanced in a representation.

This is neither parody nor mere paraphrase. Debord is saying the same thing as Marx. In fact, he puts this quotation from Ludwig Feuerbach at the beginning of the first chapter:

> And no doubt our time… prefers the image to the thing, the copy to the original, representation to reality, appearance to being… What is *sacred* for him is only *illusion,* but what is profane is *truth.* What's more, the sacred grows in his eyes as truth diminishes and illusion grows, so that *the height of illusion* is also for him *the height of the sacred.*
> Preface to the second edition of *The Essence of Christianity*, 1841

Elucidating the nature of the commodity opens the way to understanding the nature of capital, since the commodity is the "cell" of bourgeois society. The commodity, far from being a trivial thing, easy to understand, is in fact the site of a veritable metaphysical puzzle, in the truest sense of the word, for the commodity is certainly a sensible thing, with concrete qualities that make it a thing destined to satisfy particular human needs, but it is at the same time, as a value, a thing that does not fall under common sense (a "social thing", as Marx would say). For exchange to be possible, for a given quantum of commodity A to be exchanged for a given quantum of commodity B, a whole social process must be completed, stabilizing the value relationship between the two commodities at a given time and place. This is why the mystery of the commodity can only be unraveled at the end of the development of exchange. When exchange is regulated by a set of writings passed on by computer means, we have reached the end of the process of abstraction that is commodity exchange, since exchange no longer exchanges anything material, not even "hard" money, but bytes circulating on networks.

We need to develop this essential transition from the subjective to the objective, from the worker's personal activity to the objectified thing that is the commodity. For Marx, productive activity is one, if not the fundamental dimension of "human nature". In different forms, this idea is common to both his early writings—the *Manuscripts of 1844* and *The German Ideology* (1845)—and his mature writings. To produce the conditions of our existence, and thus to produce our own life, is what distinguishes man from other animals. But to produce is not to "work", if by work we mean what is most commonly understood today, namely a salaried activity whose purpose is the general equivalent of money. In productive activity, people express what they are. The starting point is subjectively experienced desire. Productive activity manifests this subjective impulse of desire and objectifies itself in the production of an object that now stands before the producer, available for enjoyment (consumption or use). The point of arrival is as much subjectivity as the point of departure. Objectivized work is merely the subject's mediation towards itself. Of course, all productive activity requires tools and means of work, which are the result of prior production, and it might seem arbitrary to make the subject the point of departure: after all, what determines (or, at least, conditions) the subject are the objective conditions he finds ready-made, which can be held to be "amassed" labor—and not only that, since nature provides the objective conditions of production free of charge. In reality, these "objective conditions" that individuals find ready-made do not determine their activity. Rather, they condition it: under similar conditions, individuals may very well embark on very different paths, each time constructing specific social relations.

From the point of view of capitalist production, that is, from the point of view of capital, the whole process is one of the self-valorization of value, from which stems the investor's own illusion that money produces or "works", an illusion that is repeated at every turn by the official economic doctrine of the "new production of value", the one that seems to emerge from nothing in financial transactions or in purely speculative operations such as the creation of crypto-currencies. This illusion had already been denounced by Aristotle under the name of "chrematistics", that "unnatural" activity in which money gives birth to money as a father gives birth to his son.

But at the same time, the capitalist must, in his calculations, "assume that constant capital is = 0", a "disconcerting operation at first sight", says Marx, who notes, however, that capitalists routinely use it to evaluate earnings. Obviously, there is no production without machines, raw materials, etc., but from the point of view of analysis, this is not the most important thing:

> For variable capital to work, constant capital must be advanced in corresponding proportions, depending on the specific technical character of the work process. But the fact that retorts and other containers are needed for a chemical process does not prevent us from disregarding the retorts at the time of analysis. (*Op. cit.*)

Marx clearly contrasts the two points of view: that of the worker and that of the capitalist. From the worker's point of view, the relationship to the means of production is not a relationship to capital, but to a mere means. As Marx puts it, "in a tannery, for example, the worker treats the hides simply as his object of labor. It is not to the capitalist that he tans the leather." But from the capitalist's point of view, that is, from the point of view of the capital valorization process, the situation is completely reversed.

> The means of production are immediately transformed into a means of monopolizing the labor of others. It is no longer the worker who employs the means of production, but the means of production that employ the worker (*Op. cit.*).

This inversion means that life is now on the side of capital. And Marx regards this transformation as a perversion.

> The simple metamorphosis of money into the objective factors of the production process, into the means of production, metamorphoses the latter into legal titles, into coercive rights to other people's labor and surplus labor. In conclusion, we'll use an example to show how this inversion, which characterizes capitalist production, how this very perversion of the relationship between dead and living labor, between value and the force that creates value, is reflected in the consciousness of capitalist skulls. (*Op. cit.*)

This is followed by a passage on the English manufacturers' revolt of 1848-1850 against the limitation of the working day. In a newspaper article, a Scottish manufacturer estimates that if the working day is reduced from 12 to 10 hours, his machines will be reduced to 10/12ths of their value. In other words, our capitalist confuses the value of his means of production with their ability to swallow a certain quantum of human labor. Life has passed from labor to the machine. Dead labor seems alive after having absorbed the vital energy of the worker. We can see why living labor seems to bring the means of production back from the realm of the dead.

This inversion and perversion of the relationship between dead and living labor only comes into full play when technical means give it its full extension, i.e. when machinismo, and in particular automatic machines, make their entry into industry. Here, we need to return to the precise analysis of the transition from manufacture to factory, and at the same time from the formal to the real submission of labor to capital. In chapter XIII, "Machinery and large-scale industry", Marx points out that "it is during the very process of labor that the means of labor, because of its transformation into an automaton, comes face to face with the worker as capital, as dead labor that dominates and sucks up the living force of labor".

This clearly shows how inseparable technology is from social relations: the worker's position in relation to the machine as a means of labor derives from the fact that the machine is not the worker's means, but the instrument by which capital pumps out living labor. But, conversely, without appropriate technology, the domination of capital over labor and the inversion of the relationship between dead and living labor cannot be achieved. This eliminates the theses of a certain Marxism that distinguishes "productive forces" (including science and technology), which are neutral and ultimately good in themselves, from capitalist "relations of production", which are to be rejected. Taken on its own, the machine is a technical object, a dead thing, but in the hands of the capitalist, i.e. when it functions as capital, it is the means of domination that comes alive with the life pumped out of the worker.

Nowhere is this perversion more visible and unbearable than in child labor. If the primary function of the machine is to supplement muscular strength, we can immediately understand how it has become the ideal means of employing workers with little muscular strength. Hence the development of women's and children's work, made possible by machinismo. Marx often compares capital to Shylock, the usurer in Shakespeare's *The Merchant of Venice*, who demands his pound of flesh. Capital is particularly fond of the tender flesh of children. If machinery revolutionizes the formal mediation of the capitalist relation from top to bottom, it's for the following reason:

On the basis of commodity exchange, the first precondition was that the capitalist and the worker faced each other as free persons, as independent possessors of commodities, one of money and the means of production, the other of labor power. But now, capital buys miners or half-miners. In the past, the worker sold his own labor power, which, as a formally free person, he had at his disposal. Now he sells his wife and children, becoming a slave trader (*Op. cit*).

Marx recalls how a special law on spinning mills exempted the children they hired from compulsory schooling. He quotes an 1846 report: "The delicacy of the fabric required a sensitivity of the fingers that could only be guaranteed by early entry into the factory", and adds: "to obtain these delicate fingers, children were completely slaughtered, as horned beasts are slaughtered in southern Russia for their fat and skin." A little further on, Marx compares capital to a vampire that sucks the blood of the worker and "does not let go as long as there is still a muscle, a nerve, a drop of blood to exploit."

Dead labor is not simply so named by virtue of a metaphorical usage, but because capital actually belongs to the world of the undead. Just as value is coagulated, solidified labor (the value of a commodity is equal to the time of social labor incorporated into it), so capital is first and foremost the expression of the past. It is what is now lifeless. Here again is a particularly telling expression: in the process of capital valorization,

> [...] the means of production appear only as vampires, only as the means of valorizing present values and thus of capitalizing them. And so, [...] the means of production, precisely for this reason, appear once again, opposite living labor, as the expression of capital eminently, and in fact, they now appear as the domination of dead past labor over living labor.
>
> *"Le chapitre VI"* [Manuscrits de 1863-1867],
> GEME-Éditions Sociales, 2010, p. 1128-129

Capital is nothing other than accumulated labor (the means of labor), and it is therefore the result of productive labor (living labor) transformed into objectified labor that stands before the worker as his master. The repetition of the verb "to appear" indicates, incidentally, what is at work in this whole "critique of political economy", namely the social genesis of the forms of consciousness. If reality appears in this way—if dead labor dominates living labor—it's because social reality has undergone a decisive transformation:

> [...] it is not living labor that is realized in object labor as in its objective organ, but it is object labor that preserves and multiplies itself through the absorption of living labor, and thus becomes valorizing value, capital, as such *(Ibid.)*.

This transformation, a veritable inversion of vital teleology, affects not only the worker. The capitalist, as a living individual, is also in some way absorbed by capital:

> [...] the functions exercised by the capitalist are only the functions exercised with the consciousness and will of capital—of the value that valorizes itself through the absorption of living labor—itself. The capitalist performs his functions only as personified capital, capital as a person, just as the worker performs his functions only as personified labor, which belongs to him in terms of suffering and effort, whereas it belongs to the capitalist as the substance that creates and multiplies value, and as such appears in fact as an element incorporated into capital in the process of production as its living, variable factor. The capitalist's domination over the worker is therefore the domination of thing over man, of dead labor over living labor, of product over producer. *(Ibid.)*

At the same time, it's obvious that this is not "really" the case: in reality, it's always the activity of living individuals that is primary, and money is not the cause of money as the father is the cause of his son, to use Aristotle's expression again. But the real world is reversed in the brains of the actors, as in a "*camera oscura*", as Marx put it. A sinister spectacle.

The expression "dead labor" is neither purely metaphorical nor hyperbolic. It concentrates a cluster of converging issues and analyses that recur throughout Marx's work, whether in the preparatory manuscripts for *Capital* or in *Capital* itself. While we can always quibble about certain concepts found in the *Grundrisse* that seem to disappear in *Capital,* we find nothing of the sort with "dead labor". It's in all his writings.

Insofar as this individual subjective activity was indissolubly linked to the producer (the worker), it formed the basis of his property. Thus, when the separation occurs between living labor, on the one hand, and the means and product of his labor, on the other, this separation is expropriation. Marxists are wont to criticize the principle of private property as the capitalist principle par excellence. But all too often, they forget that the triumph of the capitalist mode of production is conditional on the mass expropriation of independent producers, and thus the large-scale annihilation of property! There's something strange here, something that seems incoherent if you confuse Marx and Marxism. According to the Marxist vulgate, the end of small independent property (agricultural or artisanal) is the condition for the great historical advance that is the triumph of the capitalist mode of production, which, by generalizing the wage condition, would be the antechamber to communism, i.e. to the collectivism presented by orthodox Marxism as the realized communist ideal.

And yet, when Marx describes "primitive accumulation" in England, with the terrible expropriation of Scottish or Irish peasants first, he is clearly on the side of these independent peasants against the perpetrators of "capitalist progress". As Michel Henry notes:

In contrast to this state, which seems idyllic in retrospect, capitalism is judged to be in a state of decomposition, despite the tremendous boost it gives to production.

Marx, vol. 2, 1976

Capitalism is not initially on the side of life, only to become rotten, in "putrefaction", as Lenin put it, when it ages and becomes imperialism, or when we reach the "third age" of capitalism (to use Ernest Mandel's phrase)—again, this is what the Marxist vulgate says. Capitalism has been on the side of death from its very origins. Its prodigious exploits (and they are!) are ultimately a long process of preparation for what Gunther Anders called "the obsolescence of man". It follows that resistance to machines, like the "Luddite" revolts, is not a "reactionary" movement, but rather the resistance of living individuals to the death promised to them.

When the conditions of life become alien to the worker, the worker necessarily falls under the domination of dead labor. The domination of life by "things", the accumulation of commodities as the sole purpose of life, the alienation of consumer society are nothing other than different expressions of this fundamental principle of the domination of capital, i.e. the domination of value-oriented production.

Thirdly, the concept of dead labor allows us to really understand what Marx means by abstract labor. Commodity exchange assumes that all goods can be reduced to a common measure, expressed in an amount of money. If we accept Marx's thesis (taken over in part from classical political economy) that value is nothing other than coagulated labour time—or objectified, i.e. dead, labour—then we must admit that the productive labour (or rather the sum of different productive labours) required to produce a suit of clothes is rigorously comparable to the productive labour required for 20 metres of canvas (to take the examples from the first section of *Capital*). This presupposes that we disregard the qualitative differences—skill required, drudgery, possible interest—between the various jobs. When Marx speaks of abstract labor, this word must be understood in its strongest sense: abstract labor is that from which all qualities have been abstracted, that in which all trace of sensitive practical activity, of subjectivity, has been annihilated.

It's not just a theoretical formula, a word for philosophers. Theoretical categories express social relationships, and abstract labor refers to a palpable reality, that of the division of labor, its meticulous sequencing by methods offices, and Fordist or Toyotist production. Simone Weil has accurately described what labor produces in the modern factory:

> Here I am at a machine. Counting fifty coins... placing them one by one on the machine, on one side, not on the other... each time manipulating a lever... removing the coin... placing another... another... counting again... I'm not going fast enough. I'm already getting tired. I have to force myself, to prevent a moment's pause between one movement and the next. Faster, even faster! [...] How many have I done in the last ten minutes? I'm not going fast enough. I'm still pushing myself, and little by little the monotony of the task leads me to daydreaming. For a few moments, I think of many things. Sudden awakening: how much have I done? It can't be enough. Don't dream. Force it again. If only I knew how many to make! I look around me! Nobody looks up, ever. No one smiles. No one says a word. How lonely! I do 400 pieces an hour. Is that enough? As long as I keep up this pace, at least... [...] Here comes the foreman. "How many do you make? 400 an hour? You need 800. Otherwise I won't keep you on. If you make 800 from now on, I might agree to keep you on. He speaks without raising his voice. Why should he raise his voice, when one word can cause so much anguish? What can he say? "I'll try." Force. Force again. Overcome every second this disgust, this disgust that paralyzes. Faster. Double the pace.
>
> "La vie et la grève des ouvrieres métallos",
> published in *La révolution prolétarienne,* 1936

An impeccable description of the insidious transformation of the individual into a machine! The fact that Chaplin's *Modern Times* version of assembly-line work has sometimes given way to more sophisticated organization changes nothing. The "just in time" of Toyotism means the precise timing of every gesture and every word, and the implementation of procedures designed to ensure that the worker is directly involved in producing 60 seconds per minute—whereas the old Fordist organization was far less efficient (no more than 45 seconds per minute). Even sectors that seemed to be reserved for human relations (customer reception, for example) have been subjected to this cut-and-dried approach: see *call centers*, where operators, following a strict protocol, enunciate standard phrases and have to calibrate their customer relations time as precisely as possible. To ensure that instructions are carried out correctly, they are monitored from a central computer station, from which nothing escapes. This abstract work is, in the final analysis, work from which all life has been removed, reduced to mechanics. Charlie Chaplin makes us laugh in *Les temps modernes*, by applying the Bergsonian recipe for laughter: applying the mechanical to the living. But it's more like a funeral face.

Finally, the concept of dead labor, as we have sketched out, is inseparable from another concept, developed above all by Lukács and his disciples: the concept of reification. This concept of reification (the becoming thing of the living) was developed not by Marx, but by some of his less conformist followers, those who managed, at least in part, to remain free from the yoke of official Marxism, such as Lukács and certain philosophers of the Frankfurt School. For Lukács, reification means first and foremost the colonization of the lived world by the representations imposed by the domination of value. But if Marx doesn't use the word, the concept is there. Chapter I, IV of *Capital*, devoted to the analysis of commodity fetishism, clearly explains what we're talking about. Strictly speaking, fetishism consists in giving a sacred value to a being in our world. When Marx speaks of the fetish nature of the commodity, it is in relation to the anthropological analyses that deal with it. Commodity fetishism makes value and its monetary embodiment the true living power, turning living labor into a thing, with workers becoming significantly "human resources".

The question of dead labor is thus at the very heart of Marxian critical theory. It's a concept that Marx uses to understand the historical destiny of the capitalist mode of production. The law of the tendency of the rate of profit to fall is the shibboleth of scientific Marxism (or rather of those who claim to make Marxism the true science of economics). This law is not a law analogous to the laws of physics that would enable predictions to be made. The downward trend in the rate of profit is not an "economic" law discovered by experience, nor a necessary theorem derived from a theoretical system, but the inevitable consequence of the principle of the substitution of dead labor for living labor, which itself finds its ultimate origin in the dual nature of the commodity. Indeed, the accumulation of capital necessarily tends to increase the share of dead labor (constant capital, especially machinery) in relation to living labor. It is for this reason that the rate of profit must tend to fall, as the share of free labor extorted from the worker falls by fat. And the actions of capitalists can be seen essentially as a set of means implemented to counteract this fall in the rate of profit (accelerating capital turnover, increasing labor productivity through machinismo and time-hunting, etc.).

As a self-valorizing value, capital can only live by pumping out living labor and accumulating the dead labor that makes the whole of life subject to its law. That's why it's always necessary to lengthen the working day and save labor (lay-offs, down-sizing, etc.). Machines have this dual function: to make human labor work faster, and to eliminate as much of it as possible. To supply raw materials for the "energy transition" (wind turbines, solar panels, electric cars), millions of tonnes of rock have to be mined for the precious metals that are running out. Alongside the children of Kivu, we'll find monstrous construction machinery, consuming thousands of liters of fuel oil every day. To accelerate the rotation of capital, we need to multiply exchanges, multiply means of transport, multiply means of communication, multiply *data centers* and computer "farms" that consume ever more energy. We need to stimulate human inventiveness more and more, and restrict it more and more, channel it, monitor it, put intelligence at the service of stupidity, the prodigious progress of science at the service of "reality TV" and brainwashing.

Insofar as it is the subjugation of living labor to dead labor, capital is eminently mortifying. As Marx put it: it destroys the two sources of wealth, earth and labor. The only horizon it leaves is that of a planet devastated by the voracity of capital, which knows no other law than accumulation for accumulation's sake. At the same time, it heralds the obsolescence of man—something that all those who invite us to enter the "posthuman" are telling us in their own way.

The Machinery

When we say that the worker, by selling his labor power, submits to capital, which converts living labor into dead labor, or that capital converts the personal, i.e. subjective, power of the worker into the objective power of capital, we are using theoretical categories to express the patent phenomenon, felt directly by the actors, namely the submission of the worker to the machine. In the abstract, it's enough for someone to work for someone else and make him rich for us to speak of a capitalist relationship. But this is only a formal capitalist relationship. It's with machinery and large-scale industry that the "formal subsumption" of labor to capital becomes "real subsumption". This is why Marx proposes a critical history of machinery, which we won't go into here. Suffice it to note that he proposes a "Darwinian" history, with the best-adapted machines surviving... Simondon will follow a similar path in his studies of the technical object. For us, the essential point is this: the industrial revolution began with the machine tool. It is here, then, that the analysis of the machine must focus—clearly showing that the definition of the machine cannot be a purely physical one, but rather an economic and historical one. What defines a machine tool?

> [...] we are seeing the reappearance in substance, albeit often in a very modified form, of the devices and tools with which the craftsman or factory worker works; but instead of being man's tools, they are now the tools of a mechanism or mechanical tools.
>
> *Capital*, I, p. 419

Much has been made of Heidegger's analysis of the tool versus the machine, and some have even seen it as an interesting critique of Marx. But this only proves once again that Marx has not been read seriously...

In 1751, Vaucanson invented his famous "metal-framed carriage lathe", now on display at the CNAM's Musée national des techniques. The main innovation of this lathe, whose frame is made of bolted iron bars, lies in the tool carriage, which moves parallel to the axis of the points, and its prismatic guide. The carriage can machine parts up to 1 m long and 30 cm in diameter, with great precision.

> The machine tool is therefore a mechanism which, after communication of the corresponding movement, performs with its tools the same operations as those formerly performed by the workman with similar tools. Whether the driving force comes from man or from a machine again, changes nothing in the nature of the thing (*Ibid.*).

The main and most obvious difference is that the number of tools with which a man can work is limited. Marx recalls that there were very few men capable of spinning two threads at the same time; by contrast, the *mule-jenny* (1764-1767) could spin 12 to 18 spindles. The machine tool overcame all organic obstacles.

It's often said that it was the steam engine that provided the impetus for the Industrial Revolution. Marx reverses the causal order: "it was, on the contrary, much more the creation of machine tools that made the steam engine revolution necessary". The invention of the steam engine made it possible to obtain a motive force that was more regular (than wind power), less localized (than hydraulic power) and more capable of being modulated according to need. The Industrial Revolution, then, was the setting in motion of a large number of machine tools with a single driving force. Initially, the factory was no more than a juxtaposition of mechanical trades powered by the same driving force. But in a second phase, the machines form a system.

> A machine system in the strict sense of the word only replaces the isolated stand-alone machine when the object of work passes through a continuous series of different, staggered processes, performed by a chain of differentiated, but mutually complementary, machine tools. Cooperation through division of labor, characteristic of manufacturing, reappears here, but this time as a combination of partial working machines.
>
> *Capital*, I, ch. XIII

The machine system introduces an "essential difference". In manufacturing, "if the worker is adapted to the process, the process was already adapted to the worker in advance".

> This subjective principle of division does not exist in mechanical production. The overall process is analyzed here objectively, considered in itself in its constituent phases, and the problem posed by the execution of each partial process and the interconnection of the various partial processes is solved by the technical application

of mechanics, chemistry, etc., which of course does not prevent the theoretical conception from always being perfected by practical experience accumulated on a large scale. (*Ibid.*)

Marx analyzes precisely how machinism first developed on the basis of manufacturing, but how, at some point, this basis became inadequate and had to be completely revolutionized by capital. He shows how upheaval in one sphere of production necessarily spreads to other spheres. From this, it follows that :

> As machinery, the means of labor acquires a material mode of existence that implies the replacement of human strength by natural forces, and of empirical routine by the conscious use of natural science. [...] Machinery [...] functions only through immediately socialized or shared labor. The cooperative character of work thus becomes a technical necessity dictated by the nature of the means of work itself (*Ibid.*).

The radical upheaval of social relations is the product of machinery, which will only "grow and beautify" as the capitalist mode of production develops. As the aim of machinery is not to alleviate human suffering, but rather to increase profit, it is quite possible that archaic means of production will be maintained even when machines exist, insofar as the worker's wage is so low that it would be costly to replace him with a machine. For example,

> Nowhere is there a more shameless waste of human strength on trifles than in England, in the land of machines. (*Op. cit*)

Mere trifles, moreover. We know how offshoring wastes human labor in extravagant conditions in the age of robotization. We could mention the textile industry in Bangladesh or Ethiopia. Or the production of "high-tech" objects in Chinese factories, which resemble textile workshops from a century ago. We'll study how

Chapter I – Dead Capital and the Machine

children dig up from the ground the precious rare metals used for electronic technologies or for the batteries in electric cars, clamored for by the thurifers of the energy transition. But the essential point lies elsewhere. Marx asserts that large-scale mechanized industry is a revolution, the immediate effects of which must first be studied. Machinery makes muscle power superfluous. It therefore makes it possible to employ labor forces of lesser muscular strength: women's and children's work is made possible on a large scale. On the subject of child labor, Marx writes:

> Not only did forced labor for the capitalist usurp the place of children's play, it also took the place of work done freely within moral limits within the family circle for the family itself (*Op. cit.*).

It's not child labor per se that's the problem. In fact, Marx advocates a polytechnic education that includes work! But within the family circle and within "moral limits", it can be considered free work. Like the Sunday handyman or gardener.

The advantage of machinery from the point of view of capital is as follows:

> By throwing members of the working family into the labor market, machinery distributes the value of a man's labor power over the whole family (*Op. cit.*).

This considerably raises the rate of exploitation, since in the past the wage had to support the worker and his family. Now, the same wage can be used to support the worker's wife and children. This may seem like ancient history, but it's a well-known fact that low wages in industries employing a large majority of female workers are part of this logic: they are "top-up wages"… It's worth noting that all current attempts to make the labour market more "fluid" are inspired by the capitalism of two centuries ago. This integration of the whole family into the great furnace of capitalist production also transforms the wage relationship.

Marx shows how parents literally sell their children.

> The revolution triggered by machinery in the legal relationship between buyer and seller [...] means that the entire transaction loses even the appearance of a contract between free persons... (*Op. cit.*)

Marx analyzed not only physical misery, but also "the moral impoverishment resulting from capitalist exploitation of women's and children's labor", which reached such a point that Parliament was forced to intervene. Women's and children's work also helped to break down men's resistance. All this explains why, for example, the French Proudhonians, who were at the origin of trade unionism, were opposed to women's work... and also why when wages improved in the aftermath of the First World War, women massively "went back home". Feminists see this as proof of working-class "machismo", but an analysis in terms of class relations is far more enlightening.

Machinery also made it possible to extend the working day. This is made possible by the profound transformation in the relationship between the workforce and the means of work: the operations of the means of work become autonomous from the worker:

> The means of labor becomes an industrial *perpetuum mobile* that would produce indefinitely were it not for the natural limitations of its human auxiliaries: the weakness of their bodies and their own willpower. As capital, and because it is capital, the automaton has consciousness and will in the person of the capitalist, and is therefore instinctively driven by the need to reduce the natural limit of human resistance, which is highly elastic, to its minimum by force. (*Op. cit.*)

Far from freeing people from back-breaking work, machinery actually increases the degree of exploitation. It increases the

intensity of work and imposes continuous work. This intensification of work is now fairly well documented. It is particularly
aggravated by information technology. *Alternatives économiques*
(October 2012):

> Statistics, international studies and the testimonies of occupa-
> tional physicians and trade unionists all point to the same conclusion:
> work has become denser, freedom and breathing space have shrunk,
> and the scope for adopting individual and collective strategies to be
> efficient without sacrificing health has diminished. The explosion in
> musculoskeletal disorders (MSDs), a direct consequence of accelera-
> ting work rates and loss of autonomy, is one of the key indicators of
> this intensification. But it's not the only one. The upsurge in cases
> of psychological suffering in recent years is directly linked to this
> pressure on work and employees.

More specifically on the impact of Information and
Communication Technologies (ICTs), a joint report by the Centre
d'analyse stratégique (CAS) and the Direction générale du travail
(DGT) on *The impact of ICTs on working conditions* looks at the
pace and control of work. Chapter 4 of this report is devoted to
the "Impacts of ICTs on work rhythms, autonomy and control".
It shows how the use of IT can reinforce employee control while
intensifying work. Under the eye of the managerial Big Brother,
subordinates are relegated to the status of digital toilers. "Here, ICTs
play the role of a tool, finely tuning productivity standards, managerial aims, competition and the volume of activity. Similarly, ICTs
enrich the panoply of control tools", write Romain Chevallet and
Frédéric Moatty, the editors of this fourth chapter. Here, they don't
focus on IT per se, but rather on its misuse by managers obsessed
with intensifying workloads to boost profits, and with controlling
their little hands. It's this use that has led to "ICTs being blamed for
the deterioration in working conditions". For them, "as ICTs are a

means of accomplishing work, they are rarely in themselves—with
the notable exception of the increase in breakdowns—the sole and
direct cause of changes in working conditions".

The first effect of information and communication technologies
is the intensification of work. The first intensification is quantitative, and "corresponds to a Taylorian industrial logic of accelerating work rhythms". The second, qualitative, corresponds to the
addition to this quantitative logic of an imperative for productive
flexibilization linked to the vagaries of demand. We speak of intensification of work when 'industrial constraints' are combined with
'market constraints'", say the authors.

One factor comes into play: immediacy. "A first aspect of work
rhythms is the need to respond to internal or external demands
that have to be met immediately. IT tools such as messaging have
reinforced this immediacy, with the need to respond ever faster,
even if this means cutting back on the quality of the response.

Some professions suffer from this outrageous use of IT: telephone operators and order pickers. According to the authors, the
former are "subject to strict requirements in terms of call duration,
break times between two calls and, at the same time, the quality
of the relationship". The entire organization of work is defined
by IT tools: "measuring the duration of conversations, imposing
a rhythm by automatic dialing and displaying a large amount of
information on the screen". At the same time, "the system enables
double eavesdropping, as the conversation can be listened in on by
both the supervisor and the client company's representative (in the
case of subcontracting)". This has consequences for "the employee's
autonomy [which] is reduced precisely by the impossibility—or
great difficulty—of regulating the structuring dimensions of his or
her work rhythm".

Order-pickers have also seen their day-to-day working life
change with the advent of IT. With the introduction of *voice
picking*, "the modeling of the process through rigid scripts leads

to the optimization of operations from the point of view of the system, disregarding the know-how accumulated by operators". The human being must adapt to the machine more and more. Nothing has really changed since the nineteenth century, when the spread of the steam engine considerably intensified work. The machine, always presented as progress for human labor, became the new master, with man having to get down on his knees.

This new work environment of task intensification is not without consequences. According to the authors, "the acceleration of rhythms in certain sectors, such as logistics, transport and industry, is potentially going to increase the pace of work, resulting in more frequent handling, faster movements and greater repetitiveness. The risk of exposure to MSDs (musculoskeletal disorders) will increase, as will the risk of work-related accidents due to falls, cuts, etc. "Stress will also increase, as will the risk of injury. Stress will also increase, as "the rhythm imposed by a mechanical cadence creates an organizational dependency: strong time pressure and little decision-making latitude to act".

The so-called manual professions are not the only ones affected. The entire tertiary sector is also feeling the full brunt of the development of ICTs, where users are more numerous: "the increased pace of work (more numerous requests, immediacy, information overload, etc.) increases the risk of stress and the frequency of overflow situations, but also limits mutual aid and has a negative impact on forms of collective and managerial support, and even disintegrates the collectives themselves. The effects on health are fatigue, irritation and irritation, and can even lead to decompensation and loss of bearings". Alongside MSDs, psychosocial factors are therefore in the limelight.

Control is nothing new in the corporate world. It's just that "ICTs offer [...] new and effective forms of control that can be added to or substituted for those that already exist. But while ICTs add to the panoply of control tools, they are generally not at the origin of them", continue the authors. In the end, ICTs have only "sometimes been used to implement quality procedures to better meet traceability requirements".

The adage "Trust is good. Control is better" takes on its full meaning, as the authors insist:

> While ICTs offer multiple possibilities for tracking work activity, it is the organizational and managerial context that explains the use of tools and forms of control (Rosanvallon, 2009). Management has the choice of using technologies for control purposes, or to encourage operator autonomy and responsibility.

And very often, the choice seems to be quickly made.

The problem is that an all-powerful *Big Brother* affects the motivation of the troops.

> These forms of control can also have a negative impact on work commitment and motivation, insofar as they are perceived as a lack of trust on the part of the employer.

This pretty set-up of computer guards is intrusive:

> The transparency of individual results achieved by team members (sometimes in real time) is often used and enabled by ICT to boost performance. But in certain organizational and management contexts (autonomous teams, *lean management*), it leads to a peer pressure mechanism, by intensifying competition between teams, but also by reinforcing group control over individuals (*Op. cit.*).

Intensified workloads and constant control remove the subordinates' commitment to the corporate project. The apotheosis is often experienced in multinationals. Didn't Noam Chomsky refer to them as "private tyrannies" and "totalitarian institutions", where power is wielded outside any democratic control? "*Big Brother is watching you*", let's get to work...

The importance of machinery as a means of extending the working day and intensifying operations must also be stressed. The need to run machines 24 hours a day is obvious, as machines are not only worn out by use, but also by non-use—a fact well known to farmers, whose machines are often only used seasonally. There is also a kind of wear and tear that Marx calls "moral wear and tear": an identical machine can be made at a lower cost, or a machine of the same cost can offer a higher output... or both.

The greater the capital involved (and machines require a great deal of capital), the more any minute lost, any minute in which the machine is not working, appears to be a waste of capital. And with good reason: during this time, the machine is no longer sucking up living labor, which is its function par excellence for the capitalist. This is why machinery, paradoxically on the surface, goes hand in hand with the increase in the capitalist frenzy for surplus labor. Indeed:

> The law is that surplus value does not come from the labor power that the capitalist has replaced by the machine, but rather from the labor power that he employs.

Marx, Capital I

The struggle between labor and capital becomes antagonism between the worker and the means of labor, although it is necessary to distinguish between the machine and its capitalist use. Not only does machinismo reverse the relationship between man and his tools: the tool goes from being the servant of the hand to becoming the master of the worker's body. Moreover, in the capitalist mode of production, the means of labor immediately becomes the worker's competitor, since the return on capital is a direct function of the number of workers whose existence the machine destroys. The first great workers' struggles were thus often struggles against machines, as in the "Luddite" movement in the early 19th century.

It takes time and experience before the worker learns to distinguish machinery from its capitalist use, and thus to transfer his attacks from the material means of production itself, to its social form of exploitation. (*Op. cit.*)

Indeed, a major transformation is taking place. The antagonism between the worker and the capitalist is as old as the capitalist mode of production itself. But in the factory, the workers don't fight the factory per se. It's mainly individual craftsmen who oppose it, because it competes with them and throws them out into the street. Not so with machinery and large-scale industry. Now, it's machinery that's throwing workers out into the street. The means of work becomes the worker's competitor, and that's why machinery is directly responsible for creating the "industrial reserve army" of the unemployed. The means of work crushes the worker.

But we'll look in vain for Marx's condemnation of the worker's revolt against the means of labor. Thus, after noting that "world history offers no more horrible spectacle than that of the progressive decline of the English weavers" (*Op.cit.*), he draws this conclusion worth pondering:

> The autonomous configuration, alien to the worker, that the capitalist mode of production generally gives to the conditions and product of work in relation to the worker, develops with machinery in perfect opposition. Hence, for the first time in its history, the worker's brutal revolt against the means of labor.
>
> The means of work crushes the worker. This direct opposition is most obvious when the introduction of machinery competes with a traditional craft or manufacturing operation. But within large-scale industry itself, the constant improvement of machinery and the development of the automatic system produce similar effects (*Ibid.*).

Pushing exploitation to the limit, machinism also completes the process of alienation. Incidentally, the Roy translation simply speaks of the "character of independence", a more neutral and unclear expression. Rubel, in the Pléiade edition, restores the translation from the German edition, which speaks of *"Die verselbstän-digte und entfremdete Gestalt"* (independent and alienated form). Given Marx's sparing use of the notion of alienation (*Entfremdung*, to make foreign) in *Capital*, its reintroduction here is obviously no minor matter.

New Perspectives

Marx, however, remained relatively confident: in spite of everything, machinism produced greater solidarity between workers, and thus a "collective intellect" of the enterprise was to be formed, which would promote "the expropriation of the expropriators". Alas, nothing of the sort! The computer machinery is transforming the very fabric of working relationships. The "platformization" of the capitalist economy is enabling the return, on new foundations, of "contract work" in what is known as uberization, a process that is far from being confined to cab drivers—a good description of the working conditions of Uber drivers in California's high-tech paradise can be found in Douglas Kennedy's novel *Men are Afraid of the Light* (2022). The development of telecommuting—which, by necessity, cannot cover all activities—was put to the test in real life during the confinements linked to the Covid-19 epidemic (2020-2022). Gathered in Davos, big business and government representatives have been working on what one report calls the *"global reset"*, the resetting of all old social relationships. Tele-teachers, tele-doctors, even the most highly-skilled jobs can be flattened. In this way, capital no longer encounters any collective resistance or social movement, since individuals no longer have any direct contact with one another, and perceive one another only through their "avatar". Some software publishers even offer a simulation of a real office, simulating movements to the coffee machine. Guy Debord could never have imagined how spectacular this would become!

Alienation from work takes on new forms. Progressively, it's not just the working day that's given over to the capitalist, but all the rest of the day too. Cell phones and laptops are all ways of tying workers to their work when they're at home. This invasion is all the more insidious in that many people enjoy this new form of servitude: working at home means avoiding the commute to the office and enjoying greater freedom—which is perfectly illusory. At the same time, managers and intellectual intermediate professions are increasingly cut off from "real" workers, as opposed to "virtual" ones. The result is a world of increasingly isolated individuals, who increasingly relate only to simulacra of humans, machine-like simulacra that may well no longer be human at all. A spectral world, as Éric Sadin puts it (see *La vie spectrale*, Grasset, 2023).

There's no reason to believe that this trend should stop here. The more economic difficulties get in the way of business, the greater the temptation to take the next step into the construction of automata. Autonomous tractors and harvesters already exist, and their numbers are growing. Despite consumer reluctance, "intelligent objects" are about to invade our homes… to order us around. Already, cars are calling us to order: don't forget your seatbelt, you're driving too far to the left, you've been driving too long, you need a break. Your TV will pause if you've been watching too long… All these gadgets may make you smile, but they're very serious business: it's not just the worker at his machine who has become the servant of the machine, we all have to learn to obey machines in all circumstances. The "intelligent" refrigerator will be able to analyze its contents, issuing alerts because there's too much red meat and not enough insects, before denouncing to the morality police its owners who are resistant to the new diet compatible with the supposed saving of the planet!

Let's be clear about what's at stake: the multiplication of "things" invading our world is the product of the capitalist impulse to produce ever more commodities, and thus to make all those we own obsolete as quickly as possible—obsolescence is not necessarily programmed, but results from the very march of the capitalist mode of production. And to produce more and more, we need to increase labor productivity through new machines, which in turn require new industries to produce the machines. The dynamics of capital are gradually swallowing up the world that yesterday's humans knew. Consumer society is just one facet of capital accumulation. The phrase "the dead seize the living" is now valid far beyond the sphere of production, and plays a major role in shaping our ways of thinking and acting. We prefer the predictability and certainty of industrial and commercial procedures to the uncertainty of life. The living are inferior to the inert.

Günther Anders uses the expression "Promethean shame" to describe the feeling we poor humans, who are merely the random result of the laws of biology, feel when confronted with machines. Here's how he describes his first encounter with this "shame":

> T. and I visited a technical exhibition that had just opened in the area. T. behaved in the strangest way, so strange that I ended up observing him rather than the machines on display. As soon as one of the most complex machines in the exhibition began to operate, he looked down and fell silent. I was even more struck when he hid his hands behind his back, as if ashamed of having introduced his own crude, clumsy and obsolete instruments into a high society composed of devices operating with such precision and *refinement.*
>
> *L'obsolescence de l'homme,* tome I, 1956

This shame is that of the manant introduced by chance into the society of the great, with the difference that the society of the great was made up of humans and that the society of the great before which he now finds himself is made up of machines.

If I try to go deeper into this "Promethean shame", it seems to me that its fundamental object, the "fundamental opprobrium" that makes man ashamed of himself, is his *origin*. T. is ashamed of having *become* rather than of having been *made*. He is ashamed to owe his existence—unlike products, which are beyond reproach because they have been calculated down to the smallest detail—to the blind, uncalculated, ancestral process of procreation and birth. (*Ibid.*)

There's no better way to describe what drives the insane desire to make humans, or the equally insane desire to reduce one's mind to a simple, predictable mechanism. Augustine of Hippo sees the inversion of creator and creature as the very manifestation of heresy. Anders notes that a similar process characterizes the man seized by "Promethean shame": the creature (the machine) becomes the object of admiration, taking on a sacred character, and man (who is nevertheless the creator of the machine) becomes the object of contempt.

Because capital is the great machine, because we see in the machine the body of capital, we are invited to revere it almost religiously. The entire history of the capitalist mode of production is linked to this cult of the machine. Jacquard's loom, the steam engine, Le Creusot's power hammer, whose drawing we still find in elementary school children's reading books… these are all holy icons! Technical objects are sacralized and arouse passions. We all know that the automobile is something other than a means of getting from one place to another! But the passion is no longer confined to fast cars that give you the thrill of omnipotence. It has spread to cell phones and computers—you only need to have seen the scenes of people waiting for the latest Apple phone to be released, in front of those temples that are the Apple Stores,

Chapter I – Dead Capital and the Machine

to understand the nature of the phenomenon, which could be compared to the emergence of the Holy Light from the nativity grotto in Bethlehem. But this new religion, unlike the old one, is nothing more than a pitiful fetishistic religion, devoid of any spirituality. So-called "artificial intelligence" (AI) is all the rage in high-tech circles: the hesitations and errors of human intelligence are to be done away with. The difficult and uncertain heuristics used by human intelligence to solve thorny problems will finally be replaced by the single word: "let's calculate", thus fulfilling Leibniz's astonishing prophecy.

Marx defines capitalism as "the great automaton". It functions of its own accord, driving men and women, even those who believe themselves to be in control. The capitalist believes himself to be all-powerful, but for Marx, he is merely the servant of capital, dedicated to its service as a priest is dedicated to the service of God. The great automaton is powered by human sweat and intelligence, but it is he who commands. The Wachowskis' *Matrix* has been interpreted as a somewhat sophisticated dystopia, recounting the triumph of machines over men, or an allegory of the Platonic cave revisited, unless it's a development of the Cartesian "evil genius". I propose another interpretation: it's an allegory of the capitalist mode of production. The matrix is Marx's great automaton. It dominates humans and uses them to keep itself alive—it's always living human labor that gives life to dead labor. But humans enrolled in the operation of the machine must have distractions: like the matrix, capital produces a fantasy world that they mistake for the real world, distracting them from their true condition.

As mentioned above, from the Freudian point of view, work is ambivalent. The destructive drive (or the disintegrated death drive) is diverted from its objectives: by transforming nature, i.e. destroying it, man creates a new world, and Thanatos is thus placed at the service of Eros. Work creates ever larger entities with ever stronger bonds, and in this, it fulfills the work of Eros. But in absolute capitalism, as we know it today, Thanatos reigns supreme. Eros is put at the service of Thanatos (rather than Thanatos at the service of Eros), in other words, the transformation of the living individual into a death machine. All human communities are dissolved—Zygmunt Bauman's "liquid society" comes to mind. Human beings are to be nothing more than automatons driven by a few simple laws, and above all, they are to be interchangeable. Politics and warfare are no exception to this trend. Quite the contrary, in fact.

The Machinery Apocalypse

The apocalypse is the revelation of truth. The 20th century revealed the profound truth of machinery as a system of death. Auschwitz and Hiroshima showed, in a way, the culmination of capitalism's machinic development. Auschwitz—the name is emblematic of the entire Nazi concentration camp system—is not a machine for destroying humans, as one might think, but a machine for manufacturing corpses, as Günther Anders rightly points out. Humans were destroyed at the start of the process when they were crammed into freight cars and cattle cars—remember that the Nazi regime was sensitive to "animal suffering", since one of its first acts was to set standards for the transport of animals in cattle cars. The deported Jews weren't even animals, so they didn't attract the compassion of such delicate Nazis—Hitler himself was a vegetarian. The Jews were legally reduced to nothing in the early years of the regime, culminating in "Kristallnacht". The decision on the "Final Solution", finalized at the Wannsee Conference on January 20, 1942, set the wheels in motion. The Jews to be exterminated were to be "parts", so all the resources of industry had to be mobilized: it wasn't enough to arrest the Jews, they had to be shipped out, and so sufficient means of transport had to be available. The appropriate means of transport, typical of the second industrial revolution, was the railway. To "process" the "parts", the means in which German industry excelled were used, starting with chemistry and the infamous Zyclon B. Corpses are also "valorized": hair, dentures, etc. are recovered. From a military point of view, that is, from the point of view of someone who wanted to win the war against the Allies, all this was pure madness. Had Nazi Germany not "distracted" a considerable part of its economic and military forces in the extermination of the Jews, it is almost certain that the outcome of the war might have been different. But Hitler's aim was not to win the war, but to manufacture corpses. The corpse-making machine dictated to the entire system.

On a different note, Hiroshima and Nagasaki were the places where the techno-scientific power of American capitalism was tested "under real conditions". The development of the bomb required the enlistment of dozens of renowned scientists, as well as "little hands"—in all, thousands of scientists, including four Nobel Prize winners in physics. The "Manhattan Project" culminated in the two nuclear explosions that killed 70,000 people in Hiroshima and 40,000 in Nagasaki. Once again, the result was achieved by mobilizing the resources of technoscience in every field. It was during the development of the A-bomb that John von Neumann developed the basic principles of the computer, whose first fully electronic working model, the ENIAC, began operating in 1946. The military-scientific complex crystallized around the Manhattan Project, and was destined for a long posterity!

Since 1945, we've lived under this military-scientific regime: the steering wheel of the entire economic machine has been this military-scientific complex, the one that produced Monsanto's "Agent Orange" (a firm bought out by Bayer, the producer of Zyclon B), which defoliated millions of hectares of forest in Vietnam and generated disease and birth defects in droves. Between 2.1 and 4.8 million Vietnamese were exposed to Agent Orange and, sixty years after the spraying, an estimated 100,000 children have suffered congenital diseases as a result.

It was also the military-scientific complex that was behind the "conquest of space" (the creator of the V2s that the Nazis launched en masse, notably on the British Isles, was hired for this task) and the development of information technology—the Internet was born of a program launched by the Pentagon. You can look at the problem from any angle, but the development of technical power, or if you prefer techno-scientific power, has death as its ultimate goal. We'll come back to this when we talk about biotechnologies, which are triumphing as technologies of death. This is why we can say that modern techniques of death are indeed the apocalypse of capitalism.

Since the beginning of this century, we have begun to develop autonomous lethal weapons: drones piloted by AI machines capable of finding the target and destroying it without threatening the lives of the drone launchers. Face-to-face combat is disappearing: the most sophisticated machines are able to determine which target to aim at and when to shoot it. Death machines are being deployed on every battlefield. So morally terrible is this that the major powers have embarked on negotiations to ban this type of weapon, but negotiations are stalling, with everyone changing their definition of the weapons to be banned. Meanwhile, new "progress" is being made. New weapons appeared. In 1914, at the start of the great carnage that inaugurated this barbaric century (the "short twentieth century", as Eric Hobsbawm calls it), soldiers on both sides respected the Christmas truce: in the worst inhumanity, there were even fraternization movements. Thanks to the progress of technoscience, this kind of impromptu interruption of the work of death is no longer likely to occur... However, the progress of machine warfare should not lead us to believe that tomorrow we'll be able to wage machine wars that spare human lives. A war without dead humans loses much of its charm. Perhaps this is why the NATO-backed war between Ukraine and Russia so closely resembles the First World War, a war of trenches and "meat cleavers", in the delicate words of Prigogine, the late head of the Wagner mercenary group. But this war is also the occasion for a semantic innovation: we speak of "kamikaze drones", as if the drones were sacrificing themselves for their side.

The cyborg, a mix of living being and technical device, is undoubtedly a dream. But the blending of man and machine continues to progress. If there are kamikaze drones, there are also experimental exoskeletons that promise to turn soldiers into Terminators. Augmented reality, as promised by Google glass, exists for soldiers equipped with infrared goggles, while all kinds of drugs are being tested that would mean soldiers only need to sleep a few hours every four or five days. So it's human beings who are being turned into killing machines. We're not just substituting killer robots for humans.

A New Luddism?

An indictment of the machinery. You'll turn into a Luddite! Let's face it, against a solid Marxist tradition, the Luddites weren't completely wrong. That machines are not the tools of the workers, but the embodiment of their enemy, we've shown enough here. No doubt we need to make distinctions. The relationship with machines can be very different, depending on the job and the position. Excavator operators are lords and masters of their machines, which give them the power of giants. But in the vast majority of cases, the worker is subject to his machine, serving it. He is its serf. Just as Philippe Bihouix was planning to prepare *The age of low tech* (2021), we could take stock of useful, useless or harmful machines, which would presuppose at least partial "de-industrialization" of certain production processes. Following Philippe Bihouix's lead, we could put humans back into millions of jobs held by machines. The intellectual will see this as a retrograde step: what more pointless work could there be than manning a supermarket checkout counter? But the intellectual forgets that the unemployed supermarket cashier won't find a more interesting job elsewhere, and that it may be even less interesting to maintain Excel spreadsheets to satisfy the wishes of a management controller.

For a long time, machinismo held out the hope of liberating mankind. The machine was supposed to liberate man from work. It has largely become the instrument of his enslavement. Modern technology stems from science, and has nothing to do with the "knowledge immanent in action" of which Plato spoke. Machinism is inseparable from the relations of production in which it developed. Capital is "spiritual" in essence, since money is not a material reality, even if it needs, at least temporarily, a physical support like gold. But capital can only really be capital when embodied in the machinery that pumps out living labor power. Machinery also has a direct ideological function: it provides a model of efficient social organization. The capitalist mode of production as a whole functions like a great automaton (Marx). Perfect market theorists see it as a *feed-back* machine, regulating itself by successive approximations. Widespread connection via computer networks turns "global society" (if such a thing even exists) into a gigantic cybernetic machine. That this gigantic machine is essentially a means to extort surplus value, on an ever-expanding scale, independently of any properly human purpose, is no longer of any importance. Progress cannot be stopped! For Althusser, history is a "process without subject or end(s)": this is how the capitalist mode of production presents itself. It's a gigantic machine whose ends are never questioned, and which nobody directs. This makes it immune to criticism. The rationality of this machine is immune to scrutiny. It's immanent to it, and it's the model for rationality, since it's the model that determines social organization and the relationships

that individuals must maintain. For example, it is technical rationality that eliminates the counters and cash registers manned by
"human operators", replacing them with Internet applications or
automatic teller machines, and in the process transforms the user
or consumer into a cog in the machine: the customer who passes
through the automatic cash register does the work of the cashier,
who has been reduced to unemployment. The abstraction of the
commodity is pushed almost to its limit. Tomorrow, it will be the
"intelligent" refrigerator that determines the order to be placed,
which will be delivered by drone. In this way, man's relationship
with things useful to life will be reduced to a purely consumer
relationship, completely masking the entire social process of
production and circulation.

The great capitalist machinery can also be seen from another
angle, as one of Swiss artist Jean Tinguely's absurd machines, made
from bricks and mortar and operating for no other purpose than
to turn cogs. And, indeed, the great capitalist machinery recycles
everything it can get its hands on, turning it into elements of its
own functioning. The most archaic elements—extracting minerals
by hand, for example—coexist with the latest technology. A child
in Kivu can make a decent part of the machine, just as much as a
smartphone application.

The machine, as a system, is not neutral. It cannot serve
any purpose, even if that's how it presents itself. Marxists have
stubbornly defended this neutrality of the machine. Lenin was
fascinated by Taylorism and Fordism, which Gramsci more
aptly described as "passive revolution", i.e. revolution against the
proletariat. But if machinery is adequate to the capitalist mode of
production, as Marx showed, and if socialism can take it over and
run it on its own account, then socialism is in fact no more than
a kind of new capitalism, in which the capitalist is replaced by the
bureaucrat and the engineer, an evolution that has long since been
initiated by capitalism itself. But "socialist" assembly-line work is

just as alienating as capitalist assembly-line work. Computer interconnections have their own logic, which is to separate individuals ever more from each other, not to connect them, as insistent propaganda assures. To understand this is to take up anew the radical critique of technology undertaken by Jacques Ellul and Bernard Charbonneau in France, and Lewis Mumford in the United States.

No doubt it's absurd to want to break machines. Our lives depend on them so much that we would be breaking human life itself in the process. But it's high time we took an interest in their uses, their social function and the alienations they entail. A technical de-escalation is needed, which would be ruinous for the capitalist mode of production and beneficial for the majority of human beings. But, of course, a critique of technology will not spare the science from which it springs. Modern science represented the greatness of the human spirit, promising a radiant future for humanity. Today, through technology, it is used to serve its worst abasement. That's why criticism of science (and not just its misapplications) is the order of the day. Thanks to science, mankind has been liberated… from its cumbersome freedom. It's time to stop worshipping such liberators!

Günther Anders offers an iconoclastic analysis of the relationship between man and machine. He considers that in industrial society there is a real rage against machines, which finds its outlet in other objects, such as the family. But this anti-machine affect is "ignored by those who suffer from it":

> It's essential that it remains unknown to them. For if those who hate machines were to perceive their hatred and give in to it, it would undermine the very principles of production as a whole, opening the door to subversion and, quite simply, sabotage. To prevent this sabotage, we must therefore prophylactically prevent them from becoming aware of this resentment.

> *Obsolescence de l'homme*, tome II, 1980

There's a real taboo on machines, a taboo common to all classes and all economic systems. Anders says that a capitalist will always prefer a communist to a Luddite! Blindness to this resentment against machines is massive. We can confirm this by looking at developments since Anders' 1980 text. More than ever, machines are, if not adored, at least accepted as a necessity. Nothing could be better than replacing cashiers with automatic checkouts, because after all, the cashier's job is an uninteresting one! That's the main argument. The machine is always better than man. Shame on man…

CHAPTER II: MACHINE LIFE

Capitalism and modern science were born at practically the same time, at the turn of the "modern age". Everything about this story is "modern", because between the "discovery" of America by Christopher Columbus and the first advances in mathematical physical science in the 17th century, the Western world was about to tip over, dragging the rest of humanity with it. It's impossible to understand what's happened in science and philosophy without linking it to what's happened in social relations, in the broadest sense.

Categories of thought always have a social genesis: Marx is not alone in saying this. Durkheim and some other great sociologists say the same thing, and it took considerable social and mental upheaval for a new way of conceiving and understanding reality to emerge. The boldness of these men who set off on adventures across the seas, and the first developments in industry, were matched by the boldness of thinkers. De Cues, Copernicus and Bruno paved the way for Galileo to follow, while the great discoveries made the entire Earth available to "Western man", multiplying the routes of maritime trade and making possible the so-called "primitive accumulation" that would truly launch the capitalist mode of production into orbit. In the space of a century, between Galileo's first writings and Newton's "natural philosophy", the prodigious story of a colossal effort to create new knowledge and a new vision of the world unfolds. For the better, no doubt, but perhaps also, it can be said today, for the worse. This "new science" was hailed by philosophers, who sometimes contributed to it (Descartes, Leibniz) or theorized about it: Kant described it as a "revolution". More recently, Thomas Kuhn revived the concept of "scientific revolution" in his book *The Structure of Scientific Revolutions* (1962). There is much to be said for Kuhn's concept of "scientific revolution", a concept often misused in a world where the spectacle of science has replaced the patient work of knowledge. The fact remains that something revolutionary did take place between the end of the sixteenth century and the nineteenth. Something that has not been matched in the last century, despite the advances of science and, above all, technology, and the spectacle of prodigies to which we are invited on a daily basis.

Science on the Model of Physics

How can we characterize this "revolution"? Kant calls it a "Copernican revolution", but to stop there would be to reduce it to a cosmology: we swap geocentric cosmology for heliocentric cosmology, and in the end, we've changed nothing—since in a revolution, we make a complete turn to find ourselves back in the starting position. But that's not quite right. Copernicus built a heliocentric model, which he prudently presented as a useful arte-fact to simplify astronomical calculations. He took a decisive step, but remained on the sidelines, without making the big leap—he wasn't the first to imagine a heliocentric model, even if he was the first to give it serious scientific foundations. The Galilean model was not a continuation of Copernicus' model, even if Galileo defended his illustrious predecessor, for Galileo assumed an infinite universe, and in an infinite universe, there is no center! He thus followed in the footsteps of Nicolas de Cues and Giordano Bruno, some of whose work he was familiar with, and some of whose arguments he would later adopt. The transition "from the finite world to the infinite universe" (see Alexandre Koyré's book of the same name) is both prodigious and frightening. Blaise Pascal, convinced by Galilean reasons, notes that our natural knowledge leads us to see the world as "an infinite sphere whose center is everywhere, whose circumference is nowhere" (*Pensées*, "Disproportion de l'homme"). Yet it's the same Pascal who exclaims: "the silence of infinite spaces frightens me". And indeed, infinite spaces are silent. The world is silent. Copernicus was still an astrologer as well as an astronomer; Galileo was a professor of mathematics, an engineer and a philosopher. For him, the universe has no meaning: it's understandable only if you speak its language, the language of mathematics, but this mathematical language refers only to itself, it's not a sign of the world. Man no longer has to decipher this non-existent meaning, but only to understand its mechanics, which are formulated entirely in mathematical laws, for "the great book of nature is written in mathematical language." It's a nature that God has deserted. But it will be available to us, because science, which no longer has to understand, will be able to predict.

However, this aspect should not obscure another equally essential one. Galilean science aims to be objective, independent of the subjective grasp of reality that is the first knowledge we have. It replaces sensible impressions with another reality, one that can be described using mathematical idealities. Let's take a telling example: we're used to grasping reality by its varied colors, and a form without color is something we can't perceive! We need at least one line, one shadow, to draw the shape. We know how to name and distinguish a great many colors. There's blue, yellow, green and red. Kandinsky devoted much of his work to this sensual "language" of shapes and colors. But for Galilean science, none of this has any real existence. For modern science, reality is made up of light waves of a given length: red is between 625 and 740 nm, indigo between 430 and 450 nm, and so on. In other words, objective reality, the reality that is the object of science, resides in these mathematical descriptions, and our world, the world where things are red, black, indigo or white, is merely a world of appearances, marked by the famous, all-too-famous "error of the senses": I see the sun bigger in the evening than at midday, when we know that obviously its size doesn't vary. Here we return to an old story, that of Plato's cave and the division of the objects of knowledge into a sensible world that is only a kind of ever-changing copy of the real world, the world of ideas, of which mathematics is not the mode of grasping, but a kind of model, since the exercise of mathematics leads us to grasp ideas in themselves, independently of the sensible intuition we have of things that are only copies of them. It's worth noting that modern science, in its first faltering steps, found support in the revival of Platonism spurred on by Italian humanists such as Marsilio Ficino, and the renewed ties between Byzantine and Roman scholars, at a time when the Eastern Roman Empire was about to collapse under the blows of Mehmet II's troops, supported by the artillery provided by a Hungarian engineer, Orban.

Yet this science, which claims to outclass all our other modes of apprehending reality, is itself, like all other knowledge, nothing more than a product of our subjective relationship to the world. If I read on the measuring instrument the number I expect in an experiment designed to verify a physical hypothesis, I can only do so with my eyes and because I can distinguish the colors of the screen displaying the results. The litmus paper turns red, which tells me that I've soaked it in an acid solution, with a high concentration of H+ ions, but I have to be able to distinguish red from blue, otherwise I'd be confusing acid and base. There is no precise sense in which we can say that what the physical sciences teach us is truer than our immediate experiences: the expression "the rose is red" is no less true than the expression "this rose does not absorb radiation between 625 and 720 nm". Besides, this rose is a rose, not a cluster of cells whose secret lies in the DNA. Galileo is also a great advocate of experimentalism, as is Francis Bacon, the other father of modern thought, a little earlier than Descartes, but just as important as him, should our national pride suffer. However important the differences between Cartesian rationalism and Baconian experimentalism, they lie within the same problematic common to all branches of modern science.

In the first place, it's a radical mutation of the idea of truth. The propositions of the physical sciences are exact, more exact than the propositions of our immediate experience. Today, we can measure durations with a precision of eighteen decimal places, which corresponds to a shift of one second every fifteen billion years (an estimate of the approximate age of our universe). But to be more exact, disproportionately more exact, the propositions of physics are not more true! Husserl even provocatively asserts that "the Earth does not move"! The manuscript is more precisely entitled "*The arch-origin-Earth does not move.*" It moves from the point of view of Galilean astronomy—even though in Galileo's universe there is neither rest nor absolute motion, but only motion measured relative to a Galilean frame of reference—but it does not move insofar as it is "our original soil". We have no sense of the Earth's motion, since we think of all motion in terms of this original experience. Nature is not an original given, but something that is constituted on the basis of the primary gift that is the three-dimensional perception of bodies, and hence the constitution of space. In order to exist, then, science must first be constituted on the basis of a rigorous study of the ways in which its most fundamental categories—space and time—are constituted. But what characterizes today's dominant thinking is that "science" is the very manifestation of truth, and constitutes it. This is commonly referred to as scientism.

It should be added that this new science tends purely and simply to liquidate metaphysics. Beyond (*meta*) physics, there's nothing left, or at least nothing to talk about seriously. After all, if we forget the rest, this is Kant's observation. Metaphysics is a battlefield, a *Kampfsplatz*, and there can be no theoretical knowledge of what cannot be given in sensibility. Wittgenstein and the philosophers and scientists of the Vienna Circle consider metaphysical questions to be meaningless. Positivists, following in the footsteps of Auguste Comte, welcomed the fact that modern science did away with the "why"—the typically Aristotelian questioning of causes—in favor of the "how", i.e., a purely operational vision of the world. In this way, the thickness of reality dissolves into mechanics. It is also for this reason that science is no longer, as philosophy once was, the servant of theology—science has nothing to say about God—but becomes the servant of technology. Galileo is a scientist and an engineer; Huygens is a scientist and an engineer; no scientist can now do without sophisticated technical instruments, devices to make nature speak, and increasingly, tools will become applications of science—Kant still distinguishes between pure science and applied science, or "mechanical arts", but in practice this distinction is becoming increasingly blurred. We can rightly speak of "technoscience", the complete fusion of science and technology, where the ancients saw two radically separate domains.

The vast scientific and technical edifice that took shape from the seventeenth century onwards soon found institutional expression, not only in the Academies, but above all in the schools where scientists and engineers were trained. In France, the Ecole Polytechnique embodies this fusion of science, technology and state institutions. The gradual extension of the domain of science pushed aside all other forms of knowledge. What Michel Henry calls "life knowledge" predates objective scientific knowledge, however, and is its *sine qua non*. The knowledge of life is man's ability to make bodily movements and intentionality coincide in pure immanence. This practical knowledge is the condition of possibility of all theoretical knowledge. Scientific knowledge is knowledge that represents the world in front of it in a purely abstract way, but never experiences it. Yet the only reality is an experienced reality. The laws and models of physics are theoretical constructs—even atoms are theoretical constructs. The world of physics is cold and objective. Whereas the knowledge of life proceeds from the encounter between subject and object, scientific knowledge refuses to take into account the reality of subjectivity, and presents us with an object that is not the product of any gaze, that is not apprehended by any consciousness. "Nothing inside: nothing that is alive, that can speak in its own name, in the name of what it experiences, in the name of what it is. Only 'things', only death", as Michel Henry points out in *La Barbarie* (1987). In this sense, Galilean science, when transformed into the sole science and sole source of truth, leads directly to the negation of life and human subjectivity. In place of life, mechanics, i.e. death, imposes itself.

All other sciences are judged by this Galilean science, which has become the archetype of all knowledge. The "human sciences", which Wilhelm Dilthey rightly called "sciences of the mind" (*Geisteswissenschaften*), are in fact devalued because, since they deal only with the meanings and interpretations of people living in society, they do not correspond to the model of objective truth provided by mathematical physics. Objective because what it states is independent of human judgment. The scientist places himself from God's point of view—he is undoubtedly God himself!

The human sciences are therefore called upon to "take the safe road of science", i.e. to find the "Newtonian laws" of human behavior, so as to be able to act effectively on human nature, as Hume already proposed. But all attempts to do so have failed miserably. It had to be realized that, in order to understand history, it was useless to measure the average speed of Napoleon I's army between Paris and Moscow or, to put it more seriously, it had to be admitted that historical facts are not phenomena of the physical world, although there are necessarily physical phenomena that correspond to historical facts. Historical facts are not measurable—you can count the number of inhabitants, the number of soldiers, the average age, life expectancy, etc., with all these data you can make demography, which can be very useful for understanding historical events, but, in itself, it doesn't capture any historical event. The facts of the physical sciences are repeatable, whereas what characterizes the historical fact is precisely that it cannot be repeated. We can't repeat the Battle of Waterloo to see what would have happened if we'd changed one parameter: Grouchy arrived before Blücher!

The attempt to create a "social physics" from population statistics—an attempt that dates back to Adolphe Quételet (1796-1874)—has always left even its most ardent defenders with a taste of incompleteness and notorious dissatisfaction. The mathematization of economics, which obeyed the same Galilean injunctions, quickly sank into ridicule. The economist Bernard Maris, who signed his columns in *Charlie Hebdo* "Uncle Bernard" before being murdered by an Islamist commando, began his *Antimanuel d'économie* with this dedication: "To the unknown economist, who died for the economic war, who all his life magnificently explained the next day why he had been wrong the day before. To all those, alive and well, who savor the word gratuity".

Cognitive neuroscience, which I shall discuss in detail later, represents an attempt to overcome these difficulties and reduce the manifestations of the human mind (institutions, works of art, words and deeds, etc.) to physico-chemical phenomena, capable of being known by the means of physics and chemistry (in fact, physics, since chemistry can be considered a branch of physics). As we shall see, they are obviously incapable of delivering what they promise…

The final point is that sciences built on the model of mathematical physics are necessarily deterministic sciences. The fact that the rather crude determinism of Newtonian physics has been improved with the calculus of probabilities, and that remarkable sophistications have been introduced with quantum physics, changes nothing. We're still talking about determinism—I've developed this point at some length in *La matière et l'esprit* (Armand Colin, 2004). A machine built using the principles of quantum physics—a computer, for example—is a deterministic machine, even if the word "quantum" is one of those mysterious words that leave the layman speechless with admiration. The fact that the computer's components follow Heisenberg's uncertainty relations makes absolutely no difference. What's more, non-deterministic physics would be of no interest whatsoever! For physics to be a "practical science", it has to formulate laws that allow us to predict certain phenomena. And quantum physics provides remarkably accurate predictions: it can predict certain phenomena with an uncertainty of less than 10-10, something that good old classical physics is rigorously incapable of doing. Looking to Heisenberg's principle of indeterminacy for some kind of freedom immanent in nature is therefore pure fantasy. As Alan Sokal and Jean Bricmont pointed out in *Impostures intellectuelles* (Odile Jacob, 1997), it's all very well for those who indulge in the mirages of analogy.

This question encompasses another: can we reduce the causality of living beings to physical causality? Are we not led to suppose that living beings are, in reality, subject to a teleonomy, to use Jacques Monod's term (see *Chance and Necessity*)? It's easy to accept that the scientist, as a method, is "deterministic": every phenomenon studied must have a cause that we're looking for, otherwise the research stops immediately! But there's a gulf between this local determinism, specific to a limited set of reproducible phenomena, and the affirmation of a global determinism. We can imagine that such determinism has a reality, but it's the same kind of position as believing in God. I can always postulate that, knowing perfectly well the state of the universe 10 billion years ago, I could predict the collision of a meteorite with the Earth, the extinction of the

75

great saurians and the appearance of *homo sapiens* and, why not, the birth of the author of this book and the chain of circumstances that led him to write about it! This "total science" is properly a delusional idea of a religious nature. We have to admit once and for all that a finite being can only have finite knowledge, and what's more, knowledge that is that of a human being with human eyes, human ears and all sorts of other perfectly human things. It could even be argued that to claim that an infinite universe can be deterministic is a logical contradiction, since it would be tantamount to fitting an infinite chain of causes and effects into a finite discourse. In fact, it's probably more accurate to say that the universe is above all a vast chaos in which we try to bring a little order, but which quickly descends into a new chaos when our fresh theory comes up against facts that don't fit. If chance is the meeting of two independent causal series, as Augustin Cournot defined it, then we have to admit that there are an infinite number of independent causal series in our universe that will give rise to an infinite number of random phenomena. Here we find a vision of the world that more closely resembles that of the atomists (Leucippus, Democracy, Epicurus) than that of the Stoics or Aristotelians, who saw the world as the beautiful order of reason.

All these questions, which are stirring up the small world of epistemology and the philosophy of science, are, in fact, unsolvable as soon as they are posed as belonging solely to the philosophy of science or to what is often pompously called the "scientific method". If these questions seem so important, it's only because Galileo-type science has been made the sole model of truth, with all other approaches deemed weak or irretrievably perverted by "metaphysics"—the ultimate abomination! Husserl asks a good question:

> Scientific, objective truth is exclusively the observation that what the world—whether physical or spiritual—*actually* is. But is it possible for the world, and the human being within it, to have any

Becoming Machines

real meaning, if the sciences only accept as true what can be observed in this kind of objectivity, if history has nothing more to teach us than the fact that all the forms of the spiritual world, all the rules of life, all the ideals, all the norms that gave men their garb in every age, are formed like fleeting waves, and as they are undone again, so it has always been, so it will always be, so reason will always turn into unreason, and benefits into evils?

The crisis of the European sciences and transcendental
phenomenology, 1935-1936

It is easy to understand why Husserl makes this paradoxical observation: the development and success of modern science have led to a "radical crisis of life in European humanity", so that philosophy today threatens to "succumb to skepticism, irrationalism and mysticism" (*Op. cit.*, p. 9). There is much more to be said about this profound book, which is Husserl's last great work. I'll come back to it later. Suffice it to say that mathematical physics, whose great inventor was Galileo, leads, when made the archetype of all truth, to the pure and simple elimination of life in favor of mechanics. It's no coincidence that the triumph of mathematical physics, of mechanics, was accompanied by the fashion for automata, the famous automata of Vaucanson or Baron de Klempelen—including the hoax of the chess-playing Turk (see below). In 1748, La Mettrie set out the program for modern times with *L'homme-machine*. The end of life was in sight. It's not only miscreants who dare to make these analogies. Leibniz, who devoted part of his work to the "cause of God" (the subject of his *Theodicy*), defines the living being as an automaton, and the whole of creation as the work of a great architect who is above all a brilliant watchmaker who has set all his automatons so that they all correspond to each other without needing to communicate with each other. Humanity in all its history is little more than a Vaucanson duck on God's scale...

What Characterizes Life

Nothing better illustrates the triumph of the machine paradigm, and the radical transformation of human life it entails, than the development of what we call "life sciences", in the official terminology of the French Ministry of Education, or biology, which can also be translated as the science or discourse of life, our life sciences are not the sciences of a certain form of life (*bios* in Greek), but rather the science of the living (*zoè*, the simple fact of living), although this distinction, on which Giorgio Agamben builds much of his main work, *Homo sacer,* is philologically contested. We'll see shortly that the current "sciences of life" don't study life, but a certain kind of object we call "living beings". However, to constitute this "science of life", we had to repress all the ancient visions attached to this word, and ruthlessly remove all those "epistemological obstacles" that prevented us from treating life as if it were a question of geometric objects.

What we teach in schools under the name of life sciences—formerly known as "natural sciences"—could practically begin with Aristotle. Aristotle is the true initiator of this science, with his *History of Animals* and his *Treatise on the Parts of Animals.* Following in Aristotle's footsteps, an immense amount of work was carried out by naturalists, who observed, classified and described all living things. The last great specialists of this natural history were undoubtedly the Swede Carl von Linné (1707-1778) and the Frenchman Georges-Louis Leclerc de Buffon (1707-1788), whose *Histoire naturelle* (36 volumes published during his lifetime and 8 posthumous volumes) constitutes a veritable encyclopedia of all the knowledge of naturalists, and an innovative whole, if we understand the importance of the volumes Buffon devotes to that particular living being, man. While today's physicists learn nothing from reading Aristotle's physics, the naturalists' work of description and classification remains, even for us, a scientific endeavor. And Buffon's influence on Lamarck and Darwin cannot be underestimated. In short, yesterday's natural science can still matter to us, and we can't so easily establish a clear-cut separation between today's biology and yesterday's natural history. There has indeed been a scientific revolution, in Kuhn's terms, but it is far less clear-cut than the "Galilean revolution". We must, however, make the effort to understand how modern biology, with its considerable technical applications, came about, and how it marked a radical break with the natural history of the Ancients.

Aristotle proposes a method of classification and a general theory of living beings, as animate beings, i.e. with one or more souls. Plants have a vegetative soul that ensures their nourishment, growth and reproduction. Animals have, in addition to this vegetative soul, a sensitive and motor soul: animals feel the actions of the external world upon them, and they express their sensations. They are also capable of movement. Humans, on the other hand, are animals with an "intellective" soul, capable of producing concepts and exercising reason. This science of life, which drew heavily on the observation and descriptions of naturalists, was based on one premise: there is something invisible in living beings that nonetheless animates them—a soul! Or rather, three kinds of soul.

Curiously, moreover, a tripartition quite similar to Aristotle's can be found, in a very different form, in MacLean's three-brain theory, popularized by Arthur Koestler in *The Ghost in the Machine* (1967): in humans, there are several superimposed layers—the reptilian brain, the paleomammalian brain and the cortical brain— which are the successive layers laid down by evolution.

For Aristotle, being alive means being animated, but animated doesn't simply mean there's movement: the puppet is animated by the puppeteer! But that doesn't mean it's alive. To be animated is to be animated by a soul (*animus*). The soul is the form of which the body is the matter, and it is life that distinguishes the animate from the inanimate. For Aristotle, movement is not just the act of moving through space; generation and corruption, the passage from power to act, are also movement. Animate means having a soul or breath, which is nothing other than the breath of life. Breath comes from within; it is a power proper to being, its own essence, in the sense of what makes it be.

But this first definition is insufficient, because in reality, it's nature as a whole that is life for the Greek philosophers. *Physis* is first and foremost that which is born and develops, only to die. The *natura* of the Latins is an offshoot of Greek *physis*: nature is everything that is born and grows—*natura* in Latin derives from the verb *nascor* (*natum* supinum), meaning "to be born". The Stoics saw the world itself as a living being, a large animal made up of small animals such as humans, horses and ants, as well as the stars and the Earth. And to understand what happens to each and every one of us, we need to see things from the point of view of the "big animal", of the links that unite all its parts, and of the general sympathy of all living things.

However naive these early philosophers' ideas of life may seem, they are also perfectly obvious. We recognize life in the process of birth, growth and the inevitable decay of all things, in this "world of generation and corruption" of ours. Artificial flowers don't fade! Only dust can settle on it. We see that living things reproduce, and that children resemble their parents without being carbon copies. And we see that every living being pursues its own goal, its *telos*, which is first and foremost to keep itself alive and ensure as much eternity as there is power in it for such a task, even if the most elementary form of this eternity boils down to reproduction. We can easily observe that the living develop into increasingly complex organizations. Primitive forms, cells without nuclei, such as bacteria, combine to form cells with nuclei, which are the first unicellular animals; these may group together in colonies, such as coral reefs, or in more complex organizations, such as the mycelium of fungi ; The most complex form is that of man, with his large brain and billions of interconnected neurons that enable him to form an even more complex organism, a body made up of many people, which is called a society! There are waves: explosions of forms and mass extinctions. There is a history, in the truest sense of the word, of nature. Nothing ever reproduces itself identically, and if the theory of evolution proposes a general mechanism to explain descent with modification, we should perhaps go further and try to understand how evolution itself can evolve, as Anne Fagot-Largeault asked in her lecture at the Collège de France (see her lecture at the Collège de France on "The ontology of becoming" and the book of the same name). The problem raised is a thorny one: if living beings are becoming beings, is knowledge of such beings possible, and even to what extent are they beings in the strict sense of the word? They are becoming in act, if we dare use this expression, which is rather an oxymoron. Plato clearly poses the question: how is it possible to have knowledge of what is passing away? How can we call by the same name something that changes? Living is precisely that: changing, passing, and what's more, in directions that are practically impossible to predict.

We could also say that what characterizes life is that it is an impulse towards realization. The embryo is the potential adult individual, but only in potential, and each being thus possesses its own movement that leads it to realize its own essence, to become in act what it is at first only in potential. If we study the parts of animals, we can only understand them as part of the vital, finalized process, and they are characterized by their function, in the knowledge that, as Aristotle repeats, nature does nothing in vain. Beings that truly deserve to be considered as such, those that are not such or such by accident, are entelechies: there is a principle that drives them to become what they are. Inert things are nothing but what they can contribute to the production of a living being.

Bergson could be exhumed from the vault of the philosophy classroom where he was buried. In *L'évolution créatrice* (1907), he attempts a general history of life, from which human intelligence has emerged. He begins by noting that :

> [...] human intelligence feels at home as long as we leave it among inert objects, more especially among solids, where our action finds its fulcrum and our industry its working tools, that our concepts have been formed in the image of solids, that our logic is above all the logic of solids, that, by the same token, our intelligence triumphs in geometry, our intelligence triumphs in geometry, where the kinship of logical thought with inert matter is revealed, and where intelligence has only to follow its natural movement, after the lightest possible contact with experience, to go from discovery to discovery with the certainty that experience is marching behind it and will invariably prove it right.

We therefore have great difficulty in defining what life is, because our intelligence is born of practical needs and action on things. Our intelligence is oriented towards action, i.e. towards what is predictable and on which we can act, and is powerless to think about life. It's true, as Günther Anders points out, that when phenomenology speaks of the object posed by consciousness, it's not primarily a purely cognitive approach, since the first object is the prey that must be reached, and the separation of subject and object is abolished in consumption! And indeed, all sciences are born out of the need for action. *Homo faber*, the man who makes, far precedes *homo loquax*, the man who knows everything and talks about everything. But Bergson does not want to give up on delving into the meaning of life, and refuses to stick to "the mechanistic representation that understanding will always give us, a representation that is necessarily artificial and symbolic, since it reduces the total activity of life to the form of a certain human activity, which is only a partial and local manifestation of life, an effect or a residue of the vital operation" (*Op. cit.*). Understanding breaks down reality into simple, stable elements and then reconstructs their combination. But in doing

82

so, it misses the very essence of life. For Bergson, philosophy must proceed differently: it must go beyond understanding and its categories to create a theory of life that tells the story of the impetus that led to the different forms of consciousness and human intelligence. All this may seem a little nebulous, as Bergson himself admits. But this "nebulousness" stems from the difficulty of thinking the moving from the fixed, the becoming from that which does not become, for a true movement cannot be made from the summation of states, any more than duration is the summation of instants.

The ancient philosophy of life was teleological: according to all the great authors, from Aristotle to Leibniz and the vitalist scientists of the eighteenth and nineteenth centuries, living beings possess an end of their own, and their organs and structure can only be understood in relation to this end, for, as Aristotle repeats, "nature does nothing in vain". In contrast, the mechanistic thinking of modern physics recognizes only "efficient causes" and refuses to admit "final causes". This is also Darwin's method: to understand the evolution of living things by assuming neither direction nor finality. In so doing, Darwin clearly opposes Lamarck, who saw evolution as a process of adaptation and perfecting according to a predetermined direction. Bergson proposes to transcend this opposition between mechanism and teleology. The concept of élan vital articulates this transcendence. Life is this momentum, this accumulation of energy:

> [...] the whole of life, animal and vegetable, in all its essentials, appears as an effort to accumulate energy and then to release it into flexible, deformable channels, at the end of which it accomplishes infinitely varied work. (*Op. cit.*)

Life is the production of form and movement without a predefined end in view, but which follows a direction from which it can be diverted to take several different directions.

Bergson's ideas on the evolution of living things may be much criticized for being more inspired by Lamarckism, which was still very powerful in France at the beginning of the 20th century, than by Darwinian evolutionism, which he criticizes for its "mechanism". But he does make a considerable effort to think, as closely as possible, about the very nature of life, which we know in a purely intuitive way, but which we can scarcely formulate using the concepts bequeathed to us by physics and chemistry. We know perfectly well the difference between a world where life flourishes and a world of inert things. Even if life is microscopic, at first glance through the microscope, we recognize it. I can ask myself, as Descartes proposed in his experiment of "hyperbolic doubt", whether this man walking towards me is not an automaton so well made that he looks perfectly like a man. But I know that he is a man, a man like me, just as I know that the cat crossing the street is an animal, a living being and not a human artifact. There are doubtful cases: is a virus a living being or not, and *a fortiori*, should prions be classified as living beings? But in general, we know how to recognize life wherever it appears. How can we do this? Quite simply because we can feel it!

It will be objected that feeling is not a very convincing argument. Yet there's nothing more certain than the knowledge that comes from the feeling that we live, that we are life, through and through. Spinoza writes: "we feel and experience that we are eternal" (*Ethics*, V, scolie of proposition XXIII). What does he mean by this? Obviously, he doesn't mean that we will escape death. Each of us, as individuals, will eventually be overwhelmed by the power of external things. But there is something that we share with other human beings, and this something is precisely what we experience as living, immediately. It is precisely this knowledge of being living and of recognizing each other as living beings who potentially form a community that will far surpass the finitude of our individual existences. We have indeed, in a way, come to life, and we seek, as far as it is within us, to prolong this life, our own individually, but also the life of the *Nachgeborenen*, as Brecht speaks of, those who will be born after us. It was also Spinoza who asserted that "the body exists as we feel it" (*Ethics*, Part II, proposition XIII, corollary) and "By eternity, I mean existence itself, insofar as it is conceived as necessarily resulting from the sole definition of the eternal thing" (Part I, definition VIII). These three propositions do not derive from an understanding, but are immediate apprehensions of reality. The primary knowledge we have of life is therefore "knowledge of the third kind" in the Spinozist division of the kinds of knowledge, and not merely hypothetical knowledge derived from long chains of reasoning, still less knowledge by imagination or hearsay: I may imagine that I have a glass body, or that I am the King of Mexico (see Descartes, First Metaphysical Meditation), but I don't imagine that I'm alive, for the simple reason that I can't imagine that I'm not alive.

We could also follow Descartes and reflect on the strange experience of the cogito: all my beliefs having been suspended by the operation of methodical doubt, only one proposition remains that escapes doubt: "I am, I exist", and nothing can make this proposition false. Descartes could be reproached for taking a step forward without the slightest assurance when he deduces from this first proposition the definition of this ego, "I am a thing that thinks", since thought can only be deduced from the statement of what I feel in myself as a manifestation of the life of my mind. I feel that I feel, so I am life. And nothing else. Since life is nothing else, immediately, than this test of itself. And I have no reason to deduce from this that "I am a thing" of any kind.

I dwelt a little on Descartes and Spinoza, rationalist philosophers if there ever was one, but both presuppose, in different forms, this "feeling feeling", this life that experiences itself, outside of which no other knowledge is thinkable. In short, life is not a concept that can be constructed by a scientific approach, but the precondition of all conception, of all science. How do we learn the notions of true and false? Not by reading books on logic, but by comparing our perceptions with what we're told! The world is first and foremost, for this immediate perception, this relationship we create with things: theoretical constructions come later and are, in truth, much less certain than our first perceptions. What's more, to verify them, we first turn to our senses: I stopped believing in Santa Claus because I saw my parents arranging the presents at the foot of the tree, just as I saw the trace of a particle on a bubble chamber photograph. In the final analysis, it's our sensibility that validates all knowledge, because all knowledge is that of a living human being, an individual. Because I feel life within me, I am able to recognize life wherever it manifests itself. No one can seriously assume that he's not alive, that he's just a machine.

A Science of Living Beings

This understanding of life, of the primacy of life, was completely suppressed as biology became a science like any other. Not without difficulty: vitalism still dominated for a long time. Life is the set of forces that oppose death, said Bichat, a definition that was hardly scientific in truth. The great names of vitalism in the 18th century were Barthez and Bordeu. The latter is featured in Diderot's *Le rêve de d'Alembert*. In his *Nouveaux Éléments de la science de l'homme* (1778), Barthez wrote: "I call the vital principle of man the cause that produces all the phenomena of life in the human body. The name of this cause is rather indifferent and can be taken at will. If I prefer to call it the vital principle, it's because it presents a less limited idea than the name *impetum faciens* (*to énormôn*) given to it by Hippocrates, or other names by which the cause of the functions of life has been designated". The role of vitalism in the philosophy of science is twofold. On the one hand, vitalism leads to idealism: this vital principle that animates inanimate matter, it furiously resembles divine breath. On the other hand, vitalism considers that matter is, in essence, living matter, and this "vitalist" materialism erases the separation between inert and living matter, without reducing living matter to the figures and movements of Cartesian mechanism.

To make biology a science, we'll have to get rid of our immediate experience of life, but that doesn't mean it's absurd. It corresponds to the immediate knowledge we have not of nature in general, but simply of ourselves. Not without difficulty, we will also have to get rid of teleology in order to try and think of living beings solely in terms of physico-chemical causal laws.

If the seventeenth century was the century of physics and the eighteenth of chemistry, it was in the nineteenth century that biology emerged. The word, in fact, comes from the Frenchman Jean-Baptiste Lamarck, a specialist in invertebrates, whose first major course began in 1800. Until the 19th century, there was a science called "natural history", in the Greek sense of the word "histoire", which means an investigation. This natural history rested on two pillars: on the one hand, the anatomical, but also physiological and ecological description of living beings, and on the other, classification. But before the modern science of nature was consolidated—we used to speak of "natural sciences" in our school system—we need to examine its first steps. Descartes introduced mechanism into the approach to living beings and, in his own way, drew the conclusions of the new Galilean science. His "machine-animal" thesis is well known, at least by name. The body, for him, is an extended substance, fully knowable (in theory at least) by physics and chemistry, and susceptible of mathematical description, whereas the soul is a thinking substance, therefore not extended, whose knowledge is given to us directly by meditation, in that Cartesian experience of the *cogito*. The *Discourse on Method* is unambiguous:

[...] those who, knowing how many different automata, or moving machines, the industry of men can make without using very few parts, in comparison with the great multitude of bones, muscles, nerves, arteries, veins, and all the other parts that are in the body of every animal, will consider this body as a machine, which, having been made by the hands of God, is incomparably better ordered and has in itself more admirable movements, than any that can be invented by men.

[...] if there were such machines, which had the organs and figure of a monkey, or of some other animal without reason, we would have no way of recognizing that they were not in all respects of the same nature as these animals. (Part Five)

A little later, Descartes radicalized his thinking:

[...] I recognize no difference between the machines made by craftsmen and the various bodies that nature alone composes, except that the effects of machines depend only on the arrangement of certain pipes, or springs, or other instruments, which having to be in some proportion to the hands of those who make them, are always so large that their figures and movements can be seen, instead of the pipes and springs that cause the effects of natural bodies being ordinarily too small to be perceived by our senses. And it is certain that all the rules of mechanics belong to physics, so that all things that are artificial are with that natural.

Principles of Philosophy, Part 4, 1644, § 203

The thorny question remains: how can the soul and body communicate? Descartes shows the importance of the nerve system, through which fluids flow that he calls "animal spirits", and which communicate with the soul via a special part of the brain that Descartes identifies as the "pineal gland", today known as the epiphysis. We find a similar conception in Hobbes, with the difference that the great English philosopher attempts to explain mental faculties entirely in terms of bodily movements, from a very materialistic point of view.

These ingenious constructions did not last long. It was easy to see that a Vaucanson automaton was substantially different from a duck or a flute player. Hobbes, Descartes and their followers were asserting something without being able to prove it or begin to build a genuine science of the living. Harvey's pump model provided the first serious explanation of blood circulation, Descartes' "animal spirits" prefigured nerve impulses, etc., but much more was needed to build a real science of living beings. Nonetheless, these bold early attempts indicated a problem and a direction that would form the framework for many subsequent developments. The images Descartes uses to describe the human body or the anatomy of vision are often highly poetic, but virtually devoid of any scientific value.

Descartes didn't seem to grasp the real specificity of a living being, distinguishing it from a subtly engineered machine. Living beings form an organism that has, in its own perpetuation, its "vital principle". "Every being tends to persevere in its being", writes Spinoza: that's exactly what a living being does, persevere in its being. By rehabilitating the Aristotelian "entelechies" and arguing that everything is alive and that there are only individuals, in both senses of the word (forming an indivisible unity and being unique), Leibniz is not taking knowledge backwards, but paving the way for the steps forward that would be taken in the following century. Following in Leibniz's footsteps, Kant clearly defined what was at stake when dealing with living beings. In his *Critique of the Faculty of Judgment* (1790), he criticizes mechanism, showing that the comparison between a living being and a machine is radically flawed:

> In a watch, one part is the instrument of the movement of the others, but one cog is not the efficient cause of the production of another cog; one part may be there for the other, but it is not there because of that other part.

In a machine, the parts are side by side, and exist independently of each other. In a living being, the various parts of which it is composed produce one another, forming an organic unit.

It is for this reason that the cause that produces these and their form is not contained in the nature (of this matter), but outside it, in a being that, according to Ideas, can produce a whole through its causality. (*Op. cit.*)

Living beings produce themselves, according to their own internal principle, whereas machines are produced by a being that is external to them and acts according to its own ideas. This simple fact should be enough to ruin any strong artificial intelligence project. How can we computer-simulate a human brain to understand it?

This is also the reason why, in a watch, one cog cannot produce another, any more than a watch can produce other watches, by using (organizing) other materials for this purpose; it is also the reason why it does not replace the parts that have been removed from it, nor compensate for their defect in the first formation by involving the other parts, nor repair itself when it is out of order: yet all this we can expect from an organized nature. (*Op. cit.*)

Self-production, self-organization, the ability to preserve one's own structure: these are the fundamental traits that distinguish living beings. Henri Laborit defines living things in one word: a structure that preserves its structure!

The only raison d'être of a being is to be. That is, to maintain its structure. It's to keep itself alive. Without that, there would be no being. Note that plants can sustain themselves without moving. They draw their nourishment directly from the soil, right where they are. And thanks to the sun's energy, they transform the inanimate matter in the soil into their own living matter. Animals, and man as an animal, can only keep alive by consuming this solar energy, which has already been transformed by the plants. And that requires movement. They are forced to act within a space.

H. Laborit, in Mon oncle d'Amérique,
film by Alain Resnais, 1980

What Laborit is saying goes a long way—further, no doubt, than he himself envisages. A being that is in itself its raison d'être, that is an entelechy in Aristotle's thought, a being that lives to accomplish what it is in essence. And here we have a great biological scientist who, apparently without realizing it, is rehabilitating Aristotle, who had been dismissed from the scientific process in the seventeenth century. Laborit's words can also be interpreted differently: a being is alive when it possesses within itself the effort to persevere in its being, i.e. when it has a conatus in Spinoza's sense. Admittedly, Spinoza does not reserve conatus for living beings, but which beings seek to persevere in their being if not living beings? In inert things, there is nothing but the inertia that would correspond to this effort to persevere in one's being. Inert things make no effort. It's living beings who make the effort to persevere in their being.

Back to Kant, who continues:

> An organized being is therefore not a simple machine; for a machine has exclusively a *driving force*, but an organized being possesses in itself a *formative force* that it communicates to materials that do not have it (it organizes them), a driving force that is therefore transmitted and that cannot be explained by the simple power of movement (mechanism). (*Op. cit.*)

The formative force certainly evokes the old Aristotelian notions reworked by Leibniz. It also indicates that the mechanisms of causality, called efficient in old Scholasticism, are insufficient when it comes to understanding the living. We study the living world "as if" everything in it were arranged with a view to an end. This "as if" is decisive in Kantian thought, as elaborated in his theory of reflective judgment. Kant does not say that living beings are Aristotelian "entelechies". To say so would be to exceed the powers of reason, which cannot decide whether everything in nature proceeds from causality, or whether an end must be assumed. But to study living things, you have to assume an end, and act as if that end existed! This is exactly the approach taken by Jacques Monod (cf. *Le hasard et la nécessité*, 1970), who, after refuting all teleology, proposes to reintroduce a kind of teleological "as if", which he calls teleonomy.

Living, not Living

A clear separation between the fields of mechanics and the world of living beings had to be established before a true science of living beings could be created. The nineteenth century saw the birth of a new science, which emerged as an extension of natural history, but quickly distinguished itself from it. Lamarck's transformism greatly influenced French scientists for a very long time, and ultimately proved to be an obstacle to the introduction of Darwinism in France, prolonging the survival in this field of finalist or teleological conceptions, i.e. the idea of nature pursuing certain ends. But Lamarck's work, mainly his *Philosophie Zoologique*, mobilized resources and methods that would prove decisive for future science. As a specialist in invertebrates, the largest and most diverse class of animals, he rejected the rigid classifications of the naturalists and focused on "molecular variations" from one species to another. Instead of fixed essences (species), he sees the living world as a continuum that must be subjected to analysis, thereby demonstrating its profound unity.

But the founding events came after Lamarck. First came cell theory. The birth of cell theory came in 1839 with the publication of *Recherches microscopiques sur la conformité de structure et de crois-sance des animaux et des plantes* by Theodor Schwann (1810-1882). Schwann shows that the cell is the elementary structure of all living organisms, whether animal or plant, simple or complex. A cell is a structurally and functionally independent unit. Schwann identifies in animal cells the same characteristic elements (membrane, nucleus and nucleolus) of plant cells. In his view, the study of cell development should enable us to understand the morphogenesis of complex structures. Later, in 1855, the Polish cytologist Robert Remak (1815-1865), followed by the German Rudolf Virchow (1821-1902) in 1858, demonstrated that every cell originates from a pre-existing cell through division of its nucleus.

This theory does two important things:

1. it unifies the various fields of research by demonstrating the profound unity of all living things;

2. it brings to light the element of this science of the living (in this case, the cell).

Biology is not the science of life (a vague, overly polysemous term). It is the science of all those beings composed of fundamentally similar basic "bricks", the cells, which thus play a role analogous to atoms in the formation of modern chemistry. This clearly shows that a living organism can only be a self-regulating organism if it has a membrane separating the inside from the outside. This is clearly a fundamental characteristic that prohibits us from simply equating living beings, whatever their level of complexity, with machines—in a machine, there is no internal environment.

The second great foundation of modern biological science is the work of Charles Darwin. The publication of *The Origin of Species* in 1859 came after more than two decades of work and reflection before Darwin resigned himself to publishing the fruit of his meditations. If all living things are composed of the same basic elements, Darwin shows that they are all related, and that all living species are the descendants of species that have generally disappeared. And this evolution, far from being the work of a "great architect", an "intelligent design" or a benevolent providence, can only be explained by the laws of nature, causal laws that unite chance and necessity.

The third major foundation is the theory of reproduction. Here, we should mention a few milestones. The monk Gregor Mendel (1822-1884) discovered the first laws of heredity, rediscovered and developed by Hugo de Vries at the end of the 19th CENTURY. In 1871, the first observations were made on what would later be known as DNA. In 1882, Walther Flemming discovered the role of chromosomes.

With these three pillars of biological wisdom—cell theory, the theory of species evolution and the theory of heredity—we are indeed dealing with a scientific revolution in the sense of Thomas Kuhn (see *The Structure of Scientific Revolutions*): a whole swath of old knowledge is swallowed up, and a new field of knowledge emerges in a transfigured landscape. We have merely outlined a few of the crucial steps that lay the foundations of biology as a science, as a new science profoundly different from natural history. It is a modern science, because it is essentially analytical (breaking down the complex into simple elements), seeking rigorous laws of development, and in the process of linking up with chemistry and physics (molecular biology). Biological science thus presupposes, in order to exist, the objectification of manifestations of life. But, at the same time, the idea of life is disappearing. As François Jacob says, life is not a laboratory object!

Reductionism

The elimination of life by the life sciences is a coup de force, but a necessary one if we accept that Galilean physics and post-Lavoisier chemistry are the models for all natural science.

All science is reductionist. It cannot accept occult causes, mysterious "formative forces" or finality imposed from who knows where. Claude Bernard, in his *Introduction à l'étude de la médecine expérimentale* (1865), explains what the scientific approach should be:

> [...] the science of the phenomena of life can have no other basis than the science of the phenomena of gross bodies, and [...] in this respect there is no difference between the principles of the biological sciences and those of the physical-chemical sciences. (II, I, 1)

In principle, then, biology is no more than a construct based on physics and chemistry (the science of "gross bodies"). The specific characteristics of living beings appear to us as such only because our knowledge is still insufficient:

> But if we reflect on it, we will soon see that this spontaneity of living bodies is a mere appearance, and the consequence of a certain mechanism of perfectly determined environments; so that, in the end, it will be easy to prove that the manifestations of living bodies, as well as those of raw materials, are dominated by a necessary determinism that binds them to conditions of a purely physical-chemical order (II, I, 2).

We couldn't be more precise. According to Claude Bernard, the same determinism governs both "raw bodies" and living organisms. And so, there is no essential difference between what astronomers, physicists, chemists and biologists observe. So life doesn't exist, it's just an illusion that stems from our inadequate knowledge. It's worth noting, however, that Claude Bernard seeks to grasp the specificity of living beings and maintains that their fundamental characteristic is the separation between the internal and external environment, something that doesn't exist in any machine.

Living beings, in fact, if subjected to the analytical treatment of any science, never exhibit what makes them alive; they never exhibit that "formative" force of which Kant speaks, nor that internal finality of which Laborit speaks. Anatomy makes it possible to separate organs, but once the organs have been separated, the living being no longer exists; it is no more than a corpse. Tissues are made up of living cells, but once separated, these cells become dead objects, unless kept alive in a culture medium. Cells themselves are made up of molecules, but molecules only interact with each other through chemical reactions. The exchange of energy within a living being is governed by the laws of thermodynamics. And so on: knowledge of the living requires that life be eliminated as a relevant object of science. In our school system, biology and geology are wrongly called "life and earth sciences". The ideal application of biology is basically forensic medicine!

We are faced with an apparent contradiction: there is no science that does not seek to explain the complex by the simple, and that does not, in the final analysis, reduce all reality to the sequence of phenomena according to constant causal laws. But, on the other hand, we know that biology, as a physical-chemical science, ultimately misses the essential point: understanding what it means for the living to live.

Let's take a look at an excerpt from Husserl:

> Mathematical physics is an extraordinary tool for understanding the world in which we actually live, the nature that always retains its empirical and concrete unity in identity, despite changing relativities. It makes a physical technique practically possible. But it has its limits, not in that empirically we never get beyond the level of approximation, but in that only a thin layer of concreteness is effectively captured. Physiology, biophysics as the doctrine of organic bodies in the totality of the concrete organic world, can have recourse to physics as often as we like (the organism being idealizable as a mathematical body), but the fact remains that, as a matter of principle, biology can

never be cancelled out by physics. Biophysical reality and causality can never be reduced to physical reality and causality.

*The crisis of the European sciences
and transcendental phenomenology*, 1935-1936

Husserl clearly maintained that the biological is irreducible to the physical-chemical. However, the development of the life sciences over the past century seems to have proved him wrong. On the contrary, Husserl considers that physics, oblivious to its origins and the idealizations it has used to constitute itself as a science, wrongly claims to be able to reduce all concrete phenomena to its mathematical laws.

Yet many authors refute the possibility of applying the deterministic principles of physical laws to the living world. Let's take a more telling example. A dinosaur astronomer equipped with a powerful telescope could (perhaps) have foreseen the collision of the meteorite with the Earth and the upheavals this would cause. He could also have predicted the respective positions of the Sun, Earth and Moon a million years later, or even in our own time. On the other hand, a Darwinian dinosaur who knew all the laws of genetics and epigenetics could not have foreseen that the disappearance of his own species and the mass extinction at the end of the secondary era would leave the way open for mammals and, among them, the genus *homo* and the species *homo sapiens*, from which Newton and Darwin would emerge! The theory of evolution is a perfectly rational one, accurately accounting for a growing number of facts. It even appears to be one of the best-confirmed scientific theories, but it remains radically incapable of providing predictions that can be measured. It can tell us that a living organism, subjected to a given selective pressure, will "evolve" by concentrating mutations, but it can predict neither what these mutations will be, nor the final result that this evolutionary sequence will produce. If we were to apply Popper's criteria to the theory of

97

evolution, it's not certain that it would pass the test of refutability: after the fact, if an organism has survived, it's because chance had selected the right assets to survive. This is a very troublesome observation, and explains why substantive, rather than obscurantist or creationist, critiques of Darwinism are often very serious. In *What Darwin got* wrong, Jerry Fodor (an author we'll meet again later) and Massimo Piatelli-Palmarini show that evolution by natural selection is an explanation only at the margins. Internal constraints are the most important. For the most part, they use either "neutralist" arguments (evolution does not, for the most part, provide adaptive advantages), or arguments drawn from the law of forms (the forms of living beings determine their evolution), which would be a modernized and sophisticated Aristotelianism. The authors leave open the question that the standard theory of evolution is not a theory, but merely a scheme. This is obviously very embarrassing: here's a science that is definitively incapable of making predictions (in the scientific sense), just a few forecasts as reliable as the weather forecast on the TV news…

For its part, genetics, or rather the genetic theory of reproduction, seemed to have all the trappings of a rigorous science, and its mathematization provided solid guarantees. After all, we now have something constant, the gene, which seems to resist all evolution, all unpredictable transformation. We have even been able to speak of a new eleatism in this respect. The gene is! It is being par excellence. Dawkins even goes so far as to maintain that, in truth, singular living beings are nothing more than means for genes to reproduce. To the old Platonic question "How can we have knowledge of that which is only becoming?", we now have an answer: the gene is that which does not become, it is that unchanging being which alone can be the object of knowledge!

But in science, certainties don't last. In 2000, Jean-Jacques Kupiec and Pierre Sonigo published *Ni Dieu ni gène*, a book which attacked the dogmas of genetics, arguing that genetics was not a science in the sense that physics is a science, but only one theory among others, and even a "pre-Galilean" theory. This genetic theory of heredity was barely more scientific than astrology! They proposed to consider all reproductive processes not at the level of the gene, but at the level of the cell, in Darwinian fashion. For them, life is fundamentally anarchic, and Kupiec even asked the question: what if genetics were a gigantic scam? In 2007, Sylvie Pouteau published a collective work entitled *Génétiquement indéterminé*, which took stock of new research that challenged the "dogma" of genetics.

If we follow this line of new thinking in our understanding of the living world, we don't need to reintroduce metaphysical principles such as the "vital force", but we do need to abandon the idea of the living world as a deterministic machine. In physics, we can, at the very least, conceive of a world without history: the present was already contained in the past and itself contains the future. We've even been able to reconstruct "the first three minutes of the universe", thus establishing a metaphor as a rigorous scientific concept! Today, we even have the story of the gradual extinction of the Universe in the *Big Freeze*... Basically, in physics, time doesn't exist, because time creates nothing. I agree that this conception of physics is a little schematic, and perhaps here too we need to introduce more chance and indeterminacy. But it's clear that our knowledge of the living world cannot fit into this Galilean schema. The extraordinary "invention" of forms demonstrated by the living kingdom should be enough to persuade us of this. A lifeless world is hopelessly monotonous! Spinoza already sensed that we are unable to imagine all that nature can produce of its own accord. What we can't imagine often leads us to deny it the right to exist. A fatal error! Leibniz maintained that no two leaves on a tree are identical, and our world is, according to him, made up of an infinite number of living beings, all different. And, for the most part, the evolution of living things is beyond the reach of our predictions. The mutations of a being as unsophisticated as a virus escape the attention of scientists the world over, mobilized to track it down!

The attempt to reduce living beings to their physico-chemical composition undoubtedly provides a usable gain in knowledge. "Genetic scissors" techniques hold out the promise of being able, at will, to create living beings with properties known in advance. Moving from science-fiction cinema to the laboratory and from *Jurassic Park* to reality, a fund has been raised to set up a program to recreate, thanks to CRISPR, species that are now extinct, such as the dodo or the woolly mammoth... There's something quite terrifying in all this, but also perhaps one of the manifestations of the technological bluff denounced by Jacques Ellul.

We know and can only know a thin layer of reality. Life goes far beyond what can be scientifically objectified. This is the reality on which the life sciences stumble. This is why biology is so far removed from the rigorous constructs of physics. It's also why metaphors so often replace missing concepts. Normally, a science has no need of functionalist explanations, those explanations that explain nothing and merely observe what is after the fact—the nose is for wearing the glasses! And yet, biology remains part and parcel functionalist. Thus, François Jacob and his followers reject any idea of finalism in nature: evolution is not the result of the calculation of an ingenious god-engineer, who would have ensured that "everything is for the best in the best of all possible worlds". They recognize the fundamentally random dimension of evolution. But when they want to delve deeper into evolutionary mechanisms, they introduce the notion of bricolage: living beings are the result of natural bricolages in which new beings are created from existing materials and rearranged. Either. This presentation of evolution is very eloquent... but when we replace the engineer-god who graduated from Polytechnique with a nature-god, a tinkerer who specializes in recycling, we're still stuck with the same conception of a more or less finalized nature. Perhaps it's simply because it's hardly possible to speak of living beings in any other way, and because the physical-chemical vision, resolutely alien to all finalistic thinking, is incapable of saying anything interesting about living beings insofar as they are living beings, and not just conglomerates of molecules. The vision of emergent realities, constituted at different levels and thus giving rise to new properties at level N, not deducible from those of the elements at level $N-1$, is the subject of much epistemological criticism, as it struggles to explain how these properties can emerge, if we believe that any serious explanation is necessarily a reductionist, micro-macro-type explanation. We can agree with Kant and Jacques Monod (cf. *Chance and Necessity*) that the living world gives rise to a kind of finality without a predetermined end—not a teleology, but a teleonomy.

The fact remains that the most elementary observation of life, in general, shows the radical unpredictability of living beings, which don't follow agreed patterns, develop in a quite extraordinary variety of forms and leave little room for anything other than local theories, most of them highly empirical. We need only recall how everything and the opposite of everything was uttered during the incomprehensible Covid-19 epidemic, to be assured that scientists often promise more than they can deliver. A little humility, a sense of our limits and some critical thinking can't hurt.

The Body Experience

Before tackling the study of paramecia and viruses, we need to have a basic knowledge of living things, that of our own bodies. However, the objectification achieved by the creation of a science of living beings comes at the price of losing the meaning of life. As François Jacob used to say, life is not a laboratory object. Move along, there's nothing to see. But it's very boring. There's another way to rediscover the essence of life: the phenomenological approach followed by Husserl, Merleau-Ponty and Michel Henry, which has already been mentioned. If life is first and foremost the life that is experienced, its objectification is necessarily lacking. We'll return to this question in greater detail in a later chapter, when we tackle the issue of neuroscience. For now, let's stick to Spinoza's maxim: our body exists as we feel it. We are not our brains, nor are we a pure spirit that inadvertently has a body. Life is understood both as thought (I feel) and as body (I feel my body, I am this feeling body).

Everyone can say: I don't have a body, I am this body as much as I am this thought that is thought, even though the thought we have is often posited as external to us: I have a thought, a thought comes to me. We have the first, immediate, obvious experience of bodies, and of our body in particular. In fact, only bodies and their transformations can be the object of experience, if experience is the relationship between my sensibility and the things of the world. Is it possible to speak of experience outside of this experience, which is necessarily rooted in the body? How can I experience what I haven't seen, heard, smelled or touched? And, in so doing, I've seen that I saw, felt that I felt, and so on. But this experience of the body is immediately posed in a dual way, according to the very subtleties of the grammar and semantics of the French language. The preposition "de", insofar as it introduces the complement of the noun, can just as well be a mark of possession (like the Latin genitive) or a mark of origin or place, and so on. The experience of the body is thus the body's own experience, the experience that the body makes, or the experience that the subject makes of the body, this time as the object of experience.

We're not done with the polysemy of the expression "body experience". To be experienced is to have lived and not to be confronted with things as a neophyte. We learn from experience, and our bodies memorize that experience (like learning to swim or ride a bike). But experimental knowledge is something else: Fresnel's mirror experiment corroborates the thesis of the wave nature of light. So, in the same way as when we spoke of the body, we can distinguish between the subjective side of experience (Husserl's "*Erlebnis*") and the objectification that takes place in experimental knowledge.

Let's start at the beginning. The body experiences itself, because to be is to be affected. We experience ourselves, and it's only in this way that we gradually come to be-human, to be-in-the-world. Subjective life, that of the first cries, that of the soothing mother's breast, that of the first pains and pleasures, of the first caresses, is first and foremost the experience of the body in the simplest, least "epistemological" sense of the term. Right from the start, we know that pleasure and suffering are of the same nature. This is flesh, as Maurice Merleau-Ponty and Michel Henry think of it (even if they don't think of it in the same way), flesh that is not matter, but "the winding of the visible onto the seeing body, of the tangible onto the touching body" (Merleau-Ponty, *Le visible et l'invisible*, 1964). The world doesn't exist, and it doesn't need the world. We don't need to "prove" our own existence, and we don't need to engage in the extravagant exercise of withdrawing into ourselves in a reflexive act, suspending all the contents of our thoughts in order to isolate pure thought in act, the "I am, I exist" of Descartes' IInd *Metaphysical Meditation*. If the operation of the "*cogito*" were the search for this "I exist" as a primary certainty, it would be both ridiculous and pointless, and, fortunately, the meaning of Descartes' work lies elsewhere. The experience we have of ourselves is, through and through, a carnal experience. It precedes any reflexive operation, any induction, any synthesis. But in the present, in the moment when I burn myself, there is no sentence, no words, no generalization, no cognitive ambition: there is only the pure experience of burning, the experience of suffering. Flesh reveals itself to itself.

Secondly, the world is given to and by the body itself. The world "exists" precisely because I exist as a body placed at the center of the world it orders. It is insofar as I am this body, this flesh, that I come up against the world, that my gaze stops on things, not by flying over them, by describing them "objectively", from the point of view of nowhere, but by perceiving the obstacle that prevents the gaze from getting lost in pure nothingness. And all things are arranged in relation to me, they are situated in relation to me, in relation to the possibilities of my bodily organization, those that are within reach and those that are so blurred in the distance that I can barely see them. Front, back, right, left, up, down—it's my body that organizes it all. Space, and indeed space itself, can only be organized by a sensing, perceptive body. Of course, I can situate myself (I'm in the middle of the room, facing the window), but this experience, the one that assigns spatial coordinates to my own body, is a second experience, where, through abstraction, I try to see myself as if I were elsewhere, as if I were in any place... But this objectification of myself is a reflexive process, that is, strictly speaking, a return upon itself of the gaze I've cast all around me. Apart from this process of abstraction, this process of fabrication in the representation of an unreality, I cannot situate myself in the world; on the contrary, it is I who situates the world and organizes it, giving it consistency and reality. So the world is the body's experience, because it is the body's experience. The body is our "being in the world", and it is through the body that we are in the world, that we are at all.

Thirdly, we experience the body of others as we are transformed into a body-object for others. In the world, there are other bodies, those of things and those of living beings and, among living beings, other humans. In other living bodies, we spontaneously recognize the manifestations of life. And just as the subject is never a pure subject (a thought in the process of thinking) that could take its own body as an object, just as the spectator takes a look at the show, we cannot behave towards others as if they were just one thing among things. There is an immediate experience of intercorporeality, argues Merleau-Ponty.

Michel Henry, for his part, sees sexuality as revealing the essence of life and the mark of subjectivity. Sexuality engages a new form of bodily life that not only experiences the self, but also, and above all, the other. In this experience, the other is not posited as different and foreign, but as the possibility of joining life itself: "it would be through his body that we would have access to the other" (M. Henry, *Incarnation*). The erotic is to be understood here as the first, original manifestation of life, before any representation. Pornography, etymologically "the writings or drawings of prostitutes", on the other hand, proceeds from "mise en image", i.e. the substitution of image for life. In eroticism, access to others is not through seduction or control (war, violence), but through the search for coincidence.

In contrast to this coincidence-based experience of another's body, Sartre's much more agonistic thesis is based on the gaze of the other. I only become myself—a being for myself—through the other. But in the gaze of the other, I am objectified. I become a pure in-itself. The fundamental shame is the shame of being an object for another. Here, the experience of shame is the primary experience. Shame reveals to me the gaze of others and myself at the end of that gaze. To find myself, to recognize myself, I need the other. What bothers us is that the other holds the key to who we are, and that's what we're ashamed of. We're ashamed of not being our own foundation. Hence the famous line at the end of *Huis clos*: "Hell is other people". Not because they "ruin" our lives, because they disturb us, because they oppose us, but because we can't do without them to access ourselves, because the foundation of who we are is in their eyes. Hence the tendency to play them and ourselves off against each other, in bad faith. Duality, then, in the experience of the other's body: on the one hand, the search for coincidence and, on the other, the impossible coincidence.

Finally, we have the objective experience of the body in general, a body that is no longer mine or someone else's, but a body in general, a represented body, like the body of the flayed by Vesalius, author of the first *Structure of the Human Body*. This objectified body is an unreal body, since it is merely a representation or idealization of the body. The experience of the body cuts it up into functional units. It's a body in pieces, shattered. The doctor's gaze presupposes this decomposition of the body. On the one hand, the doctor has a patient, with whom he talks, whose suffering he tries to understand, but on the other, when he takes action, the doctor has only a wound to suture, no longer living, sensitive flesh. Claude Bernard used to say, perhaps in jest, that he had never found the soul under his scalpel. But neither did he find life under his scalpel, as it dissolves into physico-chemical processes. The scientific body is a lifeless body, a machine, as Descartes so aptly guessed.

As useful as it is, as vital even, this scientific, objective vision of the body does not give us the experience of our body in the strict sense of the word, but that of a "biological simulacrum", to borrow a phrase from Merleau-Ponty.

To conclude, let's ask ourselves what is so metaphysically fundamental about this experience of the body. "We feel and experience that we are eternal", says Spinoza. A mysterious phrase that becomes clearer if we take into account this definition from the *Ethics*: "By eternity, I mean existence itself." Indeed, the experience of the body is the experience of existence itself, and never of non-existence! Spinoza goes on to say that the thought of death is an inadequate thought, that is, a truncated and therefore distorted thought. Why is this? Quite simply because, not only can we say nothing serious about death other than agreed-upon nonsense and consolations for the bereaved, but also because we never have any experience of death. The experience of suffering, the worst kind of suffering, is still an experience of life. Nothing in this experience of our bodies implies the cessation of existence. Of course, we know that we will die, in a vague way, but we can never know what it is to die. In other words, if we emerge from morbid affects, from all those that diminish our power to act, we do feel that we are eternal, not because our soul is immortal (which, according to Spinoza, it cannot be), but because we experience existence itself insofar as we are body.

None of this can be objectified! None of this can be the subject of a science in the sense of the natural sciences. Biological science, which at best can help life, and at worst destroy it, is therefore unable to deal with the essential. But this "being-in-the-world" that we are is, at the same time, the "transcendental condition" of all knowledge: for there to be any knowledge whatsoever, there must be a subject, a living individual who produces this knowledge as one of the modalities of his life. Objectivity is not primary, it only comes as one of the modalities of the relationship of this subject we are to the world, just as technique is nothing other than a manifestation of life to reproduce life, to fulfill this vital teleology, which capital inverts, as Marx showed.

The Oblivion of Life

The living world as we know it in biology is no more than a structure, a set of physico-chemical phenomena in which regularities have been highlighted through functions (nutrition, respiration, reproduction…). But none of this is life. The scientific approach leads us to see living beings "too closely". Merleau-Ponty puts it clearly:

> […] a living body, seen too closely, and without any background against which it stands out, is no longer a living body, but a material mass as strange as lunar landscapes, as can be seen by looking at a segment of epidermis with a magnifying glass;—seen too far away, it

loses the value of living, and is no more than a doll or an automaton. The living body itself appears when its microstructure is neither too much nor too little visible, and this moment also determines its real shape and size.

Phenomenology of Perception, 1945, p. 346-347

All the expressions in our language that speak of life make it proceed from the subject's interiority. The person who comes back to life is aware of the world around him, whereas all that had disappeared during his fainting or coma. Others see him come back to life, but only after the fact, after he has experienced himself as alive. Life comes in all possible colors: it can be happy or sad, beautiful or hellish, a dog's life or a hobo's life, you can lose your taste for life… As we age, we wonder whether our lives have been full. However, biology is not interested in life, in this life, but in the objectified body of living beings. Michel Henry thus attempts to build a philosophy of life.

> But isn't what makes life concrete, and the reason why its mere name moves us, lost if we exclude from it determinations such as food, sexuality and all the activities that make up the substance of this life, which is everyone's and about which everyone talks? Eating, dressing, meeting and embracing others—none of these things are foreign to life; they are its primary and indisputable manifestations.
>
> Michel HENRY, "Qu'est-ce que cela que nous appelons la vie?",
Philosophiques, 5(1), 1978

Life is not external, but internal. Life is not worldly! Of course, it is the source of all externalization and objectification. Science itself is one of life's manifestations. Nowhere is this oblivion of life more evident than in the biotechnologies we'd better call technologies of death (thanatotechnologies). They are nothing more than the implementation of biology as a physical-chemical science, and they are developing because they correspond very closely to the needs of the development of the "commodification" of the world, which is simply the other name for the privatization of the living. Let's start with the most obvious. The chemical industry deals with life by killing it: insecticides, pesticides, fungicides—this is how biological technoscience has penetrated modern agriculture, with all those "-cide" products that kill insects, especially pollinating insects, and birds, which live off the food that insects unwillingly provide. And these products end in homicide—farmers, arboriculturists and winegrowers are among the main victims of this war on life. Scientists have always been there to testify that these "-cides" were harmless to man, just as the French Academy of Medicine certified in the 1950s that asbestos was a miracle product that posed no danger to man. It is striking to see how, while the harmfulness of chemical killers has now been proven beyond doubt, it is almost impossible to achieve a ban on these deadly or seriously morbid poisons. Economic considerations are advanced with the morgue of those who "know" what's good for us, confirming that it is indeed the increasingly disintegrating death drive that drives the movement of capital: kill them all, God will recognize His own.

But death is still at work in cloning research. We learn that a Chinese laboratory has produced a wolf of an extinct variety, by cloning cells from one of the last members of this species. Elsewhere, researchers have produced a mouse embryo from the gametes of two male mice... A technique which, we have no doubt, will find many adepts when it comes to applying it to the human race. At the beginning of September 2023, Israeli scientists made public their exploit: they had succeeded in producing a "model" of a human embryo without ovules or spermatozoa, from the development of stem cells. The major "invention" of natural evolution was that of sexual reproduction, which produced the fabulous explosion of diversity we know today. Science promises to overcome this unfortunate and uncertain division of living organisms. Biological science doesn't invent anything; on the contrary, it strives to mass-produce the same thing, industrially. It seeks to eliminate what occurs naturally, of its own accord, and replace it with human artifice.

Let's repeat: if the biological sciences are going in these uninviting directions, it's not because they're being misused, but because they're structurally designed to do just that! Just as physics is designed to build machines and launch projectiles. Let's be clear: there is indeed an objective knowledge of living beings produced by biology—you'd have to have lost all common sense to dispute it! But this objective knowledge, which presupposes the ability to transform living beings into objects, leaves only a *caput mortuum* in the place of the living being. It's inevitable: science begins by breaking down the whole into its parts; it studies the links between the parts, the reciprocal relationships that form a system. From this properly analytical phase, it has derived clearly defined concepts (cell, nucleus, proteins, DNA, RNA, etc.). It can then reconstruct a model of the living being, a model so well imitated that it gives the illusion of being the thing itself. But it's an illusion, the very illusion of science, an illusion all the stronger for the fact that from this model we can derive actions to be carried out that have a good chance of being followed by the expected effects. But this cartography of the living being is not the living being itself. The assembly of "parts" that makes up the biological body is no more alive than the assembly of mechanical parts that make up an automaton of any kind. The spontaneity and profound indeterminacy that characterize the living have disappeared in the reduction to the biological body. On this biological body, we can only carry out "mechanical" actions (even if chemistry takes the place of mechanics). Tissues can be repaired in the same way as clothes are mended, bones welded together, defective parts replaced—a heart, a kidney… At the very least, we could maintain a body to the point where it would be constantly reconstituted, like Theseus' boat, which the Athenians maintained with great care, replacing parts that were beginning to rot, so that the boat always looked as new as it did at the start of the expedition of the future conqueror of the Minotaur. This is the ambition of a number of "transhumanists". To escape life in order to escape death: this is the metaphysical paradox that lies at the heart of biological science.

Manipulation is not Knowledge

Modern scientific biology is frighteningly effective. Even if medical deadlocks, skilfully camouflaged, show what can be ostentatious in victory announcements. But it's very effective all the same. As far as medicine is concerned, we owe a large part of the increase in life expectancy to it—although most of it is due to improved living and working conditions, to better nutrition and hygiene. When it comes to reducing infant mortality, central heating has been a far more effective factor than paediatrics! But let's face it, medicine works quite often, and more and more cancers are being treated and cured. But life continues to elude science, however skilfully it adorns its ignorance with learned words. We continue to have to prepare for death, because it remains the horizon of the living.

It's not a question of incompleteness (we'll do better tomorrow!), but of a limit that we can't cross, because life goes far beyond the schemes of experimental science. There's no doubt about it, new knowledge will be accumulated, and rational explanations will be found for phenomena that are still mysterious. The space freed up for "alternative sciences" and "unconventional medicines" will shrink, perhaps—but nothing is less certain. Whatever we do, the question of life remains wide open.

In itself, that wouldn't be a big deal. Recognizing the limits of one's knowledge is a precious skill! No, the problem is that these limits are rarely recognized, or only in a purely formal way, as a simple polite formula designed to "pass the pill" of the unbearable arrogance of the "knowers", even where, in truth, we know no more than the sorcerer or the shaman. The paths of life in general, and of human beings in particular, remain radically unpredictable and unpredictable. And this is true, to varying degrees, of all living beings, first and foremost human beings. This is why, when it comes to "tinkering" with living things, we so often refer to the sorcerer's apprentice. We act on living things, but most of the time we don't know what we're doing.

Yet we refuse to acknowledge these limits, and we develop a whole industry and engineering of the living that destroys its autonomy and reduces it to inertness. This leads to very strange practices (agricultural, industrial or medical). When we see the development of industrial agriculture designed to produce fuel or starch for packaging, fuel to run our cars, when we convert fields into photovoltaic panels, and when we see the development of food manufactured by the chemical industry (synthetic "meat", etc.), we realize the absurdity of the techno-scientific rationality of our economic system. Could it be any clearer that we are reducing the living to the inert, and life to death? But perhaps more seriously, we are also developing potentially totalitarian conceptions of human life, since we must try to make life predictable and therefore control all manifestations of it in individuals who refuse to live like termites. The machine is no longer an epistemological model for understanding the living, but an objective to be achieved. As we shall see in the following chapters. Machinery has come out of the factories and is absorbing life.

Chapter III: Should we Eliminate the Mind?

Once living organisms have been reduced to physical-chemical machinery, the next step must be taken: thought itself can be reduced to a set of physical-chemical phenomena. The non-controllable can become controllable. In the passage of the *Discourse on Method* in which he announces that we will be able to "make ourselves as masters and possessors of nature", Descartes praises his new science (mathematical physics) not only for the promise it holds for mechanics, which will help to alleviate human suffering, but also for its consequences in medicine, since health is the greatest of all goods, and, since the soul is closely linked to the body, we will be able to make men "wiser"! The "triumphs" of physics and biology now pave the way for a genuine "science of the mind", as an extension of physics and biology. But just as biology rules out life, so these new sciences of the mind rule out the mind.

Biology even gives us good reasons to move in this direction. Ancient philosophers strove to invent philosophies of happiness. What nonsense! Today's scientist knows far more about this subject than Aristotle, Epictetus or Epicurus: there are four main happiness hormones: dopamine, serotonin, endorphin and oxytocin. To the countless writings on the virtues or dangers of love, the answer is quite simply: testosterone and oxytocin! Our feelings are chemistry and our rational mental faculties are calculation, which is what a machine can do. And, as luck would have it, we've known for a long time that our neurons are a kind of electrical circuit. Thus, George Boole invented a logical algebra, enabling the calculation of logical expressions (Boolean algebra) and Jevons, in 1869, presented the first machine to calculate Boolean equations. This led to today's computers and artificial intelligence, whose program was already outlined. In short, everything is in place to get rid of the old soul, spirit and subjectivity, and replace them with a machine model. Precisely, a machine is something we can manufacture and control for the purposes we have chosen. Thus, the devaluation of the human being, implied by molecular biology, leads to its reduction to the rank of a living machine, and is coupled, paradoxically, with *ubris*, an inflation of the feeling of power: God created man? We too can do the same!

All these questions revolve around two closely related models: firstly, the AI model, which aims to build a machine with "intellectual" performance equal to or superior to that of human beings, and secondly, the neuroscience model, which aims to understand how the neural system has biologically organized itself to be able to perform the operations we once attributed to the mind. But before we get there, we need to tackle head-on the question of whether we can theoretically eliminate the mind, i.e. whether we can do without any reference to the mind to account for thought. Those who support this position are called eliminativist materialists. But is it really possible to be an eliminativist?

Dualism

In the previous chapter, we left Descartes to grapple with dualism, i.e. the combination of a mechanistic conception of the body, which Hobbes, for example, shares with him, and a conception of the soul independent of any relationship to matter and the body, from which Hobbes is far removed. This was the main issue discussed during Descartes' lifetime, when the *Méditations métaphysiques* were published, and is reflected in the objections and responses to objections raised by this publication. It should be pointed out that Descartes does not understand spirit (or soul) in the sense of a breath that animates living beings. What he calls soul in French and *mens* in Latin is thought, thought as activity, "je pense" ("I think"). When he posits the radical separation between body and mind, body and soul, he does so not for religious reasons—although these obviously play a certain role—or because he remains attached to a kind of Platonic idealism. Purely logical reasons push him in this direction: it's perfectly possible to conceive of a body without a soul, a body that moves by itself, a well-made animal or automaton, and, conversely, it's possible to conceive of thought without any connection to the body. This last point is a little more delicate, but is nonetheless easy to understand: a thought has no physical attributes, no spatial dimensions or mass, and no sensible qualities. My imagination of a rose is not pink! A thought that is fraught with consequences weighs nothing in the balance. If we can conceive of thought without any connection to a particular body, it follows that thought cannot be the effect of a body and that "no body can think".

That thinking does not depend causally on the body is something we feel and experience—even though we know, oh how much! the state of our body conditions our thoughts and our ability to think, but to condition is not to determine causally. Plato's theory of ideas is indeed independent of Plato's body and continues to exist, in the way that ideas exist, whereas the bile produced by Plato's liver ceased to be at the same time as the rest of the Academy master's living body. Mathematical objects—what phenomenology will call "mathematical idealities"—do have a certain kind of existence, but there is nothing material about this existence, even if these mathematical idealities can give us the general forms of things that exist materially. To admit all this, we don't need to go back to the Platonic theory of ideas in its "Plato for dummies" version. There are no ideas existing in the world of ideas and material things existing in the sensible world, quite simply because there aren't two worlds, not in Descartes and not even in Plato, when you think about it and stop taking metaphors for concepts. It would be enough to admit that reality is made up of physical things with physical properties, and mental things with the properties of mental things, with both kinds of things existing in their own way—for example, assuming that reality is one, but that our mind can conceive it under different attributes.

For Descartes, things get more complicated when he tries to explain how the soul and body are linked, because it's clear that they are: the states of the soul are strongly influenced by those of the body, and the body acts according to the commands of the soul. This question lies at the heart of a philosophical debate involving Hobbes, Gassendi, Spinoza and Leibniz, among others. Thomas Hobbes rejects the Cartesian conception of an immaterial soul tied to a material body. This is how he presents the mechanism of thought in *Leviathan* (ch. III):

> When we think about something, whatever that something may be, the thought that follows it is not quite as coincidental as it seems. Every thought does not follow every [other] thought indifferently. For, just as we have no imagination of which we have not previously had the sensation, wholly or in part, we have no passage from one imagination to another, if we have not had the same previously in our sensations. Here's the reason: all phantasms are movements in us of the remains of the movements that took place in sensation, and these movements, which immediately succeeded one another in sensation, likewise remain linked after sensation, in such a way that, when the first takes place again and is predominant, the second follows,

by cohesion of the matter moved, in the same way as water, on a smooth table is attracted to the side where one of its parts is guided by the finger. But, because in sensation, one and the same thing that we perceive, sometimes one thing, sometimes another, succeeds, it happens, at certain moments, that, in the imagination of something, there is no certainty what we are going to imagine next. It is only certain that it will be something that has succeeded this thing, at one time or another.

Here, Hobbes proposes a purely mechanistic conception of the mind as nothing more than the movement of matter within the body. Moreover, Hobbes repeats that the idea of an incorporeal substance is pure nonsense. But perhaps the most radical response to Descartes was given by La Mettrie, author of *L'homme-machine*, a work whose thesis can be summed up in a few words: Descartes is right to consider the body as a machine, but he didn't have the courage to push the reasoning as far as it needed to be pushed, i.e. to recognize that the mind itself is nothing other than a manifestation of this machine. In this operation, the immortal soul sinks body and soul. Further manifestations of this liquidation of the mind can be found in Diderot's *Physiologie*, a posthumous text that sometimes seems to go off in all directions, but which also seeks to show that we have no need to postulate a soul distinct from the body.

Essentially, the problem has been with us since the 17th century, and we're still here. If we could build a machine capable of performing all the operations we attribute to our minds, we would have demonstrated that La Mettrie was right, and that there is nothing in the "human machine" that gives it any special dignity. The whole program of artificial intelligence, at least that of "strong" artificial intelligence, is closely connected to this philosophical question. At the time of writing, all the talk is of the exploits of the chatGPT conversational robot, which could be the first machine to pass the "Turing test" invented by the English mathematician Alan Turing, which is supposed to decide when a machine can be said to think. I'll come back to this famous Turing test later, when I'll argue that it is rigorously incapable of deciding whether a machine "thinks" or not.

As far as the immediate purpose of this book is concerned, if we can build a machine that thinks, it follows that, firstly, the machine is the right paradigm for understanding and rationally reconstructing what man is, insofar as this term still has any meaning. Secondly, if man is in no way substantially different from a machine, it's pointless trying to maintain the "privileges" of the body-subject: it's all an illusion we need to get rid of. We must renounce what Paul and Patricia Churchland (see below) call "carbon chauvinism". If there is no ontological difference between man and the thinking robot that has passed the Turing test, then we are left with two solutions: either treat the allegedly thinking machines as humans, granting them dignity and rights—this is the thesis of the *Real Humans* series—or treat men as machines, which is what the capitalist mode of production has known how to do from the very beginning. Dona Haraway, on the other hand, is not content to merge humans and animals into a single community (she advocates having satisfying sex with one's dog), and proposes to bring robots into this community.

There remains one last solution: to defend the advent of a human species superior to the current human species, a mix of man and machine, the cyborg of science fiction, or the surpassing of man by the transhuman or posthuman. These questions therefore have very high ethical stakes. All our ordinary moral prescriptions are based on the idea that there is, in every human being, something eminently respectable, which Kant calls "dignity", which attaches to every reasonable being and which is found neither in beasts nor in things. If robots are just as valuable as humans, then we have to admit that humans are no more valuable than robots, and that we can scrap them and replace them with more efficient robots without the slightest ethical problem. As you can see, the question of artificial intelligence is a far-reaching one, and could bring down the whole moral edifice of humanity.

Materialism in Question

We are confronted here with the limits of a radical materialism, a materialism that can be shown to be ultimately philosophically untenable. If the "hard" materialists are right, then machines can think, and philosophical humanism, that which accords a particular dignity to man (cf. Pico della Mirandola), can be discarded. But if machines can't think, if thinking is a privilege of living beings endowed with a brain like that of humans, then "hard" materialism is to be rejected, and so we must accept the enigma of the mind, admit that it's impossible to eliminate the human spirit, even if the mind is inseparable from the body.

We are therefore obliged to return, if only very provisionally, to the classical categories of philosophy, as identified by Socrates (and therefore by Plato), when he opposes the "sons of the earth" and the "friends of ideas", distinctions taken up by Leibniz under the names of idealism and materialism. Materialists hold that there is only one reality, the material reality that can be known through physics and chemistry, while idealists hold that physical realities are secondary (how they are secondary is another matter) while mental realities are primary. Here's a definition of materialism, given by Italian philosopher and philologist Sebastiano Timpanaro, in his essay *Sul materialismo* (1970):

> By materialism, we understand above all the recognition of the priority of nature over mind, or, if we prefer, of the physical level over the biological level and of the biological level over the socio-economic

and cultural levels; both in the sense of a chronological priority (the very long time that existed before the appearance of life on earth and between the origin of life and the origin of man) and in the sense of the conditioning that nature still exerts over man and will continue to exert at least for the foreseeable future.

I'd like to make it clear right away that this division between materialism and idealism is highly problematic, and that in truth there is no philosopher who is totally materialist and no philosopher who is totally idealist. For example, the materialist Marx is often closer to the idealist Hegel than to any of the materialist thinkers, or at least those stamped as materialists, of his time, even if it was long accepted by the proponents of "orthodox Marxism" that Marx was the heir to the "materialism" of the Enlightenment. Thomas Nagel argues that there is a kind of remarkable symmetry between "hard-core" materialists, who reduce all reality to the laws of physics, and theists, who maintain that the world we know is the product of a superiorly intelligent mind. A very pertinent observation…

Be that as it may, the prevailing cultural mood in the richest countries today is one of materialistic reductionism: physics is the foundation on which everything can be built. Certain arrangements of molecules in very specific circumstances gave rise to the first living beings (protobacteria) which, as they diversified and became more complex, gave rise to the prodigious diversity of living beings that we know, the mechanism leading to this speciation of beings being the blind mechanism of Darwinian evolutionism. Not everyone is convinced by this account. In one of his latest contributions to philosophy, Thomas Nagel argues that "the neo-Darwinian materialist conception of nature is most probably wrong" (see *L'esprit et le cosmos*, 2018, for the French translation). I don't know if Nagel is right. But he could be, and we can't ignore him without objection, which in no way implies that we can take biblical creationism or the "intelligent design" thesis seriously.

Today, it's in the realm of "philosophy of mind" that these different currents are unfolding. Here, the materialist tendency is largely dominant: the mind either doesn't exist, or is merely a (misleading) name for certain special phenomena that we human beings call "mental". Whether the mind is a "*res cogitans*", a thing that thinks, as Descartes would say, clearly separated from the body (an extended thing, *res extensa*), we won't find many people to defend this once-common position. Cartesian dualism hardly survives except in profoundly modified form. The main serious disputes in the philosophy of mind seem to concern the various schools of materialist monism: the supporters of eliminativist materialism versus the advocates of epiphenomenalism, the defenders of type-identity theory and their opponents, the functionalists, the externalists and so on. This is a field in which "isms" are mass-produced! But whatever the version adopted, it's clear that there's no longer any room for the soul, and that we must therefore be able to create a science of the mind analogous to the other sciences of nature. The corollary is that we could :

3. building machines that almost perfectly mimic the capabilities of a human mind ("artificial intelligences");

4. really put psychology on the safe road to science by transforming it into a branch of physics and chemistry;

5. finally make man a predictable being.

A materialist (monist, that is) should rejoice at this situation, since materialism would triumph across the board, leaving spiritualists with only a few residual strongholds. Unfortunately, for a tranquil materialist conscience, there seems to be no reason to rejoice… First, I propose to show that the way in which the central question of the philosophy of mind, the *mind/body problem*, is posed depends on the Cartesian problematic, and that it is in relation to this problematic that the various monistic materialist solutions are constructed; and that we can therefore only fall back into one form of dualism or another. Secondly, I will show that the various dominant versions of current attempts to eliminate the mind and put an end to "*mind-body*" dualism, as the Anglo-Saxons say, presuppose a "strong materialism" that one of its proponents, Yvon Quiniou, himself describes as "dogmatic". But we'll see that this materialism may not be as materialistic as it seems. And we'll conclude that it's the way in which the problem is posed that is irremediably obscure and that, despite boastful proclamations, we haven't taken a serious step towards scientific knowledge of the mind—in other words, that the theories in vogue know no more about the mind than did the classical philosophers (Descartes or Kant, Spinoza or Freud, to name but a few famous names).

More generally, we could refute materialist theses by showing that matter is nothing more than a category of thought, and that radical materialism is simply unthinkable—we'd be hard-pressed to give a definition of matter other than in relation to what is not matter: In Aristotle, who is not particularly "materialist" in the sense of the philosophical schools of thought, matter is opposed to form, and it is form that "informs" matter, the latter being eternal and uncreated, it is that of which nothing can be said other than that it is matter. We can refine this as much as we like: matter is made up of molecules, molecules of atoms and atoms of all kinds of elementary particles. There is no stopping point. When we speak of materialism, when we say that everything is matter and that it is the movements of material bodies that explain, "in the final analysis", all the phenomena and facts that fall within our understanding, we are in fact saying that ultimate reality is nothing other than what is the object of mathematical physics. But mathematical physics is concerned with bodies that have already been idealized and posited as elements, whose properties are supposed to explain the more complex compositions of matter. Such materialism is, in truth, not very different from idealism. A mass, in fact, is not something "material", any more than an electric current or pressure. A mass is a scalar from the point of view of physics, and the effect of this mass is a "force" that can be described as the product of the mass and the acceleration vector! Even the notion of "force" is abandoned in favor of that of interaction, described solely by a series of equations. This is enough to show that Plato is completely out of date when it comes to idealism, and that, contrary to Althusser's imprudent assertion, materialism is not the "natural" or "spontaneous" philosophy of the learned, unless by materialism we mean something quite different from what is commonly understood. In *La matière et l'esprit* (2004), I argued for the possibility of a "critical materialism", not an "old-fashioned" materialism of matter, but a materialism that simply rejects supernatural explanations, divine intervention or miracles. If we want to stick to Timpanaro's definition given above, we'll admit that nature existed before man and continues to condition him—in order to think, we have to breathe, eat, sleep, etc.—but these rather trivial assertions won't help us understand what thought is, and whether thought is not conditioned but determined by "physical or biological matter". Marx, following Leibniz, distinguished between "conditioning" (*bedingen*) and "determining" (*bestimmen*), and it is in this distinction that both placed the possibility of human freedom. I'm conditioned to go out for a walk rather than stay cooped up in my office. But it's impossible to determine, and therefore to predict, how I'll behave. But when it comes to material bodies, we can predict their behavior with great accuracy.

To conclude on materialism in general, I would remind you that in his eleven theses on Feuerbach, Marx criticized materialism before him:

> The main flaw in the materialism of all philosophers to date—including Feuerbach's—is that the object, reality, the sensible world, is only grasped as an object or intuition, but not as concrete human activity, as practice, in a non-subjective way. This explains why the active aspect was developed by idealism, in opposition to materialism—but

only abstractly, since idealism naturally does not know real, concrete activity as such.

*1st thesis on Feuerbach,*1845)

Precisely, what contemporary materialism proposes is to grasp reality, including that of the mind, only "in the form of the object", not as "subjective", not as "practical". And this "subjective" way of being is nothing other than the intentional activity of the living individual. In short, we are wrong to believe that we have intentions or volitions; these are merely "experiences" of movement in our bodies, obeying, in the final analysis, a physical-chemical determinism…

The Mind/Body Problem

If all reality is "material", then either the mind itself is material, or it doesn't exist. But if it is material, it exists in the same way as the body, so it must be part of the body, and can be summed up, for example, in the neuronal system. To cut a long story short, we can sum up the problem of the proponents of materialist monism in philosophy of mind by reducing it to one objective: how to get rid of Descartes? A paradoxical situation, as we shall see: on the one hand, Cartesian dualism seems both untenable, for reasons I'll come back to later, and at the same time difficult to refute if we don't reduce it to a caricature (dualism for the philosopher of the mind).

Before getting to the heart of the matter, a final remark is in order. Here, we'll be dealing mainly with "eliminativist materialism" (some authors use the term "eliminative" instead) in the strict sense, which many authors agree is now an extremely minority position. Eliminativist materialism is that which maintains that it is perfectly possible to dispense with the word "mind" and all that goes with it, and stick to an objective description of material processes. This, it can be shown, is the crux of the matter. As soon as we abandon pure eliminativist materialism—and we have good reason to do so—we fall back, whether we like it or not, on the question of mental causality (or rather, "mental causation") that constitutes the shibboleth of Cartesian thought and dualism in general: how can mental things act on the body? And so we say goodbye to pure materialism. Some authors get away with inventing the all-too-subtle epiphenomenal theory: "mental things" are merely epiphenomena of physical things, in much the same way as engine noise is the epiphenomenon of engine operation. There's no ghost in the machine, to use Gilbert Ryle's expression (*The Concept of Mind*, 1949), it's just the machine that's too noisy.

"We are body as well as spirit", said Pascal. A proposition that refutes the old Platonic idea that our soul is somehow imprisoned in the body, death being the soul's deliverance. A consoling thesis, but one that Pascal refuses to accept. It was he who said: "Man is neither angel nor beast, and misfortune wants that who wants to make the angel makes the beast. The translation would be: neither pure immaterial spirit nor mere machine. But Descartes asks a precise question: what is the relationship between body and mind? He gives a clear answer to this question: since I can clearly and distinctly think of a mind without a body and a body without a mind, body and mind are two distinct kinds of reality, different "substances". Once this has been established, the question remains as to how the mind can be affected by the body and, conversely, how it can act on the body, since body and mind are closely "conjoined", as experience convinces us. For Descartes, however, this second question is of secondary importance, and he is well aware of the difficulties inherent in his solution. The essential point is this: since the mind can be conceived independently of the body, it follows that the mind is not a property of the body and, consequently, "no body can think", as he puts it somewhat abruptly in his reply to the second objections.

Let's be clear. For Descartes, it's not a question of starting from some belief or inventing a theory of the soul. It's a question of starting from what is indubitable: what is true is what can be clearly and distinctly conceived. I can clearly and distinctly conceive of the mind as thought in action. I can form a concept of mind as effective thought, thought in act, independently of any reference to the body. It follows that mind is not an attribute of the body. Moreover, if mind were in any way an attribute of the body, it would have to be a physical attribute, i.e. visible and measurable. For example, a body has spatial measurements, possibly an electrical charge, a temperature, etc., properties that can be measured by physical devices, and none of these properties can be said to be of a spirit.

This is why "no body can think", since none of the body's attributes belong to thought. Descartes goes on to say that some hold the opinion "that the parts of the brain work together with the mind to form thoughts". To these, he replies that this opinion "is not founded on positive reasons, but only on the fact that they have never been without a body, and that quite often they have been hindered by it in their operations". We can see empirically that there is a correlation between mind and body (between thought and brain, if we want to put it another way); we can see, just as empirically, that states of the body can disturb our thoughts. But for Descartes, these are not truly "positive" reasons, simply because an empirical observation does not give reasons, but, at most, correlations. I observe that things happen in a certain way, but I don't know why this is so, i.e. I don't know whether I'm observing a contingent, accidental fact, or whether, on the contrary, it's a necessary fact. Only reason itself, examining the concepts it forms, can decide.

Let's understand what's at stake. If I examine the concept of movement, this concept cannot be thought independently of a body whose state it expresses. But I can think of a body that is not in motion. So the concept of motion does not designate a reality existing in itself, but only a quality or property of a body. Conversely, I can think the mind without reference to the body. For example, my current thought that the sum of the three angles of a triangle is two straight has no relation to the state of my own body, nor to the state of any other body—indeed, there is no such thing as a triangle in nature. If I had a body made of glass, or if I were King of Mexico, to parody Descartes, I wouldn't think any differently about triangles. Consequently, thought (the activity of the mind) is not an attribute of the body. This is why "the body cannot think". We could point out to the Cartesian philosopher that the state of the brain when I conceive of a triangle is not the same as when I conceive of a square, but on this subject we're reduced to guesswork. So it's not certain that the correlation between our mental states and the states of our bodies is given without a "positive" reason. As we shall see, there are good reasons for thinking the opposite.

The comparison between body and movement, on the one hand, and body and mind, on the other, is not arbitrary: materialists will have to try to show that mind is nothing other than a certain kind of movement of living matter. If we now take the dominant conceptual device in philosophy of mind, we'll notice that the Cartesian distinction is more or less taken up again, even if we then refute the separation of body and mind in favor of one of the versions of materialist monism. When we contrast mental states with physical states, mental properties with physical properties, or mental phenomena with physical phenomena, we are in a sense still dealing with Descartes' problematic, even if it's to refute it.

The point is to show that thought can be a property of a machine, and that there is no need to suppose a "thinking thing" distinct from the machine we would be. In his *Physiologie* (see *Éléments de physiologie* in *Œuvres I*, collection "Bouquins"), Diderot begins by refuting the need to assume a "thinking substance",

Chapter III – Should we Eliminate the Mind?

and shows that if we assume such a substance, it is impossible to conceive of its interaction with the body.

> According to the definitions we are given of the two substances, they are essentially incompatible. What connection can there be between them? Is there anything more absurd than the contact of two beings, one of which has no parts and occupies no space? Is there anything more absurd than the action of one being on another without contact?

In place of this "absurd" hypothesis, Diderot proposes another: matter is thinking and feeling:

> Why not consider sensitivity, life and movement as properties of matter: since these qualities are found in every portion, in every particle of flesh?

The link between Diderot's materialism and Leibniz's monadology is not surprising, given that Leibniz was also seeking to resolve the problem of Cartesian dualism, which he found highly enigmatic. Once this point has been made, Diderot equates our awareness of ourselves with our awareness of our own body and its various organs:

> We are only as aware of the principle of reason, or of the soul, as we are of its existence, of the existence of our foot or hand, of cold, heat, pain, pleasure; disregard all these qualities, and no more soul.

So states of the soul are states of the body, or rather, the expression of states of the body.

> Is the soul happy, sad, angry, tender, concealed, voluptuous? it is nothing without the body; I defy anyone to explain anything without the body.

I challenge anyone to explain how the passions enter the soul without bodily movements, and without starting with these movements.

And so the question of the action of the soul on the body is settled:

This is foolishness to those who descend from the soul to the body: nothing is done in man in this way. Marat doesn't know what he's saying when he talks about the action of the soul on the body; if he had looked more closely, he would have seen that the action of the soul on the body is the action of one part of the body on another, and the action of the body on the soul, the action of another part of the body on another. [...]

Reasoning can now be understood as the action of the various parts on each other:

Reasoning cannot be explained with the help of an immaterial soul, or a spirit: this spirit cannot be at two objects at once; it needs the help of memory. Memory is certainly a corporeal quality.

The difference between a sensitive soul and a reasonable soul is simply a matter of organization.

The animal is *a* whole, and it is perhaps this unity that constitutes the soul, the self, the consciousness with the help of memory.

All thoughts arise from one another; this seems obvious to me. Intellectual opinions are also linked: perception arises from sensation. Perception gives rise to reflection, meditation and judgment. There is nothing free in intellectual operations, neither in sensation, nor in the perception or view of the relations between sensations, nor in reflection or meditation, nor in greater or lesser attention to these relations, nor in judgment or acquiescence to what appears to be true [...].

Diderot concludes with the idea that man is indeed a kind of machine:

What a difference between a sensitive, living watch and one made of gold, iron, silver or copper! If a soul were attached to the latter, what would it produce? If it is possible, please tell me what the effects would be. The peasant who sees a watch moving, and who, unable to understand its mechanism, places a spirit in the needle, is no more and no less a fool than our spiritualists.

Diderot's ideas are not particularly original. La Mettrie, in *L'homme-machine*, had already replied to Descartes, reproaching him in a way for not having been consistent in prudently sticking to the body-machine thesis, when there is nothing different between human thought, a rooster crowing at dawn and a clock telling the time! If machines can perform the same functions as animals, and if human beings are similar to animals to within a degree of organization, then human beings are conceptually no different from machines, and thought can be conceived as a function performed by machines.

If we're done with dualism, we're done with the soul and all that goes with it. There's only one reality left, the tangible reality of matter and mechanisms to be elucidated. It seems, however, that on closer examination, things are a lot less clear-cut than our naive Enlightenment materialists thought. Suppose a machine does think, even if its thoughts are elementary, such as proving a fairly simple mathematical theorem or correcting the grammar of a text—even if it makes mistakes, just as humans do—then we can deduce that thought is independent of its material "support". Thought could be embodied in a machine (a being made of copper and silicon) as well as in a human being (a being made of cells made of carbon radicals). In other words, very different material beings could also think, and even have the same kind of thinking. From this we can deduce that thought can exist independently of the type of "support", provided there is one. Thinking can thus be conceptually separated from the "extended thing" or, more vulgarly, from the *hardware* of which we humans are just one possible form. Surprisingly, this materialism conceives of thought as independent of its material support. In this way, we could inadvertently fall back into a new version of Cartesian dualism. Incidentally, computer scientists who separate *hardware* from *software* are undoubtedly Cartesian dualists in their own right! As for those who believe that we could save someone's mind (their entire memory) on a computer storage device, they are, more often than not, unwittingly supporting Locke's theory of consciousness and renewing dualism: our soul could be independent of our body. In other words, a certain reductionist materialism is merely dualistic idealism in disguise! This point underlines the strength of Descartes' reasoning, and the extreme difficulty encountered by those who seek to refute it. So let's return to Descartes' position and its subtleties. It can be presented as follows:

6. the various parts of the body communicate with the brain via "spirits" or "animal spirits". Today, we would say nerve impulses;

7. these "spirits" are entities that belong to the body, and therefore, like all other parts of the body, are subject to the laws of physics, the most important of which, according to Descartes, is the law of conservation of momentum. For example, two balls colliding change speed and direction, but the sum of their quantities of motion after the collision is equal to that of the system before the collision;

8. But if the spirit, which is not corporeal, can act on animal spirits, we run the risk of finding ourselves faced with a flagrant violation of the law of conservation of momentum: we'd have a movement that doesn't arise from the transformation of other movements. Hence the dilemma: either the physical law is respected, and the mind cannot act on the body. Or the law is violated, and then physical devices would have to be able to ignore the laws of physics, which is unimaginable.

For Descartes, this law of the conservation of momentum is fundamental not only from a physical point of view, but also from a metaphysical one (it derives from Descartes' conception of God's action in the world).

Descartes came up with a clever solution: the mind cannot change the total quantity of motion, but it can, at a precise point in the brain, change the direction of animal spirits. The quantity of motion is fixed by the laws of physics, but not its direction. This was Descartes' way out of the dilemma to which we are more or less led if we accept both the separation of mind and body and the possibility of thought having physical causal power. Leibniz knew that Descartes' reasoning didn't work, and that we had to take into account not only the speed of moving bodies, but also their direction (in other words, that the quantity of motion is not an arithmetic quantity, but a vector quantity). Even if we stick to Descartes' argument, physically, it doesn't work! To change the direction of a moving body, you have to expend energy!

This story of a soul that sorts "animal spirits" according to their speed would later be found in a completely different circumstance with the invention of "Maxwell's demon": in this thought experiment, we imagine that between two gaseous enclosures of equal temperatures, a demon lets fast molecules pass through on one side, and slow molecules on the other. After a while, and contrary to the second principle of thermodynamics, the two chambers would find themselves at different temperatures, in a way moving up the arrow of time (if we identify the arrow of time with the growth of entropy). Léon Brilloin came up with the right solution: the demon must acquire information in order to carry out these sortings. However, the acquisition of information is always an expenditure of energy, and so the second principle of thermodynamics cannot be violated by the action of Maxwell's demon. For the same reasons, the soul cannot sort animal spirits without expending energy, i.e. without itself being in some way a physical thing, and so the clever Cartesian solution to the question of the union of soul and body collapses of its own accord.

Once again, it's not a question of taking Descartes' physiological conceptions at face value, nor of turning his models into rigorous theories, when in fact they have mainly heuristic value, but of understanding that he's raising an essential question here, When you delve into the abundant literature on the philosophy of mind, you realize that, as soon as it comes to explaining mental causality, we have recourse, in new forms, to solutions that are not very far removed from Descartes'. We'll come back to this a little later. The question can be summed up another way: how can physical determinism at the level of the body be reconciled with free or intentional action?

Rationalist philosophers were confronted with this difficulty and sought to provide a solution. Spinoza purely and simply eliminates the question by defending a monism of substance complemented by a dualism (in fact, an infinite pluralism) of attributes, conceived in such a way that there is no causal link between physical and mental states. It seems to me that certain theses of contemporary philosophy of mind are very close to Spinoza, notably the theories of "occurrence" or the "anomalous monism" defended by Davidson. Leibniz, too, saw the theoretical flaw in Cartesian dualism. He rightly pointed out the incomplete nature of Descartes' physical conceptions, and deduced that the Cartesian conception of the relationship between body and mind was flawed.

> 80. Descartes recognized that souls cannot give force to bodies because there is always the same amount of force in matter. However, he believed that the soul could change the direction of bodies. But that's because in his time, no one knew the law of nature that still preserves the same total direction in matter.
>
> *Monadology*, 1714

To put it in modern terms, Descartes ignores the principle of conservation of energy—which explains the errors he makes in the *Principles of Philosophy* (1644) when he sets out the laws of shocks—and the quantity of motion has yet to find its true formulation, since it is a vector quantity and not an arithmetic quantity (physicists say that not an abstract quantity of motion, but the "impulse vector", is conserved).

The Leibnizian critique of Descartes leads to another solution—that of pre-established harmony, which, fantastic as it may seem, is surely not as far removed from Spinoza's as one might think. From all eternity, body and mind have been designed by our watchmaker God, who set everything in advance so that what happens to the body finds its equivalent in a modification of the mind: if I bump into a wall and feel pain, it's not because my aching body transmits the sensation of pain to my soul, but because my soul from all eternity must have felt pain at the precise moment my body hit a wall. Body and soul lead parallel lives...

This question concentrates the problems facing the philosophy of mind. If we admit the existence of mental states distinct from physical states (roughly speaking, if we admit the experience of what we have of our consciousness), we can distinguish four kinds of causal relations:

9. physical states cause physical states;
10. physical states cause mental states;
11. mental states cause other mental states;
12. mental states cause physical states.

At first glance, there is no real difficulty in understanding the first three types of causal relationship. The first is as obvious to a dualist as to a monist. The second is just as easy to understand for a dualist as it is for a materialist who accepts that mental states are produced by physical states—insofar as we can distinguish between mental states that are distinct from physical states (as, for example, the proponents of occurrence do). The third poses no problem for a dualist, and hardly any for a monist who supports the duality of attributes, or for a materialist who accepts the theory of occurrence or emergence: if a mental state M1 occurs on a physical state P1, and P1 causes P2, then a mental state M2 will occur on state P2, and we can then consider, within certain limits, that M1 causes M2. Note, however, that this mental/mental causality may only be a pseudo-causality, a kind of epiphenomenon. This is why, as the Korean philosopher Jaegwon Kim shows (see his book *Mind in the Physical World*, 1998), theories of occurrence have a strong tendency to fall into epiphenomenalism, which may well be no more than a shameful variety of eliminativist materialism: if we go back to the scheme according to which state P1 causes state P2 and, consequently, we can say that M1 occurring at P1 causes M2 occurring at P2, the causal relationship between M1 and M2 is only an apparent causality, and we could basically eliminate M1 and M2 as mere epiphenomena…

The real difficulty begins with the fourth causal relation. It clashes with our general conception of the laws of nature. The modern conception of the natural sciences aims to give a complete explanation of all physical phenomena in terms of physical causality—this is known as "causal nomological closure". It is therefore excluded by construction that non-physical (mental) states can enter into the explanation of a physical phenomenon. Basically, if I raise my arm to greet a friend, the neurobiologist will simply study the neural systems that lead to the arm's movement. There's no room here for what we philosophers call *intentionality*. Following Michael Esfeld (see his book *The Philosophy of Mind*, 1994), we can sum up the problem as follows. We have three theses that we generally hold to be true, yet which are incompatible:

13. mental states are distinct from physical states;

14. mental states cause physical states;

15. every physical state (insofar as it is subject to laws) has complete physical causes.

Theses 1) and 2) taken together are incompatible with thesis 3). In other words, our experience of ourselves is incompatible with our belief in the validity of the natural sciences, since mental states cannot by definition be objects of the natural sciences, since they are not objects at all. The various theoretical propositions in philosophy of mind can be reduced to attempts to modify one or two of these three theses to make them compatible. Cartesian dualism, insofar as it seeks to think of the mind/body relationship as two different types of reality, accepts all three theses. Spinoza and Leibniz can be said to suppress thesis 2) and, albeit with nuances, Diderot in *Le rêve de d'Alembert* is tempted to settle for thesis 3)—I say "tempted" because Diderot's position is rather fluid. In any case, it's very difficult to understand how our subjective point of view, even when we're trying to understand the workings of the human mind scientifically, can be reconciled with the objective claims of the natural sciences. Explaining the phase transitions between the liquid and solid states, or the fusion of hydrogen atoms in the sun, is ultimately very simple—there are no real enigmas, no real mysteries in the problems of physics—but understanding what it's like to feel joy on the first beautiful spring morning, that's another matter altogether!

The Elimination of the Spirit

Since we don't want to give a complete overview of the various positions of the schools and chapels of the philosophy of mind, let's not get into the scholastic quarrels that pit one school against another, but concentrate on the theses of materialist monism.

16. These are the theses, if not dominant, at least massively widespread in this field; not because philosophers largely share them (many are reluctant to the idea of suppressing what constitutes our specificity as thinking and feeling human beings), but

because the fundamental problem of contemporary philosophy of mind revolves around this.

17. These theses are in line with an important current in 20th-century philosophy, the logical empiricism of the Vienna Circle, and particularly its physicalist variant.

18. They aim to reintegrate knowledge of the mind into the natural sciences.

19. They reduce philosophy to the discussion and clarification of scientific propositions.

We can now give a more precise definition of eliminativist materialism based on the three theses cited above:

20. mental states are different from physical states, because mental states don't exist;

21. mental states that do not exist cannot cause physical states;

22. only physical states cause physical states.

It follows, logically, that philosophy of mind should give way to neurobiology (cf. next chapter). Strangely enough, in philosophy of mind, neurobiology only comes in as supporting evidence, but even the strictest eliminativist materialists have not become neurobiologists and have remained philosophers! One wonders why: all eliminativist philosophers in truth maintain that philosophy is useless or meaningless. Books on the subject attribute eliminativist materialism to Feyerabend and Rorty, in the 1960s. But we could go further back. Hobbes' objection to Descartes (this is the second of the "third objections made by a famous English philosopher"), is expressed as follows:

> [...] a thing that thinks is something corporeal; for the subjects of all acts seem only to be understood under a corporeal reason, or under a reason of matter as he [Descartes] himself showed a little later by the example of wax, which, although its color, hardness, figure & all its other acts are changed, is always conceived to be the same thing, that is, the same matter subject to all these changes. Now it is not by another

thought that one infers that I think; for even though someone may think that he has thought (which thought is nothing other than a memory), nevertheless it is quite impossible to think that one thinks, nor to know that one knows; for this would be an interrogation that would never end: from where do you know that you know that you know, & c.?

And so, since knowledge of this proposition: *I exist*, depends on knowledge of this one: *I think*; and the knowledge of this one of the fact that we cannot separate thought from a matter that thinks, it seems that we must rather infer that a thing that thinks is rather material than immaterial.

Objections to the Metaphysical Meditations, AT IX, 135

Hobbes' critique of Descartes starts from the critique of what we might call the critique of reflexive illusion: we regard a memory and actual thought as equivalent. Immediacy (that's what intuition is)—I think and simultaneously I think that I think—is fundamentally refuted. If we think of ourselves as subjects of our thoughts, there is no reason to suppose that there is an "I" who thinks. Nietzsche would say, two centuries after Hobbes, that the good old "I" is a grammatical illusion. Remove this reflexive illusion (the "I" that accompanies all our representations, according to Kant) and we can then consider that thought is the act of something material rather than immaterial. The phrase "I think" is a rhetorical one. It would be better to say: "there's thought in there", pointing to his skull. A problem that neither Hobbes nor Nietzsche can solve: how can they know there's thought in there?

The "elimination" of the knot in Cartesian thought is absolutely essential, and underpins all eliminativist materialism. Michel Dubois (see *Le vivant et l'indéterminé*) devotes a work to these questions, to which we'll return later: how can we think about intentionality if we stand firmly on the ground of biological necessity?

Rather than looking for lice in the tonsure of English or American philosophers, we can find "at home" a good, solid defense of eliminativist materialism in the person of Jean-Pierre Changeux, made famous by *L'homme neuronal* (1983), a title that obviously echoes La Mettrie's famous *Homme machine*. But that's a question for the next chapter.

Radical Eliminativism

Paul and Patricia Churchland defend a radical materialism that is more eliminativist than that of most eliminativists. Unlike those who want to reduce thought to its biological substratum, the Churchlands believe that those who want to admit that living matter can think, but deny this privilege to machines, are demonstrating "carbon chauvinism". In today's language, such chauvinism would seem to be offensive to the silicon beings that are computers.

The brain is a kind of computer whose properties have yet to be explored, and this exploration is neither easy nor pointless. The brain computes highly complex functions, albeit in a very different way to classical artificial intelligence. Brains can be computers without necessarily being sequential or numerical, without the hardware being dissociated from the programs, and without only manipulating symbols. These are computers of a very different type from those we use today.

We don't know how the brain processes semantics, but it goes beyond human language. A small pile of deposited excrement means something to a human, just as it does to a dog: a small rodent in the vicinity. A particular echo perceived by a bat tells it that a moth is flying nearby. A theory of meaning will only emerge once researchers have discovered how neurons encode and transform sensory signals, how learning and memory circuits function, and how these cognitive capacities interact with the body's motor system.

"Les machines peuvent-elles penser?",
Pour la Science magazine, March 1990

The two central theses set out here conform to the dogmas of the strictest physicalism.

The brain is a kind of computer. To get rid of objections, P. & P. Churchland make it clear that the brain is not necessarily a digital computer, let alone a Von Neumann-type machine. Note that this way of dismissing objections is not very convincing, since (1) an analog signal can always be converted into a digital signal—analog computers even had their heyday in aviation; and (2) non-sequential processing can also be simulated on a sequential computer. In other words, all non-Von Neumann computer functions could theoretically be implemented on a Von Neumann computer; and this is exactly what we're doing with neural network programming.

The question of semantics is reduced, in a very behaviorist way, to that of behavior. Semantics "goes beyond human language" because it also concerns animal behavior, say P. & P. Churchland. I don't mind saying that a small pile of excrement means the same thing to humans as it does to dogs: "little rodent around here". But for the dog, the "meaning" is expressed in a specific behavior (the fox immediately starts chasing the little rodent). For man, the meaning will be expressed in verbal signs (emitted or simply thought), and he'll go out and buy rat poison. What P. & P. Churchland are eliminating is quite simply human language, reduced de facto to a behavioral reaction—more complex than that of the dog, admittedly, but still reducible to a combination of simple behavioral reactions of the same type.

In fact, if we follow Churchlandhuman language should simply be understood not as a system of signs, but as a code of signals. Whether the groundhog is calling out for hikers or the muezzin is calling for prayer, it's all the same. But what distinguishes a sign from a simple signal is that a sign has a meaning independent of the effects its emission triggers, whereas a signal has no meaning other than the action it aims to trigger. Churchland's eliminativism speaks only of the coding and transformation of sensory signals. To take the Churchland example again, if I see a small pile of excrement that I attribute to rodents, I may have no reaction, but it provokes thoughts of all kinds, reflections on the insalubrity of big cities, the failure of the services that ensure their cleanliness; unless it evokes the plague, Camus and so on.

As a result, the most important and difficult part of mental processes, consciousness, as interiority, simply no longer exists. For behaviorism, it cannot, in any case, be an object of science. So there's no point in trying to explain something that's just a phantom. Philosophy of mind, cognitive science and psychology are doomed to dissolve into Pavlovian mechanics.

Other Forms of Eliminativism

Let's face it, the Churchland concept is far from unanimous. There are more subtle theories of mind. CTT (Computational Theory of Mind) is a theory that holds that a number of facts about the mind can be understood as syntactic information-processing operations, based on mental representations. The computer is a typical example of a machine that processes information by performing syntactic operations. This theory met with some success because it echoed Chomsky's theory of language as the application of rules—Chomsky developed generative linguistics, but also worked at the MIT laboratory on machine translation problems.

This TCE first assumes that the human mind (we'll see later if this word has any meaning) processes information sequentially, like the processor in a computer. The problem is then to define what information is. For example, if I read a reply to a questionnaire and see the three letters O, U, I displayed, this is information, because this succession of letters tells me that the writer who answered the questionnaire has confirmed, for example, that he or she is of the right age to be registered for a particular activity. But these three letters are just lines drawn on the paper, not information in themselves. This information could have been replaced by a cross in a box, which would be the same information albeit in a very different form. When we say that, like a human mind, a computer processes symbolic information, we are verbally resolving a fundamental difficulty. A symbol is, as the etymology indicates, a link *(syn)*. If I enter the following positive or zero polarizations (for example) into the computer's 8-bit memory "box": 0V, 0V, 0V, +5V, 0V, 0V, 0V, 0V, 0V, which corresponds in binary to 10000, or 32 in decimal, and I know that if I code this working memory "box" at this point, it will correspond to a space in a text to be printed (for example). The decimal-coded "32" is a symbol for the letter "space", which is used to separate words in a sentence in our current way of writing sentences. We can therefore say that the computer, which sends the command to the printer or screen to display a space, has processed a symbol. But it's the human operator who sees things this way. In truth, the computer has done nothing more than "read" a memory cell at a given moment (on a clock pulse) and "write" the contents of that memory cell to another memory cell. If space had been omitted, the human being would still be able to read what was written (in ancient Latin documents, for example, space doesn't exist), whereas the computer, which doesn't read anything, emits an error signal for unknown words.

So, strictly speaking, we can't really say that the computer processes information, any more than the switch on my bedside lamp processes the information "I'm going to sleep now" when I turn it off. In truth, what we're doing with computers is one of the classic operations of the human mind: projecting ourselves onto external things! We call this "anthropomorphism", an intellectual attitude found in all forms of animism and fetishism. The primitive mentality is thus at work in high technology.

TCE is based on another thesis that nobody seriously defends any more: the thesis that the mind processes all information computationally, i.e. algorithmically. Even in logical or mathematical operations, the human mind does not follow algorithms. It follows that the third thesis of the TCE, that the human mind could be modelled by a computer program, is in serious trouble.

TCE can be conceived as another form of eliminativist materialism: if a machine, in this case a computer, can perform operations that are considered by an outside observer to be intelligent operations, then that machine thinks (which is the basis of the famous Turing test). The founding fathers of TCE have, for the most part, abandoned TCE. Hilary Putnam, in *Representation and Reality* (1988), and Jerry Fodor, in *The Mind Doesn't Work Like That* (2000), disowned it. TCE is generally classified with functionalist theories of mind: according to these theories, to know what there is to know, all you have to do is build a physical system capable of performing the functions ordinarily performed by the human mind. It's enough to note that the pascaline, the calculating machine Pascal developed to help his father do his job as a tax collector, obviously doesn't think. The powerful computer programs used by today's most powerful computers, however, are nothing more than an improved pascaline…

A final, albeit more indirect, form of eliminativism is developed by Daniel Dennett. His starting point is what poses a problem for eliminativist materialism, namely the question of intentionality. Dennett redefines intentionality in such a way that it can be eliminated. Roughly speaking, for Dennett, we have an intentional attitude if we can treat this system as a rational agent, i.e. if we can make predictions about its behavior by lending it beliefs and desires, and when these kinds of predictions are superior to those that might arise from other attitudes. These other attitudes are the physical attitude (I predict the behavior of a system by the knowledge I have of its physical composition and the natural laws that apply) and the design attitude (I predict behavior by the knowledge I have of its function).

For example, with a computer equipped with a program for playing chess, I can have an intentional attitude, since the explanation of the physical laws applied to the system isn't enough for me to know whether it will move the rook or the knight, and the functional explanation (it's made to play chess and win!) doesn't allow me to predict precise behavior either. So I have to lend my computer an intentional attitude, i.e. assume that it "wants" to win and "acts" rationally to that end. In other words, something is an intentional system only in relation to the strategy of someone who seeks to predict its behavior. This conception is called instrumentalism. It doesn't in itself imply the non-existence of mental states, but it does suggest that intentionality doesn't really exist, and that science might enable us to provide better explanations than intentional ones—after all, the programmer who designed the chess player's program knows that a computer running that program has no intention whatsoever.

Why can't we Support Eliminativist Materialism?

Eliminativist materialism has the great advantage of simplicity, and offers all fans of technological prowess the promise of stepping out of the minefield of philosophical discussion onto the "safe road of science". It also seems in keeping with an old philosophical materialist tradition that has its credentials: from ancient atomism to Diderot. Despite my particular fondness for these venerable authors, I cannot accept eliminativist materialism. The most fundamental reason is, at the same time, the simplest: to be an eliminativist materialist is quite simply to consider that our experience of ourselves as thinking and feeling beings is, at bottom, nothing more than an illusion—a "reflexive illusion": we are not conscious beings, it's only the way the machine works that "makes" us believe this to be the case. Let's imagine that eliminativist materialism is true, then I'd find it hard to say much more, for if I'm just a "neuronal man" or a computer, I wonder by what miracle I can still say "I". At most, I'd have to say: "the groupings of neurons A, B, C, etc. that are connected in this body called DC produce an internal state like 'I'm a neuronal man'", in the French language. That this means the same thing as "ich *bin ein neuronaler Mensch*" is only because there's a machine for translating from one language into another, and there's no point in assuming that there's anything in common between this sentence in French and this sentence in German that could be called a mental content.

Eliminativist materialism demands, in effect, that we begin by eradicating folk psychology, i.e. the idea that our behavior obeys reasons, desires, feelings and beliefs, i.e. all kinds of mental states. As physicalism, eliminativism demands that our thoughts be considered as physical phenomena. Folk psychology must then be seen as an empirical theory of the mind, and a radically false one at that. From this point of view, eliminativism is not reductionism. Reductionism holds that mental states are ultimately physical states, in the same way that a living being can be reduced to chemical combinations, but for the reductionist it is no more absurd to speak of mental states than it is for the reductionist biologist to speak of cells or white mice. For the radical eliminativist of the Churchland type, there is no possible connection between folk psychology and neuroscience. Eliminativists maintain that folk psychology has the same status as medieval demonology: the mental states it postulates have no more existence than witches.

However, there are several classic arguments against eliminativist materialism. Without claiming to be exhaustive, let's mention a few.

Firstly, "eliminativist materialism" is a theory that destroys itself by self-contradiction: if eliminativist materialism is true, then the Churchland theory is a material product of a material process, and so applying the qualifier "true" to it makes no sense. This position would therefore be a performative contradiction, like saying "I don't think".

Secondly, eliminativist materialism also fails to account for intentionality in Brentano's technical sense of the term. Intentionality is the fact that a thought is always a thought about something, that it aims at something. When I utter the sentence "The cat is on the carpet", that sentence has a semantic content. Enunciation is indeed a cerebral activity (mobilizing the language area), but it's an activity that concerns a state of the world (the fact that the cat is or isn't on the carpet). If thought is just a physical state of the brain, how can one physical state be "about" another physical state? A physical state may be caused by another physical state, but it has no semantic content in itself: physical phenomena "don't mean anything", unless we fall back into a purely animistic conception that would make physical processes signs sent to humans by who knows what or whom! A physical causal relationship is not a semantic one. If I see smoke, I think there must be a fire, but smoke is not a physical state "about" fire. It's only a human subject who, using knowledge acquired through experience, can think: "there's smoke, that means there must be a fire somewhere".

Churchland's theory is not the only one to be called into question. This self-contradiction is aimed at all attempts to "naturalize" consciousness, i.e. to dissolve the philosophy of mind into the natural sciences. Functionalist conceptions (linked to TCE, for example) can be refuted in the same way. For example, Hilary Putnam (in *Representation and Reality*), one of the earliest proponents of computational theory, has come to reject it, showing that it presupposes a functionalist conception of the mind as a machine built to perform well-defined tasks—as Fodor explains, functionalism is inseparable from artificial intelligence, since it postulates the identity or substitutability of a computer and the human mind as long as they can perform the same functions. Putnam first shows that all possible physical organisms are susceptible to an infinite number of "functional descriptions" and that, consequently, functionalism explains nothing—functionalism, in fact, takes us back to the final causes of classical Aristotelianism in a caricatured version: what is an ear? It's for hearing! As if we knew what an ear is when we know that it's used for hearing: a microphone "hears" sounds and we can then amplify or record them. Can we deduce from this that a microphone is like an ear?

More fundamentally, Putnam attacks not only the very principle of computational theory, but also the theses of J. R. Searle. The latter, while rejecting the model of the mind as a kind of computer, does not give up on "naturalizing" consciousness; he rejects the reductionism that reduces consciousness to physical states, but proposes to consider consciousness as a set of properties emerging from biological evolution, which leads him to join the theses on the connectionist model of the mind. For Putnam, it's the problem that is, at root, badly posed. When we speak or think, our words or thoughts have a reference—when I say "the cat is on the carpet", that sentence has as its reference the fact that the cat is (or isn't) on the carpet. All proponents of the naturalization of the mind have to manage to explain that this reference is a physical (or biological) relationship like any other. But if this is so, says Putnam, then we must renounce the very notion of truth... which we can hardly renounce if we want to propose a correct understanding of the human mind. We can, of course, redefine truth as the property of a neurological state in which we have reliable indications about our environment. This leads to a kind of skeptical relativism, but such a philosophical position is radically opposed to the attitude of scientific realism characteristic of computational and functionalist theories of the mind. Indeed, if truth is nothing other than a certain neurological state, then strong materialism in theory of mind is also a certain neurological state, providing more or less reliable indications as to our environment. But the indications given by strong materialism are not particularly more reliable than those given by competing theories.

Chapter III – Should we Eliminate the Mind?

Putnam recalls that these questions have already been posed philosophically, notably by Kant when he tackled the problem of schematism, i.e. the mechanism by which the understanding can relate to phenomena. "The schematism of our understanding, in relation to phenomena and their simple form, is an art hidden in the depths of the human soul, and whose true mechanism it will always be difficult to wrest from nature", says Kant, in *Critique of Pure Reason,* III (1781). The mind-machine paradigm is undoubtedly a useful idea from the point of view of technology (Fodor reminds us that the early days of artificial intelligence were engineering, not science). It's still a useful idea insofar as the simulations that machines can perform force us to develop logic and reflection on knowledge. But its scientific validity is far from proven.

Ultimate Rescue Attempt:
Jaegwon Kim and Functional Reduction

Faced with the difficulties of eliminativist materialism, Jaegwon Kim presents (see his book *L'esprit dans un monde physique. Essai sur le problème corps-esprit et la causalité mentale,* 1998) an original solution. After demonstrating the incoherence of non-reductionist conceptions in the philosophy of mind, and while rejecting eliminativist materialism, which purely and simply abolishes mind, and thus the very idea of mental states of which we nevertheless have indisputable direct experience (notably intentionality and *qualia,* i.e. the subjective content of experience), Kim defends a theory he calls "functional reduction". To achieve this, he draws on the philosophies of emergence that emerged in British philosophy in the early nineteenth century, and which have a rather bad reputation among hard-core materialists and physicalists.

Emergence (cf. above on living things) is a simple idea: there is more in the whole than in the parts. Emergentism supports an ontology that describes the world as composed of levels of complexity: either a certain organization of entities in the world at level N, this organization at level N+1 possesses emergent properties, i.e. properties that cannot be deduced from the properties at level N. For example, living organisms are "assemblies" of chemical molecules; however, the properties of these organisms are completely different from the chemical properties of their components. Emergentism promises to avoid two pitfalls: those of reductionism and those arising from the introduction of mysterious principles specific to a certain level, such as the "vital principle" that would characterize living organisms. Nevertheless, many philosophers and scientists are highly suspicious of emergentism. Indeed, there are two hypotheses. Either emergent properties can be explained by a finer understanding of the processes between components—for example, Claude Bernard maintains that we should one day be able to understand the properties of living organisms from the physico-chemical properties of their components. But in this case, emergence is only temporary: it's just a word to describe our ignorance, which is as temporary as possible, and we'll end up back in good old reductionism. Either the emergent properties are truly emergent, and are therefore irreducible to the properties of lower-level components, or we'd have to admit creation "*ex nihilo*". Or, we can say that the mind "emerges" from our biological organization, but this is simply another way of saying "then there was light".

We can see the benefits of emergentism for the philosophy of mind. Mental properties would be emergent properties at a certain level of neural complexity—this is clearly what Jean-Pierre Changeux has in mind. But Changeux's work lacks the necessary philosophical clarity—as can be seen in his book of dialogue with Paul Ricœur (see Changeux et Ricœur, *Ce qui nous fait penser. La nature et la règle*, Odile Jacob, 1998). Kim, on the other hand, is not strictly speaking an emergentist. He considers, quite rightly, that many of the properties that English emergentists held to be irreducible have in fact been reduced: we know roughly how the atomic properties of natural elements explain their chemical properties. For him, emergent properties are not intrinsic properties, but functional properties that can be "reduced". Thus, a living organism (the liver, for example) has particular properties that differ from those of its components, but (1) these properties define the organism's functions and causal power, and (2) these higher-level properties are explained by the lower-level properties. Kim asserts that this procedure can be applied to mental phenomena: they are functional properties of certain neural and physical states, therefore. As a result, we can show that mental states and physical states are the same thing. And basically, Kim, through functionalism and a rehabilitation of reductionism, finds a new way of "reducing" the mental to the physical, i.e., of eliminating it.

However, Kim does not claim to have the definitive solution. For him, his "functional reduction" should easily explain intentionality. But he does acknowledge that there is a serious problem with *qualia*, i.e. subjective perceptions. How does it feel to see a red rose? Is the red of the rose the same for you as it is for me? This problem of *qualia* has always been a thorn in the side of eliminativists. Some authors eliminate the problem: since you and I agree that this rose is red, the question of whether you see red as I see red is a false one. And Kim is not much further ahead. It's hard to see, however, that we can "reduce" intentionality without reducing *qualia*, for, unless we take up Dennett's semi-behaviorist conception of intentionality, it may well be that the two questions are more closely linked than Kim seems to think. In any case, Kim falls back on an eliminativist position, although he never states it as such. But at the same time, he has to admit that he can't hold it to the end. Indeed, there is only one direction left: pursue to the end the reduction of the mental to the physical, and then the problem of mental causality is solved… quite simply by dissolving the problem: mental causes are illusory causes, only physical causes exist. Kim shows, moreover, that all the solutions envisaged in the philosophy of mind converge towards the unreality of the mind, which is very much in line with physicalism.

The advantage of Kim's work is that he doesn't leave stone unturned by the various current doctrines in philosophy of mind, all of which claim to provide non-eliminativist solutions to the *mind-body problem*, without reverting to good old Cartesian dualism. Kim seems to be telling them that they're hiding behind their little fingers and are fundamentally incoherent. But, at the same time, everyone knows that eliminativist materialism in its various forms is ultimately a difficult doctrine to sustain seriously to the end because, as Kim remarks, "the phenomenal properties of experiences seem to resist functionalization," i.e., the process of eliminating the intrinsic character of mental properties.

Neurobiology (see below) teaches us new things about the brain, but almost nothing about the mind. And the philosophy of mind teaches us even less, since all it does is say: "the solution to all our problems lies in neurobiology", but without getting too far into this complicated subject. In fact, it's clear that neurobiology may have medical applications, but doesn't teach us much about thought. For example, knowing that depression is always linked to serotonin reuptake tells you nothing about the causes of the subject's depressive state! His unhappiness (emotional shock, for example) has nothing to do with serotonin! But unhappiness is not a physical thing: the loss of a loved one is due to physical reasons, but the fact that this loss causes unhappiness is not a physical thing, because no one is able to establish the chain of physical causality that leads from the news given to you by the surgeon (for example) to your despair. We can postulate that such a causal chain exists, but that we can't know it, which brings to mind Russell's

Chapter III – Should we Eliminate the Mind?

teapot: those who ask you to accept that there is indeed a teapot orbiting the sun, but that it's too small to be seen by telescopes, must demonstrate its existence. It's not up to those who don't believe in the teapot to show that it doesn't exist. Philosophy of mind postulates too many teapots orbiting the sun, and a healthy skepticism like Russell's is the best attitude to adopt.

So What?

Admitting, then, that the various variants of eliminativist, emergentist, epiphenomenalist, etc. theories of mind are not really convincing—some of them seem to me to be downright wrong, but others are merely debatable and incapable of gaining support—does this mean we need to return to the double ontology that separates body and soul, matter and mind as two fundamentally different realities? It's neither necessary nor useful. The Cartesian dualism of the two substances is also fraught with obscurity. What can be questioned is only the predominance of a certain materialism that ends up obscuring thinking. And just because you're not a materialist doesn't mean you have to fall into idealism. The "two camps" theory in philosophy is devastating, and almost as dangerous as in politics.

Materialism is a metaphysical position, not a science, not something that can be scientifically demonstrated. Materialism is no more susceptible to "proof" than faith in a world-ordering God. Its only advantage is that it eliminates one entity: instead of God and nature, we're left with nature. But we can't be sure that nature boils down to what is tangible and experimentable on our own scale.

There is a dogmatic, scientistic materialism that claims that the sciences, biology first and foremost, and then its extensions in the philosophy of mind, have proven the truth of materialism. No science can prove the truth of materialism. The successes of the sciences only prove that we must refuse to be dazzled and blinded by mystical ideas such as "nature is well made", "the world is ordered with a view to certain ends" and so on.

Physicalism, the doctrine that physics is the model of all science, is nothing other than this kind of dogmatic materialism disguised as an epistemological doctrine. Let's be clear: physicalism is undoubtedly wrongly equated with materialism. Physicalism maintains that nothing exists outside physical entities. It's a radical thesis. Classical materialism, methodological materialism, simply asserts the primacy of matter over mind. If you read materialist authors, they'll say that "existence determines consciousness" or that "thought depends on the brain", but few will go so far as to assert that thought doesn't exist or that it's just a physical phenomenon. Cabanis and a few others go so far as to say that the brain secretes thought like the liver secretes bile, but this type of position is relatively rare, and even often mocked by other materialists—such as Engels, who supports a very particular "dialectical materialism" (see my book, *Engels, philosophe et savant*, éditions Bréal, 2020).

For a moderate materialist, there is no world other than our world and no life of the soul after death, but a materialist of this kind can admit without difficulty the existence of mental states distinct from physical states, provided they are not the mental states of bodiless souls. Moreover, for a materialist, what we call thought is not necessarily a predicate of the body or of that part of the body called the brain. As a materialist, I have no trouble admitting that I have access to Plato's thought, even though Plato's brain hasn't existed for some time! More generally, when I communicate with another individual, I have no access to his brain (I don't have a "cerebroscope" to read the state of his brain), but I do have access to his thoughts, or at least to the part of his thoughts that he communicates, and to what I can induce from his attitudes! So you can be a materialist, and a fairly "idealist" too—like Marx, who, in his *Theses on Feuerbach*, criticizes early materialism "including Feuerbach's" for failing to grasp reality as practice, "subjectively".

So why do materialists have such a penchant for eliminativist materialism? It seems to me that it's simply because they remain entirely dependent on the Cartesian problem of body and soul, and seek to provide a materialist solution to the questions posed by Descartes. Like Cartesians, eliminativist materialists believe that the mind is "inside", in the folds of the brain, if not in the soul. Eliminativist materialists are also looking for some kind of pineal gland. But it's precisely to get away from this problematic that we need to work.

In conclusion, I would like to quote Paul Ricœur in his exchanges with Jean-Pierre Changeux:

> [As a philosopher, I profess a strong agnosticism concerning the possibility of constituting a discourse of overhang from which I would see the profound unity of what appears to me sometimes as a neuronal system, sometimes as a mental experience. In the final analysis, these are two discourses of the body.
>
> J.-P. CHANGEUX, P. RICŒUR. *Ce qui nous fait penser*, 2008

And like Ricœur, I don't see how this agnosticism about the possibility of a "third-party" discourse is a form of "idealistic prejudice". Rather, I have the impression that it's those who believe in this third-party discourse who are idealistically prejudiced: they think they're God!

The AI Debate

All the theoretical discussions we've just been talking about are now being applied to the debate on artificial intelligence. The considerable progress made in computer power has, it seems, enabled us to take a few steps towards this "artificial intelligence", which is at least as old as computing and perhaps even older! We're finally going to be able to put the mind into the machine, and show that the human mind is no different from a machine. Leibniz thought he could invent a "language of characters" (the "universal characteristic") into which we could univocally translate our natural language and, by means of defined operators to manipulate the characters, "calculate our thoughts", replacing all the dilemmas of law and morality with *"calculemus"*, and he is undoubtedly the true inventor of artificial intelligence, since he was the first to lay the foundations of a language for calculating thoughts. But we can go even further back in time, to all the mnemonic devices used to perfect memory and replace reflection wherever possible with a kind of mind mechanics manipulating "deaf thoughts", to use Leibniz's phrase. Thus, in his treatise on the soul (*De Anima*), Aristotle maintains that the soul can only think with images of concrete things, and that there is nothing in the mind that has not first been in the senses.

All the memory arts that follow are first and foremost systems of rules for forming effective images of things and words to remember. But it's not enough to memorize images; you also need to know in what order to retrieve and assemble them. Just as Simonides remembered guests by remembering their order at table, all the memory arts will propose ways of remembering the order in which memorized images should be recalled, by associating an image with a familiar (for example) or fictitious place (for example, the circles of hell), the important thing being that we can form an image of the place. In the Middle Ages, Raymond Lulle had a mystical experience: on Mount Randa on the island of Majorca, he suddenly saw all the attributes of God pervading the whole of creation. From this he derived the idea of a "universal art" based on these attributes, reduced to nine (goodness, magnanimity, eternity, power, wisdom, will, virtue, truth, glory). Representing each one by a letter, he invents a kind of machine that combines all these letters to find and memorize divine truths. This abstract combinatory system is a far cry from conventional mnemonics. We've built "Lulle machines" and they haven't been able to memorize all divine truths, but our contemporary AI prophets haven't given up hope. After Leibniz, a number of logical and philosophical works seemed to lead to decisive advances: Boolean algebra (the logic of propositions), then various logical languages such as Frege's ideography, the formalism of Russell and Whitehead in *Principia Mathematica* (1910), or Wittgenstein's attempt at a rigorous logical language in *Tractatus Logico-Philosophicus* (1921). Add to this Emil Post's theory of formal systems, or the arithmetization of number theory used by Gödel to prove his famous theorem. AI was born out of the development of logic and research into the possibility of mechanizing reasoning, precisely to avoid the errors of reasoning and paralogisms into which we so easily fall.

In its reasonable versions, AI does not claim to provide a model of how the mind works, but aims to automate a whole series of tasks, more or less tedious. Computer science itself grew out of this. The "Turing machine" is the direct result of developments based on a problem posed by David Hilbert in 1928, the problem of decidability (*Entscheidungsproblem*), i.e., is there an algorithm that decides whether a proposition stated in a logical system is valid or not? For the first time, a mathematical problem found a "technical" solution: a computable function is one that can be calculated by a Turing machine, which "completes" the calculation, even if it takes a very long time. Long before we had today's phenomenal computing power, the idea was conceived of a kind of homology between the logical calculation performed by a human mind and the operations that can be performed with a machine. There has been no fundamental change since then. Today's "intelligent" machines use the same two recipes: unlimited memory storage and algorithms. As was the case half a century ago, biological metaphors (neural networks, genetic algorithms, etc.) are flourishing, appealing to the imagination but confusing reasoned reflection.

There are many different types of computing machine. A word processor is at first sight an ultra-sophisticated typewriter, but no one has thought of presenting Word or Libre Office Writer as "intelligent" programs, and yet in the AI sense they are intelligent programs. The great and perhaps only real innovation to have developed with the microcomputer is the spreadsheet, first popularized by Lotus 1-2-3, now virtually extinct. These office machines have invaded the world of work, sometimes simplifying it and often standardizing it: PowerPoint has almost become a household name, like the moped or the fridge, and has ended up imposing "PowerPoint thinking". There's a second category: communicating machines, i.e. the entire Internet network. All these machines are already "intelligent machines" in their own way. A router finds the best route for a request. A word processor "corrects" spelling, grammar and punctuation errors. A spreadsheet makes it easy to compare scenarios. Image-editing software analyzes an image and can separate its components, correct light, etc. AI is here, as it has been for a long time, in the automatic systems that help pilots fly airplanes, in the robots used in industry and in all machines that are programmed to react to random situations. It is developing with image, handwriting and voice recognition, or with "expert systems" specialized in encoding human knowledge to make it easily accessible to everyone, or to automatically deduce "new" knowledge by means of automatic logical chaining. Cybernetics and computer science: all this is AI. It's fair to say that, right from the start, computing was conceived as "artificial intelligence", since the first computers were still referred to as "electronic brains".

In fact, we need to start by saying that AI in general doesn't exist. There are "AI machines" made up of processors, memories, acquisition or command peripherals and specific programs. There are big differences between a machine that reads written text (as in Word verification systems), a machine that recognizes faces to authorize or deny access (as is increasingly the case with smartphones) and a machine capable of extracting relevant information from an MRI scan to detect the possibility of a cancerous tumor. As many differences as between a combine harvester, a bulldozer, a racing car or an electric scooter.

We also need to distinguish between a machine and a tool. A tool is simply an extension of the hand: the carpenter works with his mallet and chisel to make his tenon. The electric saw, on the other hand, is already a machine, since the hand merely guides, while the energy comes from the electric motor. This is a first possible distinction. A second distinction could be made: the tool is in contact with the hand or any other part of the body, whereas the machine only moves with intermediate parts between the body and the part of the machine that actually acts. A spear is a tool, a thruster is already a machine—very elementary, even minimalist, but a machine nonetheless. In an older sense, a machine is a ruse (we've kept the word "machination", another name for plot), as was Ulysses' Trojan horse. The machine is intimately linked to Greek *metis*: the art of cunning that enables us to deceive others, to simulate or outwit the force of nature. The man who conceives this Trojan horse is the same one who says his name is "Nobody" when he is captured by the Cyclops Polyphemus. Polyphemus will even have to admit it when, with his eye gouged out, he cries out: "It's cunning and not strength! and who kills me: No one" (Odyssey, Canto IX).

So AIs are machines that can trick and multiply human (intellectual) strength tenfold, just as a lever or a hoist multiplies physical strength tenfold. If we adopt an idealistic point of view, we're obviously blown away by the power of these "electronic brains", whereas we're blasé about the power multiplication enabled by a simple lever—which should enable us to lift the world, provided we find a good fulcrum. An AI is a very complicated machine, made up of a very large number of components interacting with each other (the millions of transistors that make up processors and memories) at a very rapid rate. From this point of view, such a machine is a concentrate of human intelligence: intelligence of the overall design, intelligence of the physical theories that went into building the semiconductors, intelligence of the program designers, and so on.

Why are AIs more fascinating than the lever or Archimedes' screw? Obviously, because they seem to perform complex operations reserved for the human mind. But we need to keep our wits about us. Music-playing machines (Vaucanson automata, music boxes, limonaires) are machines that imitate certain functions of a human being. While the first two are hard-wired machines capable only of repeating the same operation over and over again, the limonaire is a more sophisticated machine, since it has a program in the form of perforated plates, which can be modified at will. Unlike the phonograph and its successors, the limonaire "plays", not simply transforms signals. The Jacquard loom weaves patterns on demand, according to the "program" (again, perforated plates) it is given. It will be rightly objected that these programs execute the simplest algorithms, since there is only a sequence of instructions with no test or loop, and *a fortiori* no recursive call possible. Charles Babbage's "analytical machine" project, known as "the mill", which was never completed, should have been a programmable mechanical machine (driven by a steam engine!) that prefigured the first computer.

To introduce these functions into a machine, you need testing devices (e.g. the thermostat, which defines the temperature at which the water in the washing machine is to be heated before starting the wash program). Counters are also needed (to run A for x cycles, for example). Reusable information storage devices can also be added. Self-regulating systems can be set up, like the ball regulator invented by Watt for steam engines. The machine is now becoming very complicated, but there's nothing mysterious about it, and we can control its organization and operation at every stage. The engineering of such machines is precisely what cybernetics is all about: "A science that uses the results of signal and information theory to develop a method for analyzing and synthesizing complex systems, their functional relationships and control mechanisms, in biology, economics, computer science, etc." (CNRTL). The etymology of this word would rather say: "technique of government"… Today, the machines we're dealing with are digital machines, whose triumph is only relatively recent. For a very long time, we developed analog calculators, which became quite powerful with the invention of operational amplifiers. These machines were particularly well suited to dealing with systems of differential equations. In the 1970s-1980s, the CEA in France and NASA in the United States had large analog computing centers. It wasn't until the 1980s that digital machines asserted their superiority thanks to their versatility.

What about today's AIs? It's a bit presumptuous to attempt to answer this question, since new developments will emerge that could render some of the answers obsolete. You could say that every autopilot machine is a kind of AI. It is capable of performing the task for which it was designed without the intervention of a human pilot. An autonomous lawnmower is an AI machine smart enough to save its owner from having to run behind a noisy, tiring machine. But the most fascinating machines obviously seem to be not those that act (like the washing machine programmer), but those that seem to produce knowledge. "Seem to": as such, machines don't produce knowledge, but only signals that bring us knowledge. If I turn the switches A and B on a lamp back and forth, if I press switch A when the lamp is off, it will come on, and if I press switch B, it will go off. If we have agreed to assign function F to A, then B can be assigned to non-F. A toggle switch is analogous to a logic inverter (the operation "negation which to

F corresponds non-F"). But neither the switches nor the lamp are logic machines in themselves, they are machines designed to be, in their operation, analogous to the logical operations performed by the human brain, in the same way that a suitably mounted operational amplifier can give me the derivative of the sinusoidal voltage sent in as an output, without us being able to say that the amplifier "knows how to perform" the calculation of a derivative. For these very simple examples, you won't find many minds weak enough to talk about the intelligence of switches or operational amplifiers: it's immediately obvious that they're no more intelligent than the abacus, the pascaline or Watt's ball regulator.

It's perhaps a different story with the AI machines in the news, because their complexity quickly exceeds our imagination, and imagination is limited, unlike our capacity to conceptualize, whose limits we don't experience—Descartes remarked that we can't form an image of a chiliagon, whereas we have no trouble conceiving a thousand-sided polygon. Today's AI machines are of various types. First of all, there are the so-called "expert systems". The simplest expert system is made up of a knowledge base (which is likely to evolve), primarily the result of human expertise, and an inference engine that logically links the propositions contained in the knowledge base. Computer languages such as PROLOG have been explicitly designed to implement quantified logic (order 1). AI machines are then machines capable of playing human games: chess machines and, more recently, go machines, one of the most complicated games ever (there are some 10,620 possible games), even though its basic rules are very simple. Finally, there are recognition systems (images, shapes, sound, speech, writing, etc.), as well as web search engines or web and traffic management programs.

All these machines presuppose the resolution of two types of problem: firstly, the representation of data in superimposed levels of abstraction, and secondly, calculation algorithms. Decisive progress has been made thanks to increased memory capacity, enabling access to massive data ("*big data*"), and to the computing power of machines. The "*alphago zero*" machine, which succeeded in beating the previous machine, which in turn beat the world's best go players, became champion by playing millions of games against itself in three days. The advantage of enormous computing power is obvious here. It is this enormous power that enables the implementation of self-learning processes (known as *deep learning*). But when you think about it, it's a bit like the intelligence of the shadoks, those little creatures that used to brighten up French television in the days of the ORTF: the shadoks wanted to send a rocket to the planet Gibi and, knowing that they had a one-in-a-million chance of succeeding, they would hurry up and fail the first 999,999 attempts... Without going into too much detail, these systems are largely based on selectionist algorithms: sequences of instructions are generated (randomly) and those that fail are progressively eliminated (an application of Darwinian selectionist principles), and what we call self-learning is never anything other than this type of induction-based process.

All these so-called "intelligent" techniques are so only if we reduce the word *intelligence* to its English meaning: how to obtain information? But no intelligent machine has ever shown the intelligence of even a small child, if we mean intelligence in the French sense of the ability to understand, to "take with oneself", but also astuteness, intuition and creativity. The Anglo-Saxons have distinguished between weak and strong AI. Weak AI encompasses all the computer techniques that can be put at the service of humans, while strong AI is based on the project of building a machine capable of imitating human intellectual capacities better and better. The problem is that *weak AI* is often conceived simply as a precursor to *strong AI*, which feeds all the hopes, fantasies and more or less vain fears. Conversational agents" such as Open AI, chatGPT and the like seem to cross the boundary between the two types of AI, since they not only provide information, like a common search engine, but also produce "original" texts or images. However, experience tends to prove that they are machines that don't provide any serious information at all…

Searle Critic of AI

The effectiveness of these so-called AI techniques is obvious, and there is a tendency to believe that their current limits are only temporary, and could be surpassed by the progress of methods and the power of machines. However, this is a simple belief that will be hard to substantiate. Because a machine will be able to carry out an increasingly impressive number of arithmetic and logical operations (after all, that's all a computer does), and because it will have data storage capacities beyond our imagination today, will we be able to deduce that it has become intelligent? A human brain, after all, has only limited data storage capacity (which is why we've invented all kinds of devices to serve as prostheses for our failing memory), and our computing speed is rather low: a nerve impulse propagates at around 300 m/s, whereas electrical signals in a circuit propagate at speeds on the order of the speed of light, i.e. 300,000 km/s. So, right from the start, the computer is 106 times faster than the human brain! Yet there is clearly an essential difference between the human brain and the computer, between human intelligence and the so-called "artificial intelligence" of machines. This raises the question of the real limits of AI.

Tests can be set, more or less arbitrarily, to determine whether an AI machine "thinks". The best-known is the famous "Turing test", a sophisticated version of which can be found in Philip K. Dick's novel *Do Androids Dream of Electric Sheep* (1968), adapted for the screen by Ridley Scott under the title *Blade Runner* (1982). The principle is as follows: if, in a conversation held via a telecommunications system, we can't distinguish the machine from a human interlocutor, then we can say that the machine is thinking. J. R. Searle devotes considerable space to criticizing the "Turing test", showing that it cannot prove that machines think.

Let's summarize Searle's argument. He invents another test, modelled on Turing's: a person totally ignorant of the Chinese language is locked in a room and communicates in writing with a Chinese speaker located outside. The person trapped in the room has a catalog of syntactic rules at his disposal, enabling him to choose the characters needed to answer a question formulated in Chinese characters. This is how Searle describes the genesis of his "thought experiment":

> I bought a textbook at random, whose argumentative approach stunned me with its weakness. Little did I know then that this book would be a turning point in my life. It explained how a computer could understand language. The argument was that the computer could be told a story and then be able to answer questions relating to that story, even though the answers were not explicitly given in the story. The story was as follows: a man goes to a restaurant, orders a hamburger, is served a charred hamburger, and leaves without paying. The computer is asked: "Did he eat the hamburger? The authors were very happy with this result, which was supposed to prove that the computer had the same comprehension skills as we do. It was at this point that I conceived the Chinese room argument: suppose I'm in a closed room with the ability to receive and give symbols, via a keyboard and screen, for example. I have Chinese characters and instructions to produce certain character sequences based on the characters you input into the room. You provide me with the story and then the question, both written in Chinese. Having the appropriate instructions, I can only give you the right answer, but without having understood anything, since I don't know Chinese. All I'd be doing is manipulating symbols that mean nothing to me. A computer is in exactly the same situation as

I was in the Chinese room: it only has symbols and rules governing their manipulation.

"Language, consciousness, rationality: a natural philosophy.
Interview with John R. Searle", Le Débat,
Gallimard, no 109, March-April 2000

Searle here implicitly criticizes two classic (but erroneous) conceptions in psychology: behaviorism and functionalism. Turing's idea is that a computer can be said to think if it is capable of behaving like an ordinary thinking being, i.e. a human. This idea is coupled with another: if a computer is capable of performing the same functions as a human brain, then we have no reason to deny it the quality of thinking being.

Behaviorists believe that the mind is a kind of "black box", and that only the relationships between stimuli and responses (input/output) can be investigated. A behaviorist would argue that I have no proof that other people think, other than the fact that their behavior can be interpreted in terms of thoughts. Whether, from a cognitive point of view, we are more or less reduced to observing others to know whether they think or whether they are well-made machines, is already debatable. First of all, we have more reason to believe that a goldfish spinning in its bowl or a hen crossing the road in front of a car is capable of thought than a computer. We lend animals capacities to feel that we don't lend to inert things. Our experience of other living things is in no way the same as our experience of things. It's a primary experience, prior to any reflection: I didn't need to make all kinds of observations to draw the conclusion that "this goldfish is alive". This applies *a fortiori* to other human beings. In a letter to the Marquis of Newcastle dated November 16, 1646, the latter asks how we can distinguish a man from an animal or a well-made machine. Descartes' answer to this question boiled down to one argument: we recognize a man endowed with a soul capable of thinking by the fact that he can hold a conversation, pronounce "words, or other signs made about the subjects that present themselves, without relating to any passion". The inventor of the Turing test was Descartes! But the illustrious philosopher is probably mistaken: I don't need to hold an "apropos" conversation with a mute Chinese speaker to know that he's a human like me and therefore has a "soul" like me, whereas my computer doesn't have a "soul", it seems to know so many things and can give answers to a host of questions that my Chinese friend knows nothing about. Merleau-Ponty goes in a different direction from Descartes: according to him, consciousness must be conceived as "being in the world" or as "existence". Because vision gives me a way of looking at the world, there can be a way of looking at others for me, "this expressive instrument called a face can carry an existence, just as my existence is carried by the knowing apparatus that is my body". In the encounter with another human being, there is a kind of intuition that makes me give meaning to his mimics, his gestures, that I consider his postures, his actions as actions that are possible for me. The "evidence of others", as Merleau-Ponty calls it, stems from an internal relationship that derives precisely from the fact that we are all expressive bodies in the same way.

Once again, this is not the result of reflection. Just because I compare someone else's facial expressions to my own, I don't deduce by association that they must be in the same mental state as I am when I use them. But this reasoning by analogy can explain why we perceive the feelings of others in mimics or attitudes that we have never experienced or observed. How would small children learn if they had to apply this reasoning by analogy? There's something pre-reflexive about this relationship with others.

Thus, behaviorist psychology, which appeals so much to scientists obsessed with the natural science model, misses the essential point: subjectivity, the primacy of all knowledge of the external world. The functionalist approach is no better. Functionalism consists in studying the functions that are performed in any device that could be described as intelligent, independently of the support for this intelligence. But it's highly doubtful that we can give any value whatsoever to functionalist explanations, for the reason that knowing what function an entity (machine or living being) performs is not the same as knowing what that entity is—a question that could be described as a "metaphysical question". If I say: "The function of the liver is to produce bile", I still don't know anything about the liver, since I don't have a causal explanation of the bile production system. In philosophy of mind, functionalism defines a mental state by the function it performs, knowing that mental states can cause other mental states. This concept likens the (human) mind to a calculator with a number of functional units responsible for performing certain calculations. It's something akin to the modular theory of mind once espoused by Jerry Fodor, before Fodor himself refuted it—let's say that TCE is a form of functionalism.

If we reject both behaviorism and functionalism, there's not much left of Turing's experiment (the Turing test), and so the question of the possibility of artificial intelligence analogous to human intelligence becomes highly problematic. All in all, Searle's "Chinese room" experiment does not prove that "strong" AI is an impossibility. He merely provides good arguments for rejecting the Turing test as the ultimate discriminating test.

Searle's conclusions can be summed up in a few propositions that we must accept:

23. computer programs are formal (syntactic). In fact, they only indicate the operations to be performed, and in what order;

24. human thoughts have a mental content (they have semantics). Two sentences that differ in vocabulary or syntax can have the same mental content (the same reference) and, conversely, two identical sentences can have different semantic contents, not to mention the problem of referential obscurity;

25. semantics cannot be reduced to syntax, and syntax cannot provide access to semantics. The sentence "many people mistakenly believe that Galileo was burned because he defended the Earth's rotundity" is semantically ambiguous; is it wrong to believe that he was burned or that he defended the Earth's rotundity... or both?

26. and yet it is the activity of the brain that generates thought. This last proposition is self-evident, according to Searle.

Searle's conclusions can be summarized as follows:

27. programs are neither constitutive of thought nor sufficient to produce it;

28. any system capable of generating thoughts should have a causal power at least equivalent to that of the brain. But no computer has the causal power of a human brain, not even that of a chimpanzee or sheep brain;

29. an artificial system will only produce mental phenomena if it reproduces the specific determining powers of the brain. By the same token, if such a thing could be produced artificially, it would also have the same defects as the brain and would be of no interest;

30. the formation of mental phenomena in the brain is not simply the result of executing a computer program. It presupposes a relationship with the world that is precisely called subjectivity.

For Searle, the opposition between syntax and semantics is the fundamental opposition. Machines only process syntax, not meaning. A machine never crashes because what it "says" is nonsense, but only because there has been a syntactic error in the programming, i.e. an error in the way the machine works. If I write Chomsky's famous phrase: "the green colorless ideas slept furiously", this sentence doesn't provoke any reaction from my parser, and for good reason: it's syntactically impeccable! A human, on the other hand, will quickly see that the sentence either makes no sense, or is intended for some poetic effect—rather like the Jabberwocky poem in Lewis Caroll's *Alice*—"tout flicteux allaient les borogoves…". There's a fundamental reason why machines can't handle this. Machines can only perform logical operations, whereas meaning cannot be deduced from logic, quite simply because there is no formal logic beyond the logic of propositions, i.e. beyond statements that obey the principle of analycity, i.e. statements whose logical value depends only on the logical value of the components of these statements. Let's take an example: let's consider the proposition "I believe that X". This proposition is true if I really believe that X, whatever nonsense X may contain. So the truth of "I believe that X" does not obey the principle of analyticity. This is just a small example. We can't formalize the connotation of a proposition. The truth conditions of a proposition only concern its denotation. For example, the proposition "Le vainqueur d'Austerlitz est mort à Sainte-Hélène" is rigorously equivalent to the proposition "Le vaincu de Waterloo est mort à Sainte-Hélène". From the point of view of logical calculation, one can be replaced by the other without further ado. Formal logic can be infinitely sophisticated, but meaning escapes it. Attempts to do so have produced edifices of scholastic jargon that are absolutely sterile. This is the conclusion Wittgenstein reached when he realized that the search for a purely logical language had reached an impasse, and turned to the uses of ordinary language. Formal logic, however powerful, can only account for a thin layer of linguistic statements. How can a machine that can only process formal logic be "intelligent"?

Meaning presupposes the representation of the world and of oneself in the world. But since a machine is not a "self", since a machine is merely an assembly of parts that are external to each other, it has no representation of itself or of the world, and even less of itself in the world. This is an essential difference between a machine and a living being. A living being, however crude, is a "self", possessing a certain unity that makes it an individual. It has internal regulatory mechanisms and is capable of reacting to shocks it may receive from the outside: when the gardener spades his garden, the earthworm reacts if it is disturbed, and it will not stay in the air. A machine, however complex, is an assembly of parts that do not form a single unit. If I remove the hard disk from my computer, it doesn't feel hot or cold! All this is quite obvious, and it's hard to understand why authors who often call themselves "materialists" fail to grasp that there's an ontological gulf between machines and the living, and that the most powerful computer will never have the practical and emotional intelligence of my dog.

Among all material things, Searle distinguishes between those that have an objective existence and those that exist only for a brain capable of representing them. The pain I feel is "ontologically subjective" and not susceptible of objective representation. How could a computer program model something that is "ontologically subjective"? We can always reject this kind of thing and consider it to be merely reflexive illusions that we need to get rid of in order to become true scientists of modern high-tech. We might add to Searle's remark that even things with objective existence are only known to us as such through our subjective experience, through our "presence in the world".

The problem of intentionality is central to Searle's thinking. It stems from the essential character of the mind, subjectivity, and from the fact that subjectivity is irreducible to objectivity—a very old affair: you can't simply go from "I" to "he". The statement "I think" is radically different from the statement "Man thinks" or "Descartes thinks". Intentionality expresses the fact that an action or a thing has no value in itself, but is "about something" (it has an *aboutness*, as the Anglo-Saxons say). One might be tempted to see, in this privilege given to the human mind, Searle's return to a Cartesian dualism: on the one hand, there are mechanical bodies obeying the necessity of the laws of nature, and on the other, free souls. But this is not the case for Searle. For him, the brain is a natural thing, and the mind is nothing other than the activity of the brain. But, on the one hand, there is a difference in nature between "inert" things and living beings and, on the other, within the kingdom of the living there are also several qualitative leaps. Searle belongs to the "emergence" movement, i.e. those who believe that there are different levels of organization in nature, and that the properties of a certain level cannot always be explained by the properties of lower-level components. There are therefore properties that emerge at a certain level of organization and that are properties of the organization itself. Consciousness, under the name of intentionality, would be precisely something that emerges at a high level of neuronal complexity. Searle believes that by following this path we could build a naturalistic theory of consciousness, which remains on a solid materialist foundation without falling into cognitivism or the computational theory of mind.

The Vertigo of Analogy

Let's get back to the heart of Turing's argument. It boils down to this: if a machine can simulate thought to the point where it deceives a human, then that machine thinks. Behind this lies an essential epistemological question. We frequently work with models, i.e. idealizations of a part of reality, so that we can form an idea of how things might actually be, with a view to making predictions that may or may not confirm the validity of the model. A machine can serve as a model for a scientific theory—for example, the steam engine, a model for thermodynamics. Modeling works very much by analogy: we build something we have mastered in an attempt to predict, by analogy, what should happen in the part of reality we want to understand. But this model can quickly prove cumbersome and even, in some cases, a real epistemological obstacle (see Gaston Bachelard, *La formation de l'esprit scientifique*, 1938). The Ptolemaic model of the world, which seemed perfectly intuitive, had to be rejected. Rutherford's model of the atom was replaced by Bohr's, which itself soon showed its drawbacks, notwithstanding its great pedagogical utility. These models allow us to map reality and, like all maps, if they are good models, they also allow us to navigate. Artificial intelligence functions in part as a model of neural functioning, as long as we agree to assimilate the brain to a computer-like machine. But we should be aware that when we "imitate" on a machine a certain number of operations that a human brain is capable of, firstly, we still don't know how the brain really works and, secondly, we are only "mapping" a very small part of the whole brain. As ever, the map is not the territory!

Conversely, when we study the biological functioning of the brain, we can correlate an operation that a subject can describe verbally with an arrangement of physico-chemical operations in the neurons, but nothing more. We can ask a subject to perform an operation (for example, a sequence of multiplications) and, during this time, record what is happening in the brain using a medical imaging system. But we don't see the multiplication on the screen—for example, we don't see the miscalculation our subject has made (for example, he counted 9x8=54) and obviously we have absolutely no idea what to do in the brain, which neuron to stimulate for example, to avoid this miscalculation. By observing the brain, we can understand brain physiology, but not arithmetic, quite simply because arithmetic is not a question of physiology, even if in the final analysis, it was human brains that eventually invented arithmetic. We might add that human brains invented arithmetic only when their relations with the outside world demanded it as a solution to vital problems to be solved. To be more precise, we should say not that arithmetic is an invention of human brains, but rather that arithmetic emerged from the rela-tionship between humans endowed with brains, living in society with other humans, with their vital environment, their écoumène, to use Augustin Berque's apt concept.

As for what we call, in computing, "formal neural networks" or "neural nets", it's simply an analogy of the kind that led us to speak of "electric current" by analogy with water flowing through a pipe… or as when we spoke of "electronic brains" to designate the first computers. The vertigo of analogy!

Now, let's look at the problem from a different angle: the machine can simulate a mental operation, but the fact that it's simulating in no way means that it's "doing" that mental operation. It's not active at all. When my word processor points out a grammatical error in a sentence I've just typed, it doesn't mean that "someone" has realized anything. All that happened were complicated physical operations, which could be broken down into simple operations, i.e. changes in memory state with each advance of the clock top of the microprocessors "hidden" (barely) inside my machine. You can praise the intelligence of the programmers who designed this grammar checker all you like, but there's no intelligence in the machine other than that of the… human programmers!

Can Machines Talk?

One of the touchstones of AI is the recognition of sentences spoken in "natural language". In the same category of problems, we find the age-old question of machine translation. These two issues simultaneously demonstrate both the power of dedicated AIs and the essential inability of an AI to pass the Turing test 100%, i.e. to mimic a human interlocutor so well that it can hold a conversation with him or her "about any subject that comes up", as Descartes put it in the aforementioned letter to the Marquis of Newcastle. If we go back to Descartes' words, he's saying something important. Why isn't man simply a well-made machine? Because he speaks," replies Descartes, "and this speech attests to the existence of a soul (which is simply thought in action), whereas the signals emitted by animals are due solely to their "passions" and can be explained by physical chemistry. Even if—as in my case—we don't subscribe to Cartesian dualism, we must nevertheless recognize that articulated language represents a considerable qualitative leap forward in the evolutionary process. It could even be said that this intelligent speech is the decisive adaptive advantage that has enabled the survival of the *homo genus*—and perhaps not only of *homo sapiens*, since we are fairly certain today that our *habilis* ancestors, who lived just over a million years ago, possessed Broca's area (the brain area dedicated to language) and a functionally dissymmetrical brain, two features thought to be necessary for the emergence of human intelligence, although we can't deduce that *Homo habilis* spoke. Since AIs are logical procedural machines, the question may turn into this: can human speech be reduced to a formal language like logic, since logic can be implemented on an electronic machine (or any other machine isomorphic to an electronic machine)? Although "conversational agents", such as the famous chatGPT, seem to have made prodigious leaps forward, so that machines can "understand" ordinary language, the fact remains that human language, as properly human, escapes and will continue to escape the omnipotence of algorithms.

The first reason why human language cannot be simulated in such a way that a conversation with a machine can be mistaken for a conversation with a human ("Descartes-Turing" test), is the plasticity of human language in its expression and plasticity in its comprehension. This may seem paradoxical: when Leibniz imagined his "universal characteristic", he was seeking to create a language of characters (on the model of mathematical symbolism) that would rid us of the ambiguities and misunderstandings of "natural language". If such a language can be created, Leibniz thought, then all the ambiguous and confusing reasoning in moral and legal matters could be replaced by a single word: "Let's calculate! These formal languages (e.g., the formalism of predicate logic) are perfectly suited to modeling logical reasoning, i.e., all that is computable, but stumble as soon as we want to model less formal reasoning, e.g., incomplete syllogisms (enthymemes) where one of the premises is implied. Algorithms don't like innuendo! And when there's no reasoning at all, it's even worse! There are occasions in life when we state truths without having particularly convincing reasons in favor of these assertions. We will say that they are not truths, but mere opinions, which is perfectly true, but linguistically they are stated as truths. Let's add that the understanding of a sentence exchanged between two interlocutors includes an incalculable number of non-linguistic signs (attitudes, glances, hand movements, etc.). Written exchanges obey very specific codes (those of the epistolary genre), and when the written word is molded onto the spoken word (exchanges on social networks or by e-mail), we enter the realm of misunderstandings and incomprehensions, which make these exchanges a good way of separating individuals once and for all.

No formal language can provide an accurate description of everything that natural human speech can express. Take, for example, the statement: "Jeanne is getting ready to order, but, as usual, Pierre is late". This statement is made up of two "atomic" statements, p: "Jeanne is getting ready to order" and q: "as usual, Pierre is late". These two statements are linked by the French conjunction "mais", which is nothing other than a logical "et". Indeed, the truth value of the statement depends and depends only on the truth value of the two atomic statements, and this statement is true if and only if p and q are true simultaneously. The problem is that the logical "and" is logically equivalent to the French "but", but it isn't from the point of view of meaning. And while logically, I can't draw anything from the statement, semantically, I can draw a lot of conclusions from it, for example, that

Jeanne must now be fed up with Pierre's systematic lateness, or that, fatalistically, she's saying to herself: "He's like that, we won't do it again", and so on. All the hypotheses I can put forward come from my ability to project myself into Jeanne's mind, because Jeanne is a living human being like me and lives the same inner life as I do, since I have an immediate, pre-reflexive approach to Jeanne (cf. Merleau-Ponty), which no computer program will ever be able to do. We can certainly simulate all this, i.e. develop a program that will have a repertoire of words expressing human feelings in its memory. We can build all the simulations we want, but they will never be anything more than computer simulations, in other words, false pretenses.

The plasticity of language depends on the speaker's ability to understand the context. If I say "la petite brise la glace" ("the little girl breaks the ice"), this sentence can only be broken down grammatically according to the context, since it can consider either the verb "brise" ("breaks") or "glace" ("ice"). We therefore need an understanding (and therefore semantics) of the context to determine how we should read this short sentence. There are also logically absurd sentences that we understand perfectly well: "j'ai mal à tes dents" ("I have a toothache") simply means that I share (metaphorically!) your toothache. We could go on and on. Analytical philosophy has produced thousands of pages on these issues.

Frege showed an essential difference between logic and human speech: logic is like a ruler, and speech like the hand. With the hand alone, it's hard to draw straight lines, so the ruler is very useful, but when it comes to outlining the leaf of a tree, the ruler is useless. The same applies to logic: it's very useful for reasoning straight and validating our reasoning (or denouncing our paralogisms), but it's totally useless when it comes to talking, for example, about our feelings, about what we can call our "inner life", even if this expression is highly problematic.

To get around all these difficulties, AI has found a way that is at the root of its recent successes: using the immense knowledge base provided by the Internet. For example, progress in machine translation has been meteoric since we abandoned the "Chomsky method": we stopped trying to find the logical formulas that would enable us to automatically translate one language into another (i.e. to go from the surface grammar of one language to the deep grammar common to all humans, and then to generate the same deep content in the surface grammar of another language). As long as machine power and storage capacity remained limited, it was hard to see how this could be done any other way. But suppose a certain part of a text is repeated in thousands of available documents, and translations of these documents are available, the machine translation program will detect the most likely translation and, eventually, the user will validate it, thus reinforcing the machine's learning. It's no longer a question of implementing "speech logic" in the machine, but of processing mass data and spotting similarities, just as in pattern recognition software. This means that the machine "understands nothing", "doesn't know" what the author of the text means, but selects similar sentences. So we now have high-performance translation software. But these programs can only process existing material and increase their "knowledge" with each use.

Now let's see why intelligence is not procedural. We talk about artificial intelligence, but it's hard to define intelligence. The simplest definition refers to the ability to make connections. From this point of view, AIs are indeed intelligent, since the only thing they can do with any efficiency is to establish links between masses of data processed in pattern recognition or the analysis of Internet user queries. But, on the other hand, intelligence is opposed to what is purely repetitive, what is mechanical, and then AIs are above all stupid machines, although this qualifier can hardly be something that can be said of a machine (any more than the qualifier "intelligent", for that matter).

Intelligence (human intelligence, since in truth there is no other kind), first of all, doesn't need *"big data"*. Anyone who doesn't need dozens and dozens of experiments to learn a lesson is more intelligent than someone who needs to be told the same things over and over again to get the hang of it! The *Alphago zero* program doesn't show much intelligence, since it needs several million games to learn how to play Go really well. A human being playing 10 games of go a day for 80 years wouldn't be able to play 300,000 games in a lifetime… But no program could learn to become a go champion in 300,000 games. A child, in just a few games, can sometimes show himself to be very gifted at this game and win against more experienced adults, whereas in just a few games no machine can even "know" how to play go.

The selectionist metaphor, the key to strong AI, is used to persuade us that robots can evolve and become autonomous, and perhaps one day even become good companions… or cruel enemies. In the learning of AI programs (*deep learning*), we implement this selectionist method: before launching the program into a real task, we "teach" it the right answers by rejecting the wrong ones. Only those answers validated by the program's testers pass the test. This is how chatGPT learned not to be racist or homophobic, even though its initial answers, based on what was available on certain networks, were highly politically incorrect…

But this pseudo-Darwinian metaphor is based on an impoverished and increasingly battered view of selectionist processes in nature, and doesn't demonstrate any particular intelligence of what's really at stake. The selectionism of AI fanatics inevitably brings to mind the shadocks we've already mentioned. But in that excellent 1969-1970 cartoon, the shadocks, whose language was summed up in four elementary signs—*ga, zo, bu, meu*—didn't come across as particularly intelligent beings!

An AI machine is, by construction, a procedural machine (it executes a program) and no matter how many layers of software we stack, in the final analysis, this machine can only execute logical operations step by step. The basic principle of cognitivism is that all operations performed by a mind can ultimately be broken down into these elementary logical operations. Earlier, I gave some arguments against this idea of a procedural intelligence. In *À dire vrai* (2013), I attempted a global critique of proceduralism, which unfortunately extends to many areas of thought and is nothing other than a manifestation of the one-dimensional thinking already denounced by Herbert Marcuse, a one-dimensional thinking that stems from the reduction of all knowledge to operations (operationalism), from Taylorism applied to thought. I can add a "Kantian" argument here. Intelligence presupposes not only the ability to make inferences, but also, and above all, the "faculty of judging", the object of the third Kantian critique. Let's content ourselves with the simplest judgement (if you will), which is the determining judgement: we have a rule and a particular case to examine. The problem of the judgment consists in knowing whether the particular case fits under the rule (whether it can be subsumed under the rule). This is, for example, the problem that arises in a court of law: how do we know that this particular individual has in fact committed an act that can be reduced to a general typology of acts from which a sentence can be deduced? To say that X is guilty of homicide without intent to kill, is to judge. What is the mechanism of judgment? Evidence is presented, arguments and pleadings are heard, and then the decision is made. But on what mechanism does this decision depend? We judge "in our soul and conscience". Kant maintains that this mechanism will forever remain hidden in the folds of the human soul. Assuming there is a general rule for determining how to apply a general rule to a particular case, we would need a "meta-rule" of judgment, but then we would need to be able to determine how this meta-rule applies, so as to know how the rule applies, and then necessarily a meta-meta-rule, and so on in an infinite regress. From which we would have to deduce that it is impossible to judge. But we judge, rightly or wrongly, but we judge. To the machine, we could say "X has indeed committed homicide", we could tell it the circumstances, and the algorithm would deduce the sentence. But in fact, the machine would not have judged anything: it would have been the human operator who judged beforehand, but without saying so! Despite this obvious theoretical difficulty, which has been known for at least two centuries, as these lines are being written, computer-assisted judgment is being tested, just as AIs are being tested for decision-making in a number of sectors. Like Dick's 1956 novel *Minority Report*, there are also predictive policing programs. In all cases, AI machines neither judge nor decide; they simply do what they're designed to do, performing logical operations mechanically, which we then interpret by saying: "here's a decision", but just because a screen displays "The decision is to cut off his head" doesn't mean it's really a decision. To accept as a decision what the computer screen displays, is to renounce one's own intelligence and act mechanically (i.e. exactly the opposite of acting intelligently). An AI cannot replace (human) intelligence, but it is perfectly possible for human beings to accept living and thinking like machines.

Let's add another, even more decisive argument, which we've already mentioned: human intelligence is not independent of the body. The paradox of the proponents of strong AI is this: they believe themselves to be materialists when they try to show that matter can think, but they are in fact radical idealists, Cartesian dualists of the most sectarian kind, and of a dualism that would have frightened Descartes himself, who knows how closely body and mind are linked. Indeed, to believe that a machine made of plastic, iron, aluminium, copper, silicon, etc. can think in the same way as a human being made up of tens of billions of elementary living beings and living in conjunction with billions and billions of bacteria and fungi can both be the identical "carrier" of thought, is in reality to assume that thought has no relation to matter itself. This is dualism and even radical idealism.

It's true that all the progress made by the natural sciences over the last few centuries has sought to abolish the boundary between the living and the inert (cf. above). A cell is indeed the elementary building block of the living world (Schleiden and Schwann's cell theory, 1838), and the cell is merely an organization of amino acids (organic macromolecules, i.e. based on CH radicals), but the properties of the cell are radically new and radically different from those of the molecules studied by organic chemistry. Which brings us back to the problem of emergence. A cell, as we've already said, is a "self": the membrane separates the inside from the outside, and the cell's physico-internal mechanisms preserve its unity and produce its reproduction. A computer part, on the other hand, has no "self". It is inert matter. Nor does a RAM memory, or even a microprocessor. Even the most elementary living being is affected by the surrounding world, and is capable of responding to these affections. An animal with a few hundred or a few thousand neurons is capable of far more operations and responsiveness than a very powerful computer, simply because it's alive.

Animals sense immediately, whereas computers can only pick up signals, analyze them and process them like any other digital data. It should also be pointed out that computers have only two "senses"—sight and hearing—whereas animals often have a sense of smell, touch, taste and sometimes other sensors, such as the "sonar" of dolphins or the "radar" of bats. If we leave aside the kind of immediate awareness that the most evolved animals have, and focus on man, we can immediately see the "ontological" gulf between human intelligence and the "intelligence" of the machine. The machine processes signals, but doesn't perceive, and we can't simulate all the most subjective human sensations, such as taste, smell or touch. We can imagine a computer equipped with a sensor capable of performing a chemical analysis of a glass of burgundy, but the chemical analysis of a glass of burgundy says nothing about its taste. It's also telling that we have no electronic mechanism for memorizing sensations other than visual and auditory ones. Significantly, there's nothing in the AI literature about this little "detail". If we take up Michel Henry's expression that the ontological foundation of man is "life that experiences itself", then it's obvious that no machine will ever be capable of doing this, precisely because it isn't alive!

Human intelligence is inseparable from this physicality, or rather from the flesh that constitutes its very substance. AI is merely a product of this activity of the human subjective body-mind, and at best a prosthesis like glasses, hearing aids or walking sticks. The absurd desire to build machines that equal or surpass man is nothing other than the desire for man to become a machine, i.e. the desire to return to an inorganic state, which is one of the manifestations of the death drive, if we follow Freud's analysis.

Harmful AI

In truth, the purpose of AI is that it is an intelligence technology. While AI cannot claim to equal, let alone replace, human intelligence, the fact remains that its fascinating possibilities must be delimited. While AI is a fairly old techno-scientific discipline, as old as computer science, it only broke through to public opinion relatively recently (in the 2000s). This breakthrough is due to two closely intertwined phenomena: the power of machines (both computing speed and memory capacity) and the existence of the Internet. The power of machines and the considerable drop in their production costs have enabled the expansion of the Internet, and above all of what is known as "Web 2.0". In its first version, the Internet, born of the American ARPANET project, was essentially a messaging system and a consultation or purchasing system (as was the MINITEL in France). Jean-Gabriel Ganascia (in *Intelligence artificielle. Vers une domination programmée*, Le cavalier bleu, 2017) considers that the economic model of "web 1.0" could not satisfy the hopes placed in the "startups" that promised to sell everything via the net. As it's still not much easier to book a ticket over the Internet than over the good old minitel, it's other paths that have led to the development of the Internet than the repackaging of the La Redoute catalog in electronic form!

From the early 2000s onwards, the web became more interactive, with users invited to enrich site content, evaluate services and so on. At the same time, the search tools developed by Google, which are AI tools, made it possible to diversify searches and make links between terms that are not related *a priori*. All this has led to the creation of gigantic masses of data… on Internet users, masses of data that are the most precious asset of the famous GAFAs. This *big data*, processed by the means of AI, makes it possible to statistically predict the behavior of web users, to pre-empt their desires by offering them all sorts of mirific things to buy, or to steer votes: see the "Cambridge Analytics" affair, a company that hijacked the profiles of tens of millions of Facebook users to better target candidate Trump's campaign messages in 2016. We can be reassured that this *big data* is essentially for commercial purposes, that GAFA don't want to break public trust by placing themselves too openly at the service of governments, but the truth is that, on the one hand, this means that the "system" is increasingly guiding the actions of those who are connected, and that we are therefore marching towards a society from which all spontaneity is gradually disappearing. On the other hand, no large group will put up any serious resistance when asked to do so by state intelligence services. All the more so as governments protect the interests of these major groups. But all this is only possible thanks to AI techniques, because obviously no human, no group of humans, could handle such masses of data.

A few years ago, we questioned the surveillance program of the American services, which spied even on friendly governments (the ECHELON system), but now it's the users who, voluntarily, are being recorded by the major industrial and financial companies. And, in so doing, they themselves become products. Managing the use of the personal data of several billion humans is the most massive and extraordinary success of AI—although most people know nothing about it.

AI as a set of techniques should be subject to the same scrutiny as all other techniques. Not everything that is possible is necessarily desirable: it is technically possible to destroy mankind, to use viruses as weapons of war, or to feed mankind solely with products of chemistry. But none of this is really desirable. Similarly, it is possible to modify the human genome using genetic manipulation techniques, but this possibility should never be allowed to become a reality, and those who take this path should be banned from practising without hesitation. We know that *Big Data* processing techniques are especially useful for commerce, to target potential customers and encourage them to buy, or for police surveillance of citizens according to the Chinese model. Of course, there are other possible uses, such as medical diagnostics—provided we don't take advantage of this to get rid of specialists—and others whose usefulness merits discussion, to say the least, such as autonomous cars. As for computer-assisted justice or AI-based political decision-making, their mere mention should be enough to banish them forever.

Without risking too much error, we can say that, on the side of the most disadvantaged, on the side of those who work, AI will enable increased surveillance, increased pressure from employers, the massive elimination of skilled jobs and great progress towards generalized stultification, and, on the side of the lords of our society, we'll have new means of reinforcing their domination, a domination that will be all the more accepted as the subordinate classes will find fewer means of resisting in the face of these machines that represent the supreme stage of reification.

AI tools can be precious... but just as dangerous. We know that medicines are also poisons (and vice versa), and that the same is true of all techniques (a knife can cut the meat of the animal you're feeding on just as well as the body of your neighbor). However, all tools are clearly seen as subordinate to human will; they are simply extensions of human organs ("tool" is Greek for *organon*). This is not the case with AI, since it is no longer a question of creating a tool, but something that would equal and even surpass man. In Jewish tradition, the golem, a humanoid being made of clay and set in motion by magical words, was clearly designed to help humans. Frankenstein's creature may have been inspired by the golem, but it has no utilitarian function: its primary purpose is to manifest the genius of its creator. The androids imagined by Philip K. Dick belong to the same species as the golem. With AI, we can see something else taking shape, something other than an auxiliary to man, but rather its surpassing. Proponents of "transhumanism" or "post-humanism" envisage AI as man's successor. And of course, we don't need to take this fantasy at face value. The immediate danger is not that, as in *Matrix*, machines will take over and enslave mankind. The real danger is different: since AI is supposed to produce a superior development of intelligence, it provides a model on which we should model ourselves. The transformation of human activities into "procedures" to be followed in production, in means of control, but also in relations between salespeople and their customers or in the legal system is already well advanced. Human intelligence is eliminated in favor of mechanical obedience. For want of being able to build machines that are smarter than humans, we are making great strides every day to make humans as stupid as machines. But perhaps this was the hidden aim of modern science, whose first triumphs were those of mechanics.

Let's summarize. There are two hypotheses:

31. strong AI and all the predictions of those who claim that one day a robot will have self-awareness are poppycock. Machines are only machines, and they can only be dangerous if they are used by some humans to subjugate others;

32. strong AI is possible, and then we'll be up against ruthless competitors, so we need to stop all research in this field right now and put the researchers who want to wipe out humanity out of business.

I'm obviously leaning towards the first hypothesis, but I'm not absolutely certain (there's a margin of error). If I'm wrong, then we'll have to move on to the second hypothesis. To be frankly "Luddite"! Oh horror! Theodor Kaczynski, the notorious "*Unabomber*", may have gone completely "off the rails" with his little bombs, but in his manifesto *Industrial Society and its Future* (1995), he raised essential questions when he asserted that the power of technology is greater than the aspiration to freedom:

> A lasting compromise between technology and freedom is impossible: technology is by far the most powerful social force, constantly gaining ground on freedom through repeated compromises. Consider two neighbors, each with the same amount of land, but one more powerful than the other. The powerful one demands part of the other's land. The weaker one refuses. The powerful one says: "Okay, let's compromise. Give me half of what I'm asking for." The weaker party gives in. Some time later, the more powerful demands more land, again there is compromise, and so on. By imposing a series of compromises on the weaker, the powerful eventually takes all his land. The same applies to the conflict between technology and freedom.

AI is the supreme stage of capital's machine technology. It allows us to control the herd without violence. And we find it hard to say "no". It offers so many advantages: who could refuse to have their cancer detected in time thanks to medical imaging applications? Who hasn't used automatic translators (Google Translate, DeepL) to gain easy access to texts published in a language we understand poorly or not at all? If AI works, it's because we're so thirsty for information that we no longer have time to think. We're suffering from information bulimia. Perhaps also because of an absurd desire to control everything, a late manifestation of the fantasy of infantile omnipotence. Also, because following the acceleration syndrome so well analyzed by Hartmunt Rosa (see *Acceleration*, 2014), we want to abolish time. Our era is entirely neurotic, and this neurosis is fatal. We should meditate in all its depth on La Fontaine's fable, "The Wolf and the Dog": between the remnants of his masters' sumptuous meals, on which the dog feeds, and freedom, the wolf hardly hesitates: "Master Wolf flees and runs again".

Chapter IV: Carbon Computers?

If you follow the press and editorial news, neuroscience seems to be gradually establishing itself as the most advanced science of our time. Books, broadcasts, videos, conferences, experiments and victory announcements follow one another in rapid succession. In symbiosis or in competition with AI, they promise us a new future for mankind. It's no longer a question of simulating human intelligence on a machine, but of laying bare the "biology of intelligence" of this man we'll have to call "neuronal man". In fact, after a long detour, we are invited to the return of the man-machine.

Unclear Definitions

So what are neurosciences, or what is neuroscience, since we seem to be using the singular and plural interchangeably? Let's begin our investigation by looking for definitions, or delimitations, of these neurosciences. There are so many definitions and varieties of neuroscience that the neophyte is quickly lost. Soberly, the Académie française defines neuroscience as "all the disciplines that study the nervous system". The more prolix Larousse dictionary defines neuroscience as:

All disciplines studying the nervous system (neurobiology, neurochemistry, neurohistology, neuroanatomy, neuropharmacology, neuropsychology and neurolinguistics, neuropathology, neurology, psychiatry, neuroendocrinology, neurosurgery).

All the disciplines listed here are subsets of biology, and are therefore sciences whose object is the human body, in all its various components, components which it shares with a great many animals, differing only in the high number of neurons and neuronal connections, and in the very particular organization of the brain. The disciplines that deal with neuropathologies, such as psychiatry and the specialties of what used to be called "nervous diseases", are also quite traditional medical disciplines. Drugs have been known since antiquity for their positive and negative effects on human beings. Henri Laborit, who introduced the use of neuroleptics in the treatment of certain mental disorders, is also a surgeon and specialist in the behavior of animals… and humans.

And yet, if we leave it at that, there's no question of mind or spirit. No one can seriously dispute that there is a relationship, or at least close correlations, between the body as a whole, and the neural system in particular, and the subject's emotional or cognitive mental states. But this correlation doesn't seem to be part of neurobiology.

This definition also shows that the neurosciences include branches of biology and medical disciplines, suggesting that there is no serious difference between biology and medicine. The former is a science, the latter an art, a practice or even a technique. You can be a great biologist and not be a doctor (which is quite often the case), and an excellent doctor without being a scientist. There's a human dimension to medicine that has nothing to do with biology. But, in the spirit of our times, science and technology are merging into technoscience… Neuroscience would therefore be technoscience.

However, it should be noted that there are therapies for certain mental disorders that owe nothing to neuroscience, such as psychoanalysis. There are undoubtedly scientists and essayists who consider that psychoanalysis is not scientific at all—which may be true to a certain extent, as we shall see later—and that it does not cure patients who undergo analytical treatment. While there are many controversies about the therapeutic efficacy of psychoanalysis, it would be interesting to compare it with chemical therapies and cognitive behavioural therapies. Be that as it may, there are many techniques that can be used to treat without any scientific backing. We'll come back to this later.

The Unique Character of Neuroscience

From a neuroscientific point of view, there's no doubt that the brain is the seat of intelligence, the center of thought production. The decisive point in this configuration is the recognition of the brain's central role. Neuroscience is "encephalocentric". The ancients, if they were materialists, wondered where the soul was located, and the Epicureans or Stoics placed it in the chest (the heart), although Democritus had already highlighted the role of the brain as the seat of intelligence, with ailments localized in the heart, liver and other organs. The localization of thought, spirit, soul, intelligence—whatever the precise appellation—in the brain provides a stable foundation for a materialistic "philosophy of mind", and this is the essential point. It remains to be seen which sciences will concern themselves with knowledge of the brain as the "seat of thought".

The Encyclopedia universalis does not give a generic definition of neuroscience; it simply defines cognitive neuroscience, alongside other categories of neuroscience, as the sciences that study the nervous system and cognition. So, as soon as we start trying to define neuroscience, we find ourselves with a whole swarm of neurosciences! We have cognitive neuroscience, social neuroscience, computational neuroscience and so on. For the definition of cognitive neuroscience, we find this:

> The aim of cognitive neuroscience is to identify the cerebral processes at the origin of our mental capacities and to evaluate, in neurobiological terms, the plausibility of the models proposed in cognitive science. How does the functioning of our brain underlie our immaterial mind? Perceiving, recognizing, deciding, acting, memorizing, speaking, reasoning, being aware of, paying attention to… What brain organization, what neural processes, what neural coding allow us to account for the great cognitive capacities of humans and animals? Cognitive neuroscience lies at the interface between neuroscience, psychology, computational neuroscience, cognitive science and philosophy.

If we understand correctly, we're looking for causal links, if any, between the structures of the brain (and the neuronal apparatus as a whole) and mental states, characteristic of an "immaterial" mind. In other words, this definition is dualistic (there are "extended" things—the brain, neurons, etc.—and a "mental" thing, the mind, which is non-extended because it is non-material. Moreover, cognitive neuroscience (which is therefore a subset of neuroscience in general) is an interface between many disciplines, including psychology and philosophy.

The Brain Institute, an organization dedicated to raising funds for medical research into neurological pathologies (including neurodegenerative diseases such as Alzheimer's), defines neuroscience as follows:

> Neuroscience encompasses all scientific research into the nervous system, i.e. the brain, spinal cord and nerves. The different scales of study give rise to different fields of research, such as molecular and cellular neuroscience, neurophysiology and cognitive neuroscience.

It's still a very confusing definition: it talks about different scales of study such as molecular neuroscience, cellular neuroscience and cognitive neuroscience. In the end, everything is called neuroscience, even though we already have molecular biology, which deals with the internal molecular chemistry of cells, cell biology, etc., the biology of the brain (which isn't just made up of neurons!) and so on. But how do we get from the biology of the neuronal system as a whole to "cognition"? That's a profound mystery.

In fact, it seems that every field of study must now be called "neuro + something"! For example, there is "neuroeconomics", which deals with decision-making mechanisms in economics. There is neuropsychiatry, which has difficulty distinguishing itself from psychiatry. There are even specialists in neuroeroticism! Even advocates of neuroscience are not without reticence. For example, Benoit Dubreuil, a Quebec neuroscience and "neurophilosophy" researcher, writes:

> [...] we maintain that neuroeconomics has a bright future ahead of it, since it offers essential tools for explaining decision-making. At the same time, however, we are skeptical about its ability to contribute to the study of most of the phenomena that traditionally attract the attention of economists, including, above all, prices and market equilibria. Using the example of social preferences, we give reasons to believe that neuroeconomics is unlikely to make a better contribution to modeling the utility functions of real economic agents than behavioral economics and cognitive psychology already do.
>
> "Neuroeconomics: essential, but for whom?"
> in *Économie et instituions*, 16/2011

In other words, neuroeconomics is probably of no interest to economics. Which is unfortunate... As we shall see, neuro-economics is not alone in this respect. Some authors position neuroscience within the cognitive sciences as a whole. Jean-Paul

Thomas (in *Raison présente*, 2017) defines the field of knowledge of cognitive science as follows:

> Under the name of cognitive science, six disciplines have been grouped together: neuroscience, computer science (including artificial intelligence), cognitive psychology, linguistics, anthropology and philosophy of mind. These disciplines form a whole, but this whole does not absorb its parts: it is not completely unified. This is primarily because these disciplines were not born with the common conceptual framework that binds them together today. They have their own histories, and some parts of them remain far removed from the assumptions and tools on which they are based.

Where can we find a consensus definition? Stanislas Dehaene, professor of cognitive psychology, in his inaugural lecture at the Collège de France (2006) sets out his own definition after quoting William James, who describes psychology as the science of mental life:

> Cognitive psychology] sees itself as an integral part of the life sciences, exploiting the full panoply of biological methods, from genetics to brain imaging, but also as a science of mental life, attempting to set out the general laws of thought, an intimate and subjective domain that might have been thought inaccessible to the scientific method. Its aims are broad. How is the chain of command organized, from perception to motor action? In what form are our memories stored? What is a word? A concept? An emotion? An intention? A decision? An introspection? What rules govern the syntax of cognitive operations? How can we distinguish between conscious and non-conscious information? The challenge of cognitive psychology is to formulate general laws in response to each of these questions, and to understand their origins, at the intersection of constraints imposed both by the biology of the brain and by the environment and culture in which it flourishes.

Dehaene is not talking about neuroscience, but about cognitive psychology, which seems to cover the whole field of neuroscience and appears as a field of life sciences, exploiting "the panoply of biological methods". The aim, then, is to make the "science of mental life" one of the natural sciences in the same way as physiology, anatomy and so on. The expressions used by Dehaene are revealing: the notion of a "chain of command" to replace the expression of the will indicates that the paradigm of this science of mental life is indeed the paradigm of "mechanistic" origin, and the aim is to set out the laws of mental life in the same way as the other laws of nature. Dehaene is part of an ancient current of psychology, born in the 19th century. And as ideology is never far away, the "chain of command" points to a political-military model for understanding human psychology, an analogy between the living body and the body politic that already played an important role among ideologists, and which we find again in Auguste Comte.

It's true that behaviorism, based on the experimental study of human behavior including physical measurements, has always been of great importance since the 19th century, and philosophers have taken it seriously, whether Bergson in his *Essai sur les données immédiates de la conscience* or, a little later, Merleau-Ponty in the *Phénoménologie de la perception*, to cite just two of the best-known examples. Yet these philosophers refused to make behavior the alpha and omega of the human mind.

With Dehaene, as with the psychologists integrated into the cognitive sciences, we have moved beyond the still rudimentary methods of experimental psychology. What's new is the contribution of medical imaging to intimate knowledge of the brain, enabling him to argue that the subjective domain is no longer inaccessible to the scientific method. The question is to what extent people like Dehaene are right, i.e. to what extent psychology can be transformed into a science of nature, which is none other than the question of whether subjectivity can be reduced to a set of natural, and therefore objectifiable, phenomena. For Dehaene, the answer is a resounding yes.

If we now seek a synthesis of all these definitions, we'll remember that neuroscience goes far beyond neurobiology, since it aims to elucidate mental life, properly spiritual activities and the most abstract of cognitive activities through knowledge of the neuronal system.

At Last Changeux Came...

In this panoramic view of the transition from neurology to neuroscience, Jean-Pierre Changeux occupies a special place. He is one of the most important precursors of contemporary neuroscience. He published the results of his work in a 1983 book, *L'homme neuronal*, and produced a synthesis that sets out the founding theses of neuroscience. Jean-Pierre Changeux sets the stakes when he deplores the fact that the human sciences are ignoring the brain and are thus uprooted from their "biological soil", including disciplines such as psychoanalysis, which were originally "physicalist". While the human sciences in general remain fairly indifferent to knowledge of the brain as a biological organ, the general trend is to link psychic phenomena to the brain's physiological processes, including in the treatment of "mental illnesses", which we try to classify on the basis of the chemical elements involved.

However, in the very way neuroscience conceives itself, things seem a little more complicated. Commenting on the various aspects of cognition, Michel Imbert writes: "It is obvious, and no one can reasonably doubt it, that these cognitive processes are represented, embodied in the nervous system; that they are, in the final analysis, manifestations and expressions of the functioning of the brain" ("Neurosciences et sciences cognitives", in *Introduction aux sciences cognitives*, 1992).

In the same sentence, it is explained that the nervous system is "the embodiment of cognitive processes" and, on the other hand, that these processes are "the expression of brain function"; on the one hand, we have a strong spiritualist or idealist connotation and, on the other, a more materialistic-looking connotation. This duality—or internal contradiction—constantly runs through the field of neuroscience. "Incarnation": the spirit becomes flesh, but "expression" indicates something that is inside (of what?) and finds expression in a material device. Beyond a primordial materialism that reduces the processes attributed to the soul to material (chemical) processes, the models through which neuroscience expresses itself are marked by a profound ambiguity. Michel Imbert, in the article quoted, refuses to open a debate "full of pitfalls, obscured by ideological quarrels" on whether cognitive processes depend on brain function.

He goes on to explain: "Cognitive phenomena depend on cerebral mechanisms in the sense that, by analogy, the processing of information by a computer program depends on the details of the computer's electronic circuits" (*Op. cit.*).

However, the dependence between information processing and computer circuits is much closer than Michel Imbert suggests. It's based on principles identified by Boole, which lead to the isomorphism between logical algebra and electrical circuits considered as operating in "all-or-nothing" mode. And that's why computers (at least, today's computers and those envisaged for the years to come) can only process information that can be coded using Boolean algebra. So it's not just a vaguely heuristic analogy we're talking about, but a central question: the identity of thought and the material processes it expresses. The back-and-forth between neuroscience and cognitive science mentioned by Michel Imbert no doubt describes the empirical workings of research, but tells us nothing about this "dependence", "embodiment" or "expression". Posed in this way, the question is insoluble. Whether or not the "mental" depends on the "physical" is a quarrel that materialists refuse to accept, since it's a question of maintaining the duality between an extended substance and a non-extended substance, thought. Materialism is not about making Descartes' pineal gland work in reverse. For Lucretius, the soul is not something different from the body; it is itself matter. So the question is not whether it depends on the body or not. If we posit that thought is nothing other than the cognitive functioning of the human brain, then "ideological quarrels" have no reason to exist. But to leave it at that is to stick to a presupposition that can't be proven. We need to demonstrate that "it works", i.e. that we can explain by a chain of reasons and verified facts how thought is formed from elementary biological processes. This is the path chosen by Jean-Pierre Changeux with his "neuronal man".

The starting point of J.-P. Changeux's conception is the eradication of the term "thought", which refers to an immaterial entity or non-corporeal substance (as in Descartes). J.-P. Changeux implements "an analytical approach that consists in breaking down the anatomical substrate or function into simple elements" (*L'homme neuronal*, 1983).

But we can't simply put the brain into "spare parts". We need to reassemble the machine and study how it works in concrete terms, how the various parts communicate with each other; this is the fundamental role of neurotransmitters, which convert chemical energy into electrical signals. However, if the study remains at this level, we can validate the Cartesian theory of animal machines, but not understand the specificity of human mental processes. This is because,

> [...] in terms of the elementary mechanisms of nerve communication, nothing distinguishes man from animals, and no receptor or ion channel is unique to man (*Op.cit.*).

Mental states or behaviors cannot be connected to precise physical devices, to a well-defined, individualized chain of neurons.

We can only say that the neuron graph mobilized by a given behavior or sensation includes one or more critical links that make privileged use of a particular neurotransmitter. (*Op. cit.*)

Changeux analyzes a machine of "formidable complexity". However, functional specializations enable this machine to be broken down into "cogs-neurons", whose "movements-pulses" can be grasped, thus "justifying the reckless commitment of the mechanists of the eighteenth century" (*Op. cit.*, p.160). Nevertheless, this claimed mechanism does not imply a brain/computer analogy. There are two reasons for this.

One of the characteristic features of the brain machine is that its internal coding involves both [...] a topological coding of connections described by a neuron graph, and a coding of electrical impulses or chemical signals. Here, the classic "hardware/software" distinction doesn't hold. On the other hand, it's obvious that the human brain is capable of developing strategies on its own. Anticipating events, it builds its own programs. This faculty of self-organization is one of the most striking features of the human brain machine, whose supreme product is thought (*Op. cit.*).

We still need to explain what this faculty is. Changeux first demonstrates the materiality of mental images. In an approach close to that of the Epicureans, he asserts that there is a "neural kinship, a material congruence between the percept and the memory image." From this stems the hypothesis of "mental objects" as diverse states of material units of mental representation. The next step is to carry out a biological analysis of the interactions between these mental objects, and of the operations performed on them by the "surveillance system". In Changeux's analysis, we have a passage of levels, from an elementary level with its own regulations to a higher level with modes of operation that have a certain autonomy in relation to the rules of the lower level. However, Changeux rejects the thesis of emergence—very common in contemporary thinking on science, and which can often function like the dormant virtue of Molière's opium for doctors—and asserts that if consciousness "emerges", we must take the comparison literally, in the way an iceberg emerges. We need to consider the functioning of the cerebral machine as a whole, as an interlocking of "spider webs" with a global regulatory system. Hence the important conclusion here:

> [...] Consciousness is this system of functioning regulations. From then on, man no longer needs to concern himself with "Spirit"; he need only be a Neuronal Man. (*Op.cit.*)

An extremely radical conclusion! But even if we accept Changeux's explanation, it's not certain that we've reached the end of our tether. Human experience is not simply the experience of the external world, it is also the experience of our own experience, the experience of our own subjectivity, which appears chronologically second, but is then posited as the presupposition of all sensible experience and all speech. This raises the problem of modeling self-reflection or self-reference. Changeux evokes the self-organizing capacity of the human brain machine; is this explanation sufficient? The "*is*" emphasized by Changeux can be seen as a trompe-l'œil solution. To identify consciousness and a functioning regulatory system is first to identify two mental objects through a mental operation. Here we find the fundamental paradoxes of materialism: the assertion that everything is matter, that everything can be explained by material operations and interactions, is first and foremost a "thought" that fails to think of itself as matter. If Changeux's methodological materialism is effective in the scientific field, we may well ask whether its philosophical scope is as important as it first appears, and whether man really no longer has anything to do with Spirit. Presumably, such a discovery should have settled a number of thorny questions once and for all. But it has to be said that we are no further ahead than we were when Changeux's book was published.

Core Technologies and Ontology

Neuroscience is based on brain imaging technologies, and this is what fundamentally distinguishes it from old-fashioned experimental psychology. Before brain imaging, brain areas could only be located on the basis of brain-damaged patients—which is how Broca's famous area was discovered. Medical imaging makes it possible to "directly" observe the brains of healthy individuals. Functional Magnetic Resonance Imaging (fMRI) does not directly measure neuronal activity, but reveals which areas of the brain are active by measuring blood flow, since blood supplies the brain with the elements it needs for activation, notably oxygen. As a subject performs a given task, a greater volume of oxygenated blood flows to active brain areas, and the BOLD (*blood oxygenation level-dependent*) signal reflects these changes in flow. This technique has been rapidly adopted by cognitive neuroscience researchers, as it enables certain mental activities to be associated with changes in the subject's brain. This applies both to purely cognitive activities (perception and pattern recognition, calculation, reasoning, decision-making, etc.) and to emotions and affects. This makes it possible to break down the brain—Jean-Pierre Changeux calls it a "brain in pieces". Imaging, in the first instance, presupposes that the subject is able to state what he or she perceives subjectively. We then began to construct a kind of brain code that would enable us to know what the subject is thinking about when we observe a given brain configuration. Some scientists claim to have developed a method that uses fMRI brain recordings to reconstruct continuous speech (see *The Scientist*, 4/10/2022). In a *preprint* published in September 2022 on *bioRxiv*, a team from the University of Texas at Austin describes a "decoder", or algorithm, capable of "reading" the words a person hears or thinks during a brain scan using functional magnetic resonance imaging (fMRI). While other teams had previously reported some success in reconstructing language or images from signals from brain implants, the new decoder is the first to use a non-invasive method to achieve this. "If you had asked any cognitive neuroscientist in the world twenty years ago if this was feasible, they would have run you out of the room laughing," says Alexander Huth, a neuroscientist at the University of Texas at Austin and co-author of the study.

Yukiyasu Kamitani, a computational neuroscientist at Kyoto University, who was not involved in the research, writes in an e-mail to *The Scientist* that it is "exciting" to see intelligible language sequences generated by a non-invasive decoder. "This study... lays a solid foundation for [brain-computer interface] applications," he adds.

These technologies make it possible to establish a correlation between physically observable brain states and mental states as perceived by the subject. We could thus conclude that a mental state corresponds to a physical state of the body, in this case the brain. At this point, we could say that body and mind (*mens*) are the same thing considered under two different attributes, to use Spinoza's expression. We'll see how much we can learn from the author of the *Ethics* later on. But for now, there's a clear difference: the principle of neuroscience is to consider that physical phenomena are the causes of mental states and that, consequently, the laws of the brain's physical phenomena (if any can be found) explain mental states. Assuming that a certain brain configuration A is regularly followed, by virtue of a natural law, by a configuration B, the mental state X that "decodes" A will necessarily be followed by a mental state Y which "decodes" B. There would be a psychic (or mental) determinism which would be nothing in itself, which would not be a psychic determinism strictly speaking, but an epiphenomenon of a physiological determinism. This is generally what the advocates of cognitive neuroscience think, with nuances and "it's more complicated than that", but it's basically their position. The idea that neuroscience can help us improve our mental capacities is similar to the idea that knowledge of the laws of physics can increase our efficiency in our interactions with nature. We'll see later that this thesis actually presents inextricable difficulties.

Time Travel

"Neuro" is in vogue, underpinned by the thesis that mental life can be fully explained by the laws of biological nature! The idea common to all this serious and less serious research is a "mechanistic" vision in which, starting from the lowest level, that of the molecule and the cell, we believe we can explain not only the functioning of the neuronal system as a whole, but also—and this is where things get complicated—the mental states of human subjects, from emotions to complex reasoning and decision-making. This widespread desire to unify a whole range of research fields, which must disappear behind the prefix "neuro", is already a global model unifying the human body and mind in a resolutely reductionist perspective. When we speak of changes of scale—"Different scales of study give rise to different fields of research", says one of the definitions quoted above—we find ourselves faced with an attempt at a micro-macro explanation, entirely in line with the development of the natural sciences since the seventeenth century. The fundamental direction of scientific research is reductionism: reducing the complex to a combination of simple elements, obtained by analysis (to analyze is to decompose).

So, reductionism implies systematically seeking to explain complex levels of organization by combining simpler elements, biology by chemistry (a cell is fundamentally a combination of mostly carbonaceous macromolecules) and chemistry by physics (knowledge of particle physics makes it possible to account for chemical reactions), and quite naturally the idea of reducing mental creations (including God!) to particular combinations of atoms, "populations of neurons", as neuroscientists sometimes say. Materialism asserts the primacy of matter, eternal and uncreated; reductionism, by seeking to explain all phenomena on the basis of the combination of the simplest and least differentiated elements, moves in the same direction. And indeed, the project, or rather projects, that come under the heading of neuroscience are fundamentally materialistic, in the sense that, ultimately, everything is matter and nothing else.

Although the term neuroscience is fairly recent (circa late 1960s), there's nothing new about the project. It can be traced back to antiquity, with the work of Hippocrates and Egyptian physicians, who were the first to associate the brain with mental functions. Galen made a number of decisive contributions, based on the examination of the many chariot drivers and gladiators he had to treat. Galen can be considered the initiator of what has become the clinico-pathological procedure in neurology, whereby correlations are sought between abnormal behavior and a pathological state of the body. In this way, he demonstrated the central role played by the brain. In the 4th century, Nemesius, a bishop and reader of Plato, extended Galen's work. In his treatise *On the Nature of Man*, he set out to understand the links between the soul and the body, and linked the main faculties of the mind to locations in the brain. Thus, "the organs of the imagination are the anterior ventricles of the brain, the vital spirit contained in them, the nerves that depend on them, and which are impregnated with vital spirit, finally, the entire apparatus of the sense organs" (ch. VI). Avicenna extends Nemesius, whom he had read and commented on, and confirms this localization of intellectual functions in the lower ventricles.

Renaissance physician-anatomists such as Laurent Joubert, who showed that learning to speak was a process of imitation, and thus depended on hearing rather than on the metaphysical properties of the human soul, Vesalius, the great anatomist, and many others contributed greatly to our knowledge of the nervous system. Descartes, in his *Traité de l'homme*, offers a global description of the human body. He elucidated the reflex act, and tried to understand the mechanism of vision. He tried to understand the links between bodily processes—the movements of "animal spirits"—and mental activities. But he maintained a clear separation between body and soul, and his explanations of their links met with powerful objections right from the publication of the *Méditations métaphysiques*. The most radical objections came from Hobbes. After noting, rather unkindly, that Descartes, in questioning the testimony of the senses or the difficulty of distinguishing dream from wakefulness, was merely recounting "old wives' tales" going back to Plato, Hobbes attacked the root of the *cogito*. Certainly, since I think and I know that I think, I can deduce without dispute that I am, but, Hobbes adds,

> [...] where our author adds, i.e. a mind, a soul, an understanding, a reason: from this arises a doubt. For this reasoning does not seem to me well deduced, to say I am thinking, therefore I am a thought; or I am intelligent, therefore I am an understanding. For in the same way I could say, I am walking, therefore I am a walk.
>
> Objection to *Meditation II*, 1641

Hobbes' entire attack focuses on one point: it is impossible to separate thought from the body. Thus, Descartes would commit a logical error by confusing reality with the act it performs, whereas "all philosophers", says Hobbes, distinguish the subject from its acts.

It is very certain that the knowledge of this proposition, I exist, depends on this one, I think, as he has taught us very well: but where does the knowledge of this one, I think, come from? Certainly, it is from nothing else than from the fact that we cannot conceive of any act without its subject, like thought without a thing that thinks, science without a thing that knows, and a walk without a thing that walks.

And from this it seems to follow that a thing that thinks is something corporeal; for the subjects of all acts seem to be understood only under a corporeal reason, or under a reason of matter, as he himself showed a little later by the example of wax, which, though its color, hardness, figure, and all its other acts are changed, is still conceived to be the same thing, that is, the same matter subject to all these changes. Now it is not by another thought that I infer that I think: for even though someone may think that he has thought, which thought is nothing other than a memory, nevertheless it is quite impossible to think that one thinks, nor to know that one knows: for this would be an interrogation that would never end, from where do you know that you know that you know, and so on ad infinitum?

Where Descartes carefully distinguishes between imagination and conception, Hobbes sees this as no more than a collection of words. In short, the certain foundation of our knowledge lies not in some "thinking substance", but in the corporeal subject that we are. This position makes Hobbes a materialist, who regards the idea of incorporeal substance as absurd as a square circle.

In terms of physiology, it was Thomas Willis, again in the 17th century, who made the most important advances. He distinguished between brain and cerebellum, gray matter and white matter; he linked certain disorders to specific areas of the brain, etc. He was one of the first to use the microscope as an anatomical observation tool. He was one of the first to use the microscope as a tool for anatomical observation. In their book on *the philosophical foundations of neuroscience* (2003), Bennett and Hacker note:

It was the quality of Willis's meticulous observations that enabled him to identify cortical lesions as opposed to organs such as the spleen and lungs, which others had suggested were at the root of behavioral disorders. When Willis had fully established his clinico-pathological correlations, accompanied by detailed anatomical drawings, there was no doubt that a normal cortex was necessary for normal behavior. But although the ventricles had been displaced as the focus of interest in this respect, the question of which part of a normally functioning cortex correlates with the behavioral manifestations of particular psychological powers had not been elucidated.

But it was with Galvani and his work on "bioelectricity" that the first advances were made, concerning not only anatomy, but also the functioning of the nervous system. Galvani showed that nerves conduct electricity in the same way as metallic conductors. He therefore assumed the existence of "animal electricity", and for him, it was the brain that secreted the "electric fluid". The theory of electric fluid was refuted by another Italian, Volta, without being totally invalidated. It was a far-reaching discovery: a machine switching electrical circuits could resemble a brain, and so a machine could think!

However, for a time, particularly following the statements of the great Buffon, whose authority was asserted even when he was wrong, the idea of locating thought in the brain was abandoned. It was Gall, the inventor of phrenology, who revived this idea: the "geography" of the cranium would make it possible to localize the various functions of the brain, such as memory behind the orbits, etc. This theory was to have a sad descendant when it was invented. This theory would have a sad descendant when it combined with the racist delusions taken up by the Nazis, who classified individuals according to the shape of their skulls. Hegel rejected Gall's suppositions with a word that, although not a decisive argument, should remain in the memory of every researcher: the mind is not a bone!

Since then, knowledge of the nervous system has advanced enormously, with Santiago Ramon y Cajal's 1888 discovery of the cells that make up the "nerves", i.e. the neurons, the establishment of the brain's geography and the precise observations made possible by medical imaging. But, for a long time, it was above all the clinic that guided theory: Broca's discovery of the localization of language functions (Broca's area), the work of Charcot—who also had a decisive influence on Freud—were all milestones that led to today's neurobiology and the considerable progress made in the treatment of brain pathologies.

Neuroscience, Biology and Computer Science

The neurosciences attempt to synthesize biology and computer science: computational neuroscience relies on computer modeling to understand the mental workings of the human brain. The neural system of a human being can be coupled to electronic devices in such a way that the brain directly controls a machine. In this way, quadriplegics could be equipped with an artificial exoskeleton that they could control directly by thought. The team led by Alim-Louis Benabid, Professor Emeritus at Grenoble Alpes University, has designed an implantable device (WIMAGINE®) which collects, at the level of the sensorimotor cortex, the brain signals emitted during a person's movement intentions. Without the need for an external command to provoke movement, the tetraplegic person can move thanks to the exoskeleton's mental control. According to Prof. Benabid, "this device is a major step forward for the autonomy of disabled people. We're very proud of this proof of concept, and are already thinking about new applications to make daily life easier for people with severe motor disabilities".

To achieve these results, we had to build *brain-to-computer* interfaces (BCIs), which can be described as systems that enable brain activity to command an action in "real time", bypassing traditional interfaces such as the keyboard or mouse. These systems do not work on their own. Their users must learn to use them, just as infants learn to explore their sensorimotor system.

In 2019, Chinese researchers succeeded in building a network of human brains using a BBI (*Brain to brain interface*) capable of cooperating with each other to solve problems. Linxing Jiang and his team present their work (*Nature* journal, 16/04/2019) thus:

> The interface combines electroencephalography [EEG] to record brain signals and transcranial magnetic stimulation [TMS] to deliver information non-invasively to the brain. The interface enables three human subjects to collaborate and solve a task using direct brain-to-brain communication. Two of the three subjects are designated as "senders" whose brain signals are decoded using real-time EEG data analysis. The decoding process extracts each sender's decision whether or not to rotate a block in a Tetris-like game before it is removed to fill a line. The senders' decisions are transmitted via the Internet to the brain of a third subject, the "receiver", who cannot see the game screen. The senders' decisions are transmitted to the receiver's brain by magnetic stimulation of the occipital cortex. The receiver integrates the information received from the two senders and uses an EEG interface to make the decision to turn the block or keep it in the same orientation. A second round of the game offers an additional chance for the senders to evaluate the receiver's decision and send feedback to the receiver's brain, and for the receiver to rectify any incorrect decision made in the first round. We evaluated BrainNet's performance in terms of [1] group-level performance during the game, [2] positive true/false rate of subjects' decisions, and [3] mutual information between subjects. Five groups, each with three human subjects, successfully used BrainNet to perform the collaborative task, with an average accuracy of 81.25%. Furthermore, by varying the reliability of sender information by artificially injecting noise into a sender's signal, we studied how the receiver learns to integrate noisy signals in order to make a correct decision. We found that, like

conventional social networks, BrainNet enables recipients to learn to trust the more reliable sender, in this case, based solely on information transmitted directly to their brain. Our results pave the way for future brain-to-brain interfaces that enable cooperative problem-solving by humans using a "social network" of connected brains.

What these researchers are proposing is nothing less than the creation of an Internet network linking not computers, but human brains, suitably equipped with an electromagnetic signal transmission interface. Evil minds might see in this research the goal of remote brain control, the dream of all totalitarian systems. But the researchers' intentions are good, and the medical and social benefits of all these experiments are emphasized.

Paul Thagard notes the importance of computer technology in the development of neuroscience:

> As far as experimentation is concerned, the cognitive science of science has made extensive use of computational models, which have been theoretically and methodologically important since the 1950s. Theoretical usefulness comes from the fruitfulness of the hypothesis that thinking is a kind of computation: thinking consists in applying processes to representations, just as computation consists in applying algorithms to data structures [...]. This hypothesis was far more powerful than previous attempts to understand the mind in terms of familiar mechanisms such as clocks, vibrating strings, hydraulic systems or telephone switchboards.
>
> *The cognitive Science of Science,* MIT Press, 2012

He adds that "computer modeling has provided an invaluable tool for developing and testing ideas about mental processes". Admittedly, Thagard remains cautious and does not fail to point out the limitations of this model—he must note, somewhat ruefully, that hypothetico-deductive reasoning works rather poorly in biology or the human sciences.

Despite the cautions and reservations of philosophers like Thagard—cautions and reservations that do not encumber the minds of *"new age"* propagandists like Laurent Alexandre—there is general agreement that the cyborg is just around the corner. And we can only profit from it! All this seems all the more obvious as advances in computer systems and so-called "artificial intelligence" (AI) seem to make it possible to manufacture "intelligent robots". A TV series took up the subject to promote recognition of the rights of robots, almost our brothers (*Real Humans*, a Swedish series broadcast between 2012 and 2014).

Another line of research is being pursued by *Blue Brain*, a Swiss project led by the École Polytechnique Fédérale de Lausanne. The aim of *Blue Brain* is to establish "simulation neuroscience" as a complementary approach to experimental, theoretical and clinical neuroscience for understanding the brain. The *"blue brain"* project aims to simulate a part of the brain, replicating the activity of thousands of cells (10,000 cells, billions of synapses) in a computer. The project should make it possible to model the brain of an autistic or schizophrenic person and eventually "test" treatments by simulation before applying them to real patients. A bit like how student pilots learn on a flight simulator before taking the controls of a real aircraft.

Computational neuroscience starts from the idea (already formulated by Hobbes and Leibniz!) that "to think is to calculate", which is also the central thesis of the advocates of "strong artificial intelligence"—the advocates of strong AI maintain that even if today's machines don't think, they will nevertheless be able to think at a later stage of technological progress, while the advocates of weak AI believe that the word "intelligence" applied to a machine has only metaphorical value, but that a very intelligently designed machine doesn't think and indeed will never think, whatever the subsequent technological progress (cf. above). The *blue brain project* puts this question on a new footing: if we can simulate brain function on a computer—advances have been made in this direction—then the question arises of the value of this simulation: does it tell us what human thought really is in certain operations or, on the contrary, is it only a partial pedagogical model? To continue the flight simulator analogy, a flight simulator is not a flight, and no one is transported in a flight simulator. It's true that some science-fiction writers have imagined that quantum teleportation could be perfected, enabling a person to be transported without a plane or a boat, but that's just science fiction. Once again, the question arises: is simulation knowledge? See what was said above about Searle's reflections.

However, the machine direction of neuroscience is not the only possible path. Another direction refutes the possibility of computer modeling of the human mind, and seeks to stand firmly on the ground of biology, medicine and psychology. Basically, the question is whether (biological) knowledge of the brain will be an auxiliary to the complete machinization of human relations, or whether machines are destined to be mere adjuncts to the brain, enabling it to increase its capacities, in much the same way as a spade increases the capacity of the gardener's hand when turning over the soil, but is of no use to him when pruning roses.

The fascination with the transformation of the brain into a machine is based on fantasies that are almost as old as humanity itself. The question of whether we can hope (or fear) that our memories can be recorded on a computer medium is a serious one. There's even a *start-up* offering to save our memories in the cloud. Nectome, a company founded in 2016 by two MIT-educated engineers, wants to preserve the brains of deceased humans in order to safeguard their memories and recreate their "minds". The company has even opened a waiting list for its storage service, with a $10,000 deposit, refundable if the person changes their mind. To save memories, we first need to know what a memory is: we know what a spoken or written word is, an image, etc., but we don't really know what a memory is. Secondly, we know that memories are not "stored" in a corner of the brain like we save our vacation photos on a USB stick. Researchers working on memory storage are well aware of these problems. In a way, they are proposing to save the configuration of the connections of 86 billion neurons and 1.5×10^{14} synaptic connections… As we shall see, this is a classic approach in neuroscience: solutions are put forward even though we have no precise knowledge of the problem. But the key to the mystery is revealed by Laurent Alexandre, one of the ardent propagandists of transhumanism, who proclaims that he would prefer to live millions of years in a silicon "chip" to see the extraordinary future that awaits us. It's hard to imagine a sillier proclamation, especially from someone with a medical background. Of course, even if our brain data (but it's not clear what that is) could be stored on a silicon memory chip, silicon sees nothing, hears nothing and couldn't possibly be amazed by the future world…

Dizzying Promises

Neuroscience, then, is already heralding far-reaching applications. Knowledge of the functioning of the neural apparatus, of what Jean-Pierre Changeux called *Neuronal Man*, coupled with other disciplines, such as cognitive behaviorist theories (CBT) or artificial intelligence research, is supposed to unlock the secrets of the human mind and thus increase our power by treating, correcting and properly training our brains. In other words, understanding our brain as the "seat" of thought would finally enable us to produce scientific knowledge of the human being in all its dimensions. Paul Thagard and other researchers, working in the same direction as him, are seeking to build a scientific knowledge of scientific knowledge. *Cognitive Science of Science* (2012) attempts to draw conclusions from the experience of an "artificial brain" of 2.5 million "neurons", *Spaun*, which serves as a model. The ambition of Paul Thagard, who is a philosopher, is quite simply to solve the problems of the philosophy of knowledge using cognitive science. If such a project could be carried out, not only would it be possible to draw a rigorous line between science and non-science, but it would also be possible to provide answers to the questions that have made philosophy a "battlefield", to use Kant's phrase. However, Thagard has to note that we don't arrive at a satisfactory model. He notes:

> It's possible that certain specific types of representations are embedded in the brain, for example those that may lead us to think that the world is made up of objects linked by causal relationships. However, it is often difficult to say whether the knowledge that appears very early in babies is there because it has been inscribed in the brain by evolution, or whether there is simply a tendency to acquire the appropriate types of information through learning. I tend to hypothesize innate mechanisms when they are the best explanation for the ability of humans and other animals to develop representations and behaviors. For particular representations such as concepts, rules and emotions, I recommend asking the following questions. Are they culturally universal, or only present in certain societies? Are there specific brain areas where they are present?
>
> *From Neurons to Consciousness and Creativity,*
> Oxford University Press, 2019

Despite the gigantic promises and victory announcements of the neurosciences, here's an eminent representative of cognitive neuroscience going back to Descartes' good old innate ideas! But how does one observe innate ideas in the brain? Like everyone else, Thagard hasn't the faintest idea of what it would take to observe innate ideas.

To get an idea of the field occupied by neuroscience today, we need to draw up a (non-exhaustive) list. Let's start with cognitive neuroscience, as presented in the *Encyclopédia Universalis*, by Michèle Fabre-Thorpe, director of research at the CNRS:

> The aim of cognitive neuroscience is to identify the cerebral processes at the origin of our mental capacities and to evaluate, in neurobiological terms, the plausibility of the models proposed in cognitive science. How does the functioning of our brain underlie our immaterial mind? Perceiving, recognizing, deciding, acting, memorizing, speaking, reasoning, being aware of, paying attention to… what brain organization, what neural processes, what neural coding allow us to account for the great cognitive capacities of humans and animals? Cognitive neuroscience lies at the interface between neuroscience, psychology, computational neuroscience, cognitive science and philosophy. Researchers often combine cognitive psychology paradigms with approaches specific to the study of the brain and neuronal functioning. The spectacular technical developments of the last thirty years have led to a colossal boom in cognitive neuroscience.

These lines should be analyzed in detail, as they raise so many complicated problems. They do, however, point the way for cognitive neuroscience: to identify the brain processes at the origin of our mental capacities. But what does the word "origin" mean? Does it refer to the cause that produces our mental capacities, or simply to the necessary but not sufficient condition for us to develop our mental capacities? We also need to define what we mean by mental capacities: are they the faculties of traditional psychology? Or something else? We'll come back to these questions later. The author adds that cognitive neuroscience lies at the interface with other neurosciences and cognitive psychology. It all adds up to a very vast program. But don't confuse cognitive neuroscience with cognitive science and cognitive psychology. What an accumulation of terms! Cognitive science describes the mechanisms of cognition. But what have modern philosophers, from Hobbes to Kant, done if not try to elucidate the "mechanisms of cognition"? Apart from the word "science", it's hard to see how this differs from the good old theory of knowledge, developed by Kant's heirs, notably neo-Kantians like Hermann Cohen, or specialists in the philosophy of science like Bachelard, Canguilhem and others, or logicians or psychologists who described and detailed the mechanisms of learning like Jean Piaget. As far as cognitive psychology is concerned, it has moved on from the study of higher "functions" (reasoning, conceptualization) to that of sensory capacities. Nothing really new, you might say, and rightly so. What do neurosciences bring to this work? The neurological substrate of learning and knowledge mechanisms. We can correlate certain mental operations with neurological processes, and no doubt we can hope for better treatment of neurodegenerative diseases, accident-related disorders, hemiplegia and so on. All these would undoubtedly be very positive advances, but for all that we still don't know what the mind is, or what words like freedom, necessity, truth and other categories of thought mean.

Among other neurosciences, we find computational neuroscience, which seeks to "discover the computational principles of brain function and neural activity, i.e., generic algorithms that allow us to understand the implementation in our central nervous system of the information processing associated with our cognitive functions", according to Wikipedia's definition, based on David Marr's "founding" articles. This presupposes that we can understand "brain functions" in terms of calculation, i.e. algorithms. If we add that the aim is to study how information processing is implemented in our central nervous system, we take the human central nervous system to be a simple machine, like any other, in which an information-processing function is implemented in the same way as information-processing functions are implemented in a computer. The paradigm of computational neuroscience is exactly the same as that of artificial intelligence.

Then there's social neuroscience. Their aim is to explore the neural bases of love, altruism, moral judgment and generosity.

Advocates of social neuroscience present it as a transdisciplinary field. Here again, we are struck by the vagueness of the terms used. "Neural bases"? What else? Do we mean to say that our moral judgments are determined by biochemical processes in our brains, or that our moral judgments encompass a whole series of neural processes which, however, are not their cause? If the second hypothesis is correct, then social neuroscience contributes absolutely nothing to our knowledge of moral judgments (to stick to this example), but if it's the first hypothesis that we have to follow, then we're back to the good old "naturalistic fallacy" that G.E. Moore criticized in his day (see *Principia Ethica*, 1903). Defenders of social neuroscience will protest: they propose a multi-level analysis—from the genetic level to that of social interactions—and defend "multiple determinism". What's more, they don't limit themselves to human beings, but include animals in their research. We are ready to admit that empathy has a neural basis, for example. The ability to put oneself in another's shoes has certainly been a selected trait in the evolution of our lineage—primates are capable of clearly displaying empathy—and this trait has obviously strengthened human sociability, which has played a decisive role for our species, given the terrible challenges it has faced in the course of its history. However, empathy is not a moral judgment, but a feeling, and perhaps only an emotion. Social neuroscience may well be just another version of sociobiology, the doctrine that seeks to synthesize evolutionary theory, in its strictest versions, with sociology, or evolutionary psychology.

In addition to the social neurosciences, there are other more or less far-fetched neurosciences, which we'll talk about along the way. But no matter how you look at the relationship between biological neuroscience and the other disciplines encompassed by neuroscience, a sort of continuum is established between the human body and various electronic component-based devices. Once upon a time, it was thought that listening to the spoken word was the key to understanding the human soul. Now, it's techno-scientific equipment that will unlock its secrets. A man-machine continuum, the cyborg, is emerging as a central element of transhumanist or posthumanist ideas, although undoubtedly few scientists would admit to adhering to the transhumanist project or ideology.

For it is the human being who must be overcome in the project of cognitive, emotional or social neuroscience. Browsing the scientific and literary output on the subject is extremely enlightening. One suggests "*Biohacking* and Neuroscience techniques to increase your discipline, build positive habits and combat the impulsive and distracted nature of your brain". Others propose reinventing our training with neuroscience. These are offered as a guide to pedagogical practices. They'll also help you feel "good in your head", they'll help you concentrate, and here they are, mobilized for your "slimming program"; they'll activate individual talents and collective intelligence; for managers, they'll give you "the power to change", and you'll be able to overcome fear and guilt, and even avoid human errors at work! Don't throw away any more! One wonders why the world continues to go wrong with all that neuroscience is supposed to bring us. Indeed, while neurobiology (not to be confused with neuroscience in the broadest sense) has produced many advances in the treatment of pathologies, and while the promise of the brain-machine connection helping to make advanced prostheses work seems interesting and useful, neuroscience has contributed nothing serious to our knowledge of the human mind, at least nothing we don't already know simply from observation and good old psychology.

The Quantum Canticle

It's pretty obvious that if we remain within the theoretical framework of molecular biology, which is in fact just a branch of physics-chemistry, we won't be able to think about the specific properties of the human body-mind. As we saw earlier, with regard to artificial intelligence, we can try to reduce the problem posed to a single question, that of intentionality. If we can resolve this question, then we can claim to have reduced the mind to the brain. Michel J.-F. Dubois, an agronomist with a doctorate in molecular biology, tackles this question with the great advantage of tackling it head-on, in a large work that is actually his doctoral thesis in philosophy, *Le vivant et l'indéterminé* (Éditions universitaires européennes, 2014).

The starting point, and the purpose of Volume 1, is to try and understand what intentional action is, and how it relates to the brain. Intentional action (perhaps) exists insofar as we generally believe that we can act intentionally, i.e. without our actions being the result of a succession of physical processes.

Yet there seems to be an incompatibility between the basic methodological principle of the natural sciences, the principle of determinism, and the possibility of intentional actions—these actions presuppose something that can be called subjectivity, and it is in these actions that the subject recognizes himself as a subject. Dubois recalls the eliminativist positions of Jean-Pierre Changeux, but also the epiphenomenalist positions that see mental facts as mere epiphenomena of physical facts: consciousness would be like the noise of the engine. If the engine makes noise, this noise has no functional role, and besides, we prefer low-noise engines! Nevertheless, Changeux's thinking is more complex: rather than denying intentional action, he makes it a result of certain neuronal configurations, which are in a way the causes of thoughts, thus returning to Cabanis's position: it's neuronal configurations that produce thought. Dubois examines Henri Atlan's theses (a little too quickly!) and concludes that complexity theory is "a smoke-screen for our inability to admit the contradictions we don't want to face". He also shows that Dennett's subtle proposals offer no real solutions.

Several authors (Changeux, Dennett, etc.) are trying to explain intentional action as the result of an evolutionary process, which is tantamount to recognizing its effectiveness against epiphenomenalist and eliminativist dogmas. In truth, we must admit intentional action, and we admit it simply when we hold a certain proposition to be true. Dubois rightly states that truth and falsity are impossible to admit when we admit that we are determined (cf. above).

Intention is first and foremost what the subject affirms: intention and subjectivity could thus be the same thing, and consequently, the author's desire to limit his work to intention is largely outdated… Dubois relies on the ordinary way in which we distinguish our acts: by chance or on purpose, right or wrong. He gives all sorts of good reasons for admitting intentionality, and shows that biological determinism, like determinism in general, is incapable of conceiving invention, the appearance of the new. In a deterministic conception, everything is already in the initial conditions, so there is never really anything new or unexpected, except when there are hidden causes that we hadn't perceived. Using Cournot's definition of chance (the meeting of two independent causal chains), he admits that invention can be the result of chance. In short, the Darwinian scheme could admit invention—we might think here of Monod's reflections on *Chance and Necessity*. But, in practice, it's very difficult to distinguish between what comes from objective elements and what comes from interpretations. In fact, it's virtually impossible to prove that an invention is the result of chance. Intentionality must therefore be accepted.

Indeed, all inventions and discoveries of any complexity presuppose intentionality, and most creations cannot be considered as the random result of independent causal chains. However, there is determinism. It was Schrödinger who postulated the identity of the laws of biology with the laws of molecular chemistry and physics. However, this is only a theoretical program. In fact, physics does not provide the elements needed to understand molecular biology.

Dubois makes an interesting point about the notion of "code" used in molecular biology:

> The concept of code in molecular biology is both a metaphor and a means of processing results. From transcribed and translated DNA sequences, we can deduce the sequence of the corresponding protein. This does not mean that DNA is a language. Transcription and the succession of nitrogenous bases are deterministic in their operation, as is RNA translation. This determinism may be limited by random events, but calculations show that an extremely low error rate is necessary for the system to maintain itself. There is no meaning in the succession of base pairs in the DNA double helix, except what we want to put there. Deciphering nature means that nature doesn't speak. There may be a code, but there's no meaning; no biologist will say there's an intention. To say that DNA is the book of life is no more than a metaphor that does not call into question the determinism of molecular biology. (*Op. cit.*)

Determinism therefore operates at biochemical, molecular chemical, physiological and neurological levels. This determinism is even necessary for the realization of intentional activity. It is only the origin (not the functioning) of intentional activity that is not accessible to biological determinism. Orientation and purpose (finalization) are the fundamental characteristics of intentional activity. Purpose functions as a bondage (in the cybernetic sense) to the (deterministic) functioning of intentional activity.

Dubois therefore proposes to look for the presence of indeterminacy in the human body. First, he asserts that the laws of Newtonian mechanics are not strictly deterministic, which is incorrect. The three-body problem is invoked: what are the mathematical solutions to the differential equations describing the orbits of three mutually attracting celestial bodies? There is no stable long-term solution to this problem. But this in no way implies that Newton's laws are not deterministic. They fall into the category of "deterministic chaos", which applies to all systems that are sensitive to initial conditions—as, for example, to the systems used to model atmospheric movements, about which the famous "butterfly effect" has been imagined. These are systems of equations in which a minimal variation in initial parameters can lead to unpredictable variations. Strictly speaking, these systems are not indeterministic. What is poorly determined are the measurements of the initial conditions—any measurement inevitably involves some degree of error.

Dubois adds that cybernetics as a means of describing the living world assumes an indeterminism independent of intentional activity. The indeterminism of cybernetic systems is nothing more than their ability to adapt to their environment (self-regulation). But this is not indeterminism. The same applies to the concept of self-organization. Finally, information theory introduces randomness, but again independently of any intentional activity. Information theory does introduce the notion of noise, but this cannot be seen as an essential indeterminacy that could be used to explain intentionality.

After analyzing all forms of indeterminacy, Dubois comes to the conclusion that the indeterminacy that can produce intentional activity is located in the central nervous system, which is so particular that it somehow escapes general deterministic laws. So Dubois, too, is an "encephalocentrist", and has little chance of solving the problem he himself posed! He's looking for the "pineal gland", i.e. the biological device that enables us to move from biology to thought. But for him, it's a pineal gland that's not locally determined—it involves all the areas of the brain that process information or control movement. He assumes that the brain is not an organ like any other. This assumption is bound to confuse the reader of good will.

How does Michel Dubois go about saving his "store" by confining himself to the cerebral domain? He accepts the neurobiological principle of looking for "cerebral functions" in a biological substratum, but for him intentionality is not a function—like the functions of recognition, memorization and so on. It's in quantum physics that he's going to find his Grail! According to him, quantum physics discovers indeterminism! Epicurus and Lucretius introduced a random element into the universal determinism of atoms: the clinamen, that random deviation in the course of atoms that gives rise to novelty and, on the basis of this random element, the Epicureans founded the possibility of a will that makes it possible not to suffer destiny. The problem is that we shouldn't take all this literally. Atomists don't base their moral and psychological conceptions on their physics; on the contrary, it's physics that serves as an image for their psycho-moral conception.

Even if we admit that Alain Aspect (see Aspect's experiment) proved that indeterminism is fundamental and not the result of our ignorance of hidden variables, as Einstein implied with his famous "God doesn't play dice", he didn't deny determinism at the macrophysical level. It's hard to understand how we get from the quantum level to the biological level of neurons. That elementary particles are fundamentally indeterminate, that the quantum fluctuation of the vacuum is at the origin of the "big bang", etc., says nothing about our ordinary experience. If a stone falls according to deterministic laws, we know in advance that it is in a given state and that it will reach the ground after a calculable time. A cat enclosed in a box will remain in a living state for a certain period of time, but it could end up in a "dead" state if left to starve to death! Real cats don't behave like Schrödinger's cats.

Moreover, Michel Dubois acknowledges that indeterminism at the microphysical level gives way to determinism at the macrophysical level. It remains to be shown that indeterminacy **also** exists at the neuronal level. Michel Dubois seems to be reiterating Eccles' thesis, taken up by Henry Margenau, that the junction between mind and brain takes place in microsites at the neuronal level. We can, of course, accept that there are quantum phenomena governed by the principle of indeterminacy at the level of synapses, although nothing says that this is so, but to deduce that this is the birthplace of consciousness and intentionality seems to me a leap into the void as arbitrary as Descartes'. Incidentally, Eccles calls himself a proponent of a "dualist-interactionist" philosophy. And Dubois seems to be following in his footsteps. But then he changes his mind and wonders whether he's following the same erroneous path as Descartes.

He then questions the hypothesis that neurons themselves are non-deterministic. He examines the hypothesis of a homology between the cerebral magnetic field and states of consciousness. Some authors see the indeterminacy of this field as the "explanation" of free will! As an aside, it's worth noting that Dubois always expresses himself by assuming analogies and using conditionals, but no definite thesis, for the good reason that it would have been necessary to define consciousness and intentionality directly, and eventually show how this would or would not correlate with mental states.

The author remains cautious:

> We can't say that quantum mechanics explains intentional activity. We have only concluded that the existence of intentional activity leads to the necessity of non-determination, where intention acts, i.e. on the brain, and that quantum physics, the backbone of the sciences of matter, does indeed allow it to exist, or even allows it a place. This place does exist at the cerebral level (*Op. cit.*).

He recognizes that subjectivity can no more be explained by quantum mechanics than by neurology. The homology between intention and quantum indeterminacy is only a homology, not an explanation.

The only things that are certain are :

33. the existence of intentional activity cannot be denied;

34. this assumes indeterminacy at the neuronal level;

35. quantum mechanics makes this indeterminacy thinkable.

But the whole thing remains unconvincing. If we admit that quantum mechanics is a description of reality at a certain level and classical physics (the physics of our world) is a description at another level, there's nothing to do but show that the micro description is compatible with the macro description, but it's not possible to deduce that the "micro" level causes the "macro" level in the sense of a cause having effects. If I put a pan of water on the fire and after a certain time it comes to the boil, I know that there are all sorts of quantum phenomena occurring and expressing themselves in the transformation of the water's state, but they are not the "cause", which remains that I put the pan on the fire! This discussion of the problem of cause brings us back to an old debate already raised by the Stoics: does the ball roll because it's round, or because I pushed it?

It is to be feared that it is encephalocentrism that is causing the difficulties in which Michel Dubois is embroiled. Does the brain determine our thoughts? Yes and no! Yes, because without a brain we wouldn't be able to think, because without this hypercomplex organization our thoughts wouldn't be what they are, etc. But no, because our thoughts are formed by the brain. But no, because our thoughts are formed in the interaction between our body and the outside world, including other human beings who "think like us" or more or less. The indeterminacy needed to understand intentionality could be sought in this direction without having to mobilize those costly and unconvincing quantum foundations.

Once again, it must be stressed that "micro" indeterminacy does not translate into "macro" indeterminacy! In a semiconductor, there's a quantum phenomenon: electrons pass "under" the transistor's potential barrier through a quantum effect, but this doesn't mean that the semiconductor has a non-deterministic effect (fortunately, otherwise we'd hardly know what to think of the results of running a program: 2 +2 gives 4, not the superposition of 4 and 5 or whatever. Transferring the problem to the level of synapses doesn't change this observation. Incidentally, Michel Dubois himself doesn't believe it, and notes that the various hypotheses are only weak explanatory hypotheses, and nothing more. Let's not forget that he makes a few references to authors, sometimes good authors, who have been known to rave: he cites, among others, some of the stars of the "Cordoba Colloquium" (October 1979), without mentioning the event itself. Under the generic title of "Science and Consciousness", it was a question of whether paranormal phenomena could be explained by quantum mechanics…

So we're perplexed, and so is the author. He maintains his central thesis, that of the reality of intentionality. Intentionality is effective and acts causally on the body. Dubois thus opposes the theses of philosophers like Nietzsche, who don't give it any real efficacy: if "I want to do X", it would be because, in reality, all sorts of processes are already engaged in my body, leading to this X action. So my "will" would be no more than an epiphenomenon, grafted onto physiological processes. Dubois wants to anchor intentionality in the indeterminacy of the brain. If, indeed, the brain is deterministic, there is no real intention… So we have to admit that the brain is quantum, but not entirely quantum. It's a strange proposition, which he acknowledges will meet with "resistance". After all, all phenomena are quantum and non-quantum, depending on the level of description at which they are described! But at a given level, the phenomenon is quantum and not non-quantum, or vice versa. A woman cannot simultaneously be pregnant and not pregnant.

We must therefore try to overcome these difficulties. If we admit that intentional action exists—and how could we not—how is this compatible with "the data emerging from modern physical and biological sciences"? When you read this from the pen of Michel Dubois, you can't help but think that no progress has been made since Descartes! Indeed, the (mental) representation of a goal is ineffective, unless you believe in magic. Action necessarily involves the body—the body itself, or what we might call the "self". The problem is that our body is a material object of the same nature as the bodies on which it acts, but then intentionality, which cannot act directly on bodies, becomes inexplicable. And yet, it undoubtedly exists. Michel Dubois compares the two theories (dualist and monist), which he sets out with an apt metaphor ("on the one hand the artist playing an instrument, on the other hand the robot-instrument, an adaptive and creative automaton"), and shows that the two theories cannot be separated by the facts—a case of underdetermination of the theory by the facts. Monism denies intentionality, and dualism is unable to explain how intention acts on the body. As for emergentist theories, they have the disadvantage of being difficult to falsify (in Popper's sense).

After a long peregrination, Michel Dubois concedes that quantum mechanics meets some of the requirements of intentionality, but does not explain it! We can only say that in a world governed by the laws of physics (including those of quantum physics), intentionality can exist. This also enables us to understand why intentionality cannot be explained.

In conclusion, we agree with the author that he is not trying to sweep under the carpet the difficulties of his attempt to give a scientific theory of the mind. His work contains precise refutations of all the shortcuts we are fed by neuroscientific theorists. But we're not much further ahead: we do have a global theory, often diabolically precise, of the objective world, i.e. the world as grasped by subjects like ourselves, but we can't reintegrate the subject into this objective world. We can probably explain what's going on in the brain of someone we could observe and who would say to us "I intend to learn quantum physics", but we can't deduce what intention is when we ourselves can say to ourselves "I intend to understand Michel Dubois' theory of intentionality."

Once again, we're not much further ahead on these issues than Descartes, Spinoza and Leibniz were. This may seem hopeless for those who "believe" in the definitive victory of the scientific conception of the world. But it will not despair anyone who, refusing to play God, knows that something essential will always elude us, and so renounces scientistic beliefs—beliefs that are no better than any others, and may even, in some respects, prove worse in their consequences than the good old religious superstitions of yesteryear.

Illusions, Disillusions and Threats

A detour through the work of Michel Dubois shows how the honest researcher quickly becomes confused when he wants to clarify the relationship between the biological and the psychological, and link our mental states to neuronal states.

It's easy to see, then, that all this literature extolling the applications of neuroscience is singularly lacking in scientific seriousness. From a certain point of view, it's reassuring that all this "manage your team better with neuroscience" literature is close to pure and simple quackery. Because, conversely, if neuroscience could deliver what it promises, mind control techniques would find a way to control individuals as in the most frightening dystopias. And there's something wrong with these dystopias: if the sciences of brain manipulation can transform humans into termites in their termite mounds, then some humans must have had this intention, and must somehow escape the scientific determinism that allows them to control others…

It could well be that neuroscience will suffer the same fate as its cousin, artificial intelligence, which has had to lower its sights and is now, more often than not, reduced to powerful techniques for the massive processing of digitized data and images.

Already, some of the promises of neuroscience appear to be mere marketing ploys. NM (neuro-marketing) is precisely marketing. The use of neuroscience in forensic science appears, if not ethically questionable, at least useless in determining the liability of a defendant. Some researchers, however, are proclaiming that we are close to the biological identification of "violent brains", an unexpected return to the old theories of criminologist Cesare Lombroso, who in 1876 published *The Criminal Man*, a work in which he argued that born criminals could be identified from certain physical traits. We'll no longer say he has a criminal's head, but a criminal's neurons. What fabulous progress!

For the time being, Stanislas Dehaene's work on reading or learning mathematics doesn't seem to have enthused teachers, and convincing experimental results are yet to come. Perhaps neuroscience will promise us a moral education for pupils in the future?

If the proof of the pudding is in the eating, let's face it, we haven't yet had any substantial dishes on our plates to validate the findings of neuroscience. It will be objected that cognitive science and neuroscience are still in their infancy, that practitioners in the various sectors that could be interested in them are largely unaware of them, and that we must be patient in awaiting results that will win over the most recalcitrant. These arguments are not lacking in relevance; disappointments in the face of inordinate or absurd ambitions cannot constitute a valid objection against the neuroscientific project.

In fact, the ambition of neuroscience is to put an end to the absurd belief (according to neuroscience) that man is free. If we could show that an individual's intentions and volitions are determined by his or her neuronal state, it would follow, firstly, that individuals never act freely and can therefore hardly be held morally responsible for their actions, and, secondly, that judicious interventions on this neuronal state would make it possible to eliminate crime, perversions and all the horrible things that our societies, denying the tragic nature of the human condition, have decided to eradicate. Thanks to neuroscience, we're going to become happy, happy with an "unbearable happiness" (see Ira Levin's book, *Unbearable Happiness*, 1970).

This in no way diminishes the importance of neurobiology. For example, if we could really cure cancerous tumors in the brain, nobody would complain. If we could delay senile dementia, that would undoubtedly be a good thing! Similarly, advances in pain medication would be welcome. But no medicine is going to take us away from the anguish of death, which is always certain even if the time is uncertain. Posthumanist or transhumanist nightmares are in fact in line with neuroscientific madness.

Indeed, neuroscience, functioning as an ideology, reinforces the idea that man can be made malleable at will, that he can become whatever we want him to become, and that he can also be the object of unlimited experimentation. By the same token, we can give a certain legitimacy to all operations of conditioning or "reconditioning" human beings. In this way, psychology is gradually being transformed into a series of techniques aimed at adapting individuals to the functioning of society as it is—which is one of the reasons why cognitive behavioral therapies (CBT) are favored over good old-fashioned psychotherapy, not to mention psychoanalysis.

This does not invalidate the traditional criticism of free will as an illusion—which can be found in Spinoza and Diderot. For the same reasons that the dualistic thesis cannot be proven, the monistic materialist thesis cannot be refuted. It's easy to admit that our decisions, our intentions and all our self-perceptions are conditioned by the material and social world and by the state of our bodies, and that our free will is therefore not all that free! Spinoza asserts that we believe we are free because we don't know what determines us to want this or that, but he doesn't deduce that freedom is an illusion! In fact, the last part of the *Ethics* is entitled "On the Freedom of Man". But this freedom can be gained by working on ourselves, by understanding the dynamics of our own affects, not by suppressing them.

In other words, the "monist" position of Spinoza or Diderot remains entirely within the framework of humanist thinking, i.e. thinking that builds on the potentialities of human nature, whereas the neuroscience project, when followed through to its conclusion, aims at a radical transformation of man, through reconditioning or reformatting techniques, i.e. it is anti-humanism.

In Between

We'd like to show that these disappointments and absurdities derive not from the insufficient progress of the neuroscience project, but from the project itself—again, not confusing neuroscience with neurobiology. The thesis I'd like to put forward now is that knowledge of the brain can tell us nothing about thought, precisely because thought is not a product of the brain in the same way as bile is a product of the liver, because thought is not produced in the braincase, and because, fundamentally, it cannot be objectified, even though it is the condition of all objectification.

What makes us subjective—that is, what makes us subjects capable of becoming aware of ourselves as we are in the world—is called consciousness. Consciousness is neither a part of the brain (like Broca's area) nor a property of the brain. A first approach can be made when we look at memory, since memory is an essential dimension of self-awareness. We spontaneously believe that our own memories are buried in our brains. Like photographs in old albums or in boxes piled in the dust of an attic, we believe that memory is a certain part of our brain assigned to storage, like the equivalent of a computer's hard disk. But this metaphor works very poorly. We have no unified description of memory. We can build sophisticated models of psychological memory, but these models cannot be superimposed on those being constructed by the neurosciences. We can't repeat here the mountain of philosophical or scientific texts devoted to memory (see our book, *La mémoire*, published by Bréal, 2018). Let's content ourselves with taking up Antonio Damasio's concept of "extended consciousness", which is the capacity we have to tell ourselves our own story.

And yet, this extended consciousness can only arise in the interaction between the subject and the world, and more specifically in interaction with others. Self-awareness, as Hegel had already masterfully shown, is born of this relationship with the world (why do children like to make circles in the water while throwing pebbles?) and with other human beings, whom they recognize and through whom they know themselves. We can only think, and say what we want to say, because we speak. But speech is a gift from others, and we don't speak the language we've invented; we settle into a language that's already there, and which will forge our thoughts and the categories through which we'll apprehend the world. The brain does not produce speech—even if, damaged, it can cause us to lose it. Classical philosophy and phenomenology have demonstrated all this admirably, whereas neuroscience is incapable of saying such simple and obvious things as soon as you stop to think about it.

But to avoid getting bogged down in old-fashioned thinking, let's take a look at some of the more contemporary thinkers who have put these questions on a new footing. Ludwig Wittgenstein, for example, writes:

> The main reason why we tend to locate thought in the brain is that we use the terms "speak" and "write" to describe bodily activity, in conjunction with the terms "think" or "penser", which leads us to regard thought as an analogous activity. When terms in everyday

language at first glance present a certain analogy in their grammatical function, we tend to understand them within the same system of interpretation: in other words, we strive to maintain the analogy at all costs. Thought," we say, "is something other than the sentence, for the same thought will be expressed in French and English in quite different terms. However, since we can see where sentences are, we're looking for a place where thought might be. (It's a bit like trying to move the King on a chessboard by applying the rules of checkers). "But thought," you may say, "exists; it's not a 'nothing'." To this, we can simply reply that we don't use the word "thought" at all in the same way we use the word "sentence".

Would it be absurd, then, to speak of a place where thought takes place? By no means. But the expression has no other meaning than the one we intend to attribute to it. When we say: "The brain is the place where thought is located". What does that mean? Simply that physiological processes are correlated with thought, and that we assume that their observation will enable us to discover thoughts. But what meaning can we give to this correlation, and in what sense can we say that observing the brain will enable us to reach thoughts?

We can probably assume that the correspondence has been observed experimentally. Let's imagine this kind of experiment. It involves observing the brain of a subject who is thinking. But the explanation is likely to be inadequate, as the observer will only know the thoughts indirectly, through the intermediary of the subject who must somehow *express* them. To overcome this objection, let's assume that the subject and the observer are one and the same—a man who could look into a mirror, for example, to see what's going on in his brain. (This simplistic image does not detract from the logical force of the argument).

But what does the subject observe? A single phenomenon, or two separate phenomena? (And don't tell me he's observing the same phenomenon in its double guise, *internal* and external, because that doesn't make the difficulty go away. But we'll come back to this question of inside and outside later). The observation concerns a relationship between two types of phenomena. One, which we'll call "thought": a series of images, impressions, or a series of visual, tactile or kinaesthetic sensations, experienced when writing a sentence or speaking words; and, on the other hand, a phenomenon of another kind: the sight of contractions or cellular movements of the brain. Of course, we can say that in both cases we are dealing with a process of "expressing thought", but we must avoid asking: "But where is the thought? to avoid confusion. However, if we use the expression "the brain is the seat of thought", we should be aware that this is a *hypothesis* that can only be verified by observing thought in the brain.

This long excerpt from Le *Cahier bleu* (1958) has the immense advantage of unravelling a number of issues confused by the misuse of language. In a completely different direction, and building on Gibson's work, Japanese philosopher Tetsuya Kono derives a conception of the "extended mind": the mind is neither in the brain nor in the body, but in the body/brain/environment relationship.

The identification of the mind with the brain widely practiced in neuroscience obviously poses all kinds of ethical challenges (e.g., that of improving brain performance, "reading" the brain, etc.). Tetsuya Kono is part of the movement calling for a neuroethics. But if the concept of the extended mind—that the mind actually exists within the complex of brain/body/environment relation-ships—is true, then the very project of neuroscience is in jeopardy.

If this conception is true, not only the brain-reading project, but also the mind-brain identity theory that neuroscientists presuppose are fundamental errors. They are internalist prejudices in the eyes of the extended mind.

And he adds:

Psychologization is a trend of thought that seeks the cause of all problematic behavior in the mind or interiority of the individual. It tends to reduce all social and political problems to the level of the mind and individual behavior. According to this thinking, psychologists and psychiatrists have the power to solve all society's problems.

Lectures at EHESS

All these reflections lead to the same point: the project of a scientific knowledge of the mind by means of a scientific knowledge of the brain is a dead end in theory, but it is part of a global vision, born in the seventeenth century, that wants to turn man into a machine. We can clearly see the link between the emergence of the machine, which was to invade all production, and a new general model of thought, imposing itself on knowledge of living organisms and of human thought itself. The practical efficiency of this mechanical model enabled it to impose itself and gradually invade the whole of social life, transforming the human condition from top to bottom. For millennia, the domination of man over man involved brute force, the balance of power, the struggle (to the death) between master and slave—a struggle that never ended, since the slave could always regain the upper hand through new circumstances. Neuroscience promises to bring humans into line with current social norms in a non-violent and sustainable way. If man is no more than a cluster of neurons, there is obviously no moral objection to this project. But if man is just a cluster of neurons, all morality is just noise produced by this cluster of neurons, and, by the same token, all scientific theories are just noise, including those that reduce man to a cluster of neurons. Nevertheless, if we are willing to admit that others are nothing but a cluster of neurons, no one can think of himself as a cluster of neurons.

CHAPTER V: THE ULTIMATE STAGE OF REIFICATION

Subjectivity is the enemy! The whole of modernity is built around the frantic quest for objectivity. Instead of our hesitations, our impulses, our feelings, only the calculus decides. *Calculemus*, as Leibniz put it. Ancient values were all subjective: honor, courage, loyalty, all came from the *thymos*. And our weaknesses, our greed, our laziness, our cowardice, our depravities, all came from the *epithymia*, i.e. from a part of our soul. With modernity, obsolete values can be replaced by a value that can be measured, a neutral value, money, which alone gives true power. Commodity fetishism is the overthrow of the human world. Marx's essential contribution is to have analyzed this reversal.

We used to foolishly believe that man could be educated, by word and example and through human relationships. But nay, he must become modifiable by neuroscience, *upgradable* like software, transformable by the addition of "intelligent" prostheses. When Sartre speaks of the inertia of social groups, he precisely uses the term "serialization": modern machinery and even mega-machinery (cf. below) aim at this general serialization of humanity, which has become predictable.

Indeed, machinism is the means by which all individuals are transformed into interchangeable "human resources" or consumers dedicated to maximizing their utility. First and foremost, machinismo has enabled our world to be invaded by machines that claim to do just about everything for us. Far from enabling us to emancipate ourselves from natural determinisms, the machines built by science have subjected us to their own determinisms. Charlie Chaplin's famous film, *Modern Times,* is rightly regarded as the best representation of our times.

But what's on the horizon is nothing less than man becoming a machine. Transhumanism and cyborg theories are not science-fiction themes (or at least no longer are), but well-advanced projects to surpass the human in such a way that those who refuse this inevitable evolution will be "the chimpanzees of the future", as Kevin Warwick put it in 2002 in his appeal against techno-totalitarianism.

Finally, our relationship with the world and with other human beings is radically subjected to the machine. We are doomed to talk to "conversational robots", but this is perhaps only a secondary aspect of the evolution of the human condition: we are condemned, throughout our professional and personal lives, to "follow procedures", i.e. to execute a program, exactly as a machine does. More and more often, the images we are offered are computer-generated images, or "virtual images" as they are bizarrely called, images produced by machines that not only imitate reality, but substitute themselves for it.

Commodification

Reification is the transformation of living things into inert things. The process of commodification as the fundamental process of modern society is analyzed by Marx, notably in the first section of *Capital.* But it is Lukács who is responsible for the systematic use of the term reification and its corollary, reified consciousness. He developed these themes in *Histoire et conscience de classe (History and Class Consciousness*), a book published in 1923 that earned him condemnation from the summits of the Communist International for non-conformity with Marxism, as codified in those years. In 1930, the author repudiated his book. But the fruitfulness of ideas transcends the vagaries of history. For it is indeed under the emblem of reification that our world presents itself, but understood in a much broader sense than Lukács could have suspected.

The idea of reification is already present in Marx's work, even before the developments concerning the transformation of living labor into dead labor, and the inverted relationship established by machinismo. In his polemic against Proudhon, *Misère de la philosophie* (1847), Marx writes:

> The mere quantity of labor serving as a measure of value without regard to quality assumes in turn that simple labor has become the pivot of industry. It assumes that work has been equalized by the subordination of man to machine, or by the extreme division of labor; that men have faded before work; that the pendulum of the clock has become the exact measure of the relative activity of two workers, as it is of the celerity of two locomotives. So we shouldn't say that one man's hour is worth another man's hour, but rather that one man's hour is worth another man's hour. Time is everything, man is nothing; he is at most the carcass of time. Quality is no longer an issue. Quantity alone decides everything: hour for hour, day for day; but this equalization of work is not the work of Proudhon's eternal justice; it is quite simply the fact of modern industry.

We could multiply quotations from Marx along the same lines. The development of machinismo (cf. first chapter) pushes the commodification of workers to its extremes. Man is no longer the master of his tools, but the servant of the machine. The worker's knowledge and skills have been transferred to the machine. The organization of work is now "scientific" (OST), and what could one object to a scientific organization? This OST reaches a new stage when Artificial Intelligence devices are used to directly control Amazon warehouse workers, to direct their movements, thus transforming them into robots of human flesh.

But commodification doesn't just concern the worker at work. All relations between humans now appear as relations between things, insofar as things useful to life, but also useless things, become commodities with an exchange value.

Reification is the consequence of the fact that, in the capitalist mode of production, human beings are subjected to abstraction: decomposed concrete labor has become abstract labor, the pure expenditure of labor power, and the commodity itself is not worth its perceptible qualities, but the labor time coagulated within it. Quality is reduced to quantity. From then on, all differences disappear, all distinctions lose all meaning. Culture is reduced to the production of cultural goods—Adorno devoted many pages to the culture industry, the ultimate expression of this reification. How can we still appreciate Vivaldi when it has been arch-used as music on hold in telephone call centers? Undifferentiation affects all fields: in schools, we no longer study works or even texts, but documents, even if we don't hesitate to call a motley collection of "documents" a "corpus".

Treating Humans like Things

Treating human beings as things is the ABC of capital. Human beings are merely means for the accumulation of capital. In commodity exchange, goods face each other, seemingly endowed with a life of their own, when in fact they are no more than the materialization of living labor, of the personal power of men. And we've made progress, if I dare say, since "personnel management" in companies has given way to "human resources management": human beings are no longer people, but resources at the service of the production process. This transformation has the merit of being frank!

But humans are unpredictable and often whimsical: you can't really count on them. If it were just a case of bad heads being spotted by the police (public or private), it wouldn't be such a big deal. All you have to do is contain the bad heads and order will reign. But, alas, any human can become a bad head. Circumstances sometimes turn cowards into heroes, submissives into rebels. You can force people to say what you want them to say, but how can you force them to think? Spinoza, the optimistic thinker, was well aware that you can force languages, but not brains! It is precisely this supposedly impossible task that the neurosciences have tackled (see above). We must make man predictable at all costs, otherwise it will be forever impossible to govern him scientifically, as Auguste Comte dreamed. In the absence of rigorous scientific means, we've had to make do with good old-fashioned propaganda techniques, as theorized by Walter Lippman and Edward Bernays, a nephew of Freud, with the practical exercises of propaganda in favor of the United States' entry into the war (1917) and a major advertising campaign to encourage women to consume *Lucky Strike* cigarettes...

But propaganda alone is not enough. Bernays' Nazi disciples knew this, and complemented it with ruthless surveillance and repression of anyone suspected of not sharing in the adoration of the beloved Führer. Conditioning and beast-training remain basic techniques of government. All these techniques are, however, costly, and their effectiveness is ultimately rather mediocre, if we expect agents to be not simply automatons, but human beings capable of reflection and appropriate decision-making in unforeseen situations. This is where the "human sciences" come in, instrumentalized as a technique for controlling humans.

The human sciences should, according to the program of the natural sciences, become the equal of the natural sciences—to find the "Newton's law" of human affairs, demanded David Hume. The neurosciences, as we have said, propose to realize this program in the most radical way, by reducing, as the Papuans reduced heads, the human mind to inert nature. These are promises and even marketing speeches, rather than tangible realities. So, for the time being, we have to make do with the instrumentalization of existing human sciences. Unintentionally, Émile Durkheim had indicated the direction to follow: "social facts must be treated as things" is the most important of the "rules of sociological method". Durkheim certainly didn't consider men to be things, beings deprived of spontaneity and freedom. But, in his view, the social fact is or must be considered as independent of the individual psyche, and imposes itself on individuals—this is what characterizes it as a social fact. There are countless examples of social facts, sufficiently widespread in a given society, which impose themselves on individuals and develop their own causal relations—language, but also religion, are classic examples. If we confine ourselves to attempting to describe social facts with no pretension other than to offer a particular insight that is not exclusive of other insights, we have nothing to reproach these "sociologies of constraint", which insist on the existence of these social determinisms or conditionings, the reality of which is hardly in doubt. On the other hand, this sociology of constraint can easily be instrumentalized to reinforce population control and surveillance systems. The enormous amount of information that computer systems gather on each and every one of us is used to draw inductive rules to guide individual choices. Commerce is already using it: an online book or music sales site makes purchase proposals to its customers by researching what other customers, who have made the same purchase, have bought elsewhere. For one thing, repeated political polls on a fairly small sample make it possible, through inductive processes, to obtain relatively reliable predictions of electoral behavior.

Apprehended through these grids of statistical behavioral studies, individuals lose all thickness. They become calculable automatons. The computer processing of personal data makes it possible to draw up a graph of all the relationships of each person and all the transactions carried out by that person, and to do this, it is no longer necessary to have a police officer behind each citizen and a police supervisor behind each police officer. Individuals have voluntarily enrolled themselves in the system and, when they have refused to do so, maintaining relations outside the system has become legally impossible—you have to have a bank account to be paid and an identity card is compulsory—or things have been made so complex that, war-weary, almost everyone has bought a computer or a "smartphone" and initiated themselves into computer hell. And hell it is: between forgotten passwords, which are increasingly complicated, and malfunctioning connections, performing even the slightest operation can feel like entering a still-unknown annex of Kafka's world.

Treating social facts as things: here we go! Man as a "political living being" or social animal is entirely objectified, not by the pure cognitive mechanism of Durkheimian science, but by the very development of this gigantic social machinery into which we are inserted as one of its components. Marx believed that nature is the non-organic body of man. He was wrong, in view of the real situation: it's the social machinery, its computer networks and its procedures that constitute man's non-organic body, or rather, it's man who is the properly organic part of the social machinery.

Nothing I write here is profoundly new. Marcuse had already made an important contribution to the analysis of modern industrial totalitarianism, which is entirely subject to the principle of efficiency. I can only refer the reader to my book devoted to Marcuse (Max Milo, 2017). From a slightly different perspective, Jean Chesneaux's essay *De la modernité*, published in 1983, begins by describing the thirteen perverse effects of modernity.

Under the heading of modernity, the author analyzes the profound social transformations that France underwent in the post-war period. With hindsight, however, we need to give these early descriptions their true meaning, which, it seems to me, still eluded Jean Chesneaux. Indeed, it seems that the years 1970-1980 were a turning point. These were the years in which we entered "the crisis" (1973, the first oil shock), and we may well wonder whether "modernity" will mark time, or even regress, or whether, on the contrary, it will envelop us ever more deeply. The ensuing four decades have provided the author with answers to the questions that still seem unanswered. Chesneaux defined modernity as the combination of "two globalities". Firstly, that denounced by Sartre (see *Critique de la Raison dialectique*, 1960), with the serialization of beings, objects, conditions and mechanisms, and the reduction of trivialized life to a single model. On the other hand, the generalized "wiring" of the planet, the universal interdependence of economies, communication networks and political and social structures—in a word, "the despotism of the global market". As you can see, all our themes are already clearly delineated in this 1983 book.

The thirteen perverse effects of modernity, according to Chesneaux, begin to describe very precisely the ravages in the world of life, correlative to the indefinite extension of the domain of machinery. Let's take a look at a few of these "perverse effects", noting that while they may have appeared to Chesneaux as perverse effects, today we see very clearly that they are the very essence of the system, and flow quite naturally from a history spanning several centuries.

First perverse effect: standards. It is modern, highly productive capitalist industry—as we shall see in greater detail, this is not as true as it seems—that produces standards. If you want to mass-produce goods, you need standards. Electrical outlets must all be identical, so as to be able to plug in all the appliances that might be connected to them, including those that don't yet exist, those that we haven't yet thought of, but which, when they're built, will have to obey electrical connection standards. It's not for vice that we're going to calibrate apples, which naturally come in all possible sizes: we need to be able to store apples in the little boxes of six apples that will be placed on the display and will enable the customer to pick apples without having to feel them, choose them and weigh them or have them weighed. Some supermarkets even sell peeled bananas in plastic packaging… Mechanization produces the norm, but the norm calls for mechanization and produces "mechanical" behavior in the consumer sphere, i.e. behavior that is less and less spontaneous. Things produced in accordance with the norm are indistinguishable, distinguished only by their serial numbers. In Leibniz's sense, these things are not individuated, which is why as such they no longer have any value, and can be substituted for one another without the slightest regret. On the piece of furniture I've got from my grandmother, who got it from her mother, nothing is standardized, and the craftsman's name still appears on it, nothing to do with the earthly condition of furniture from a certain Swedish brand. What applies to things must also apply to living beings. Animals are classified into "breeds", a highly dubious classification (as Jean-Pierre Berlan has clearly shown), which expresses the standardization of the living world imposed by machinery. The absurd ideal of the clone has no other origin. The bull crowned at the Salon de l'Agriculture deserves to be cloned: it will serve as a model for future bulls.

Here, the contradiction is clear. What has enabled the domestication, breeding and selection of species (both animal and plant) is the contradictory property of living organisms—their variability/reproducibility. Reproduction, obeying the laws of genetics, can only reproduce the same thing, but this reproduction is subject to unpredictable variability—in fact, it is variability that is the general law of living things, identical reproduction being the result of the production of viable variants. By eliminating the "bastards", selection seeks to eliminate variability, in other words, to kill the "goose that lays the golden eggs". In other words, it seeks to eliminate life. Just as standardization in general kills inventiveness. By exhibiting manufactured products as works of art, artists such as Duchamp and Warhol have revealed the great secret of our age: the incompatibility of *ready-made* and life.

The second perverse effect of modernity, according to Jean Chesneaux: flows and circuits. Gilles Deleuze's description of "desiring machines" is the connection of flows and circuits. From this point of view, *L'Anti-Œdipe* (1972) must be considered the most emblematic text of our modernity: human beings and their relationships are transformed into machines, and life is nothing other than the movement of the machine. Chesneaux is primarily interested in the organization of urban space. But circuits and flows do much more than organize movement; they organize the whole of social and personal life. Exchanges via the Internet weave a complex network of relationships, which are not just virtual, but rely on the material support of cables and satellites that criss-cross the entire Earth. These are not simply "circulatory prostheses" that invade and crush space. Augmented reality" goggles and "virtual reality" helmets are sold: the designations of these devices are absurd, since reality cannot be "augmented", otherwise it would no longer be reality, and above all, "virtual reality" is a contradiction in terms, something like a square circle. The moderate success of these devices is due to the fact that they have had a terrible competitor: the cell phone or, more precisely, the "smartphone", which comes to our rescue in any situation and infallibly guides us where it wants to guide us. At the end of each month, Google offers us a detailed map of all our movements… Circuits and flows: no machine exists without them, without all these connections, and no machine exists without all its components being in motion. The "bougisme" of which Pierre-André Taguieff has made one of the dominant forms of contemporary ideology, translates exactly the machine imperative of movement. The social megamachine resembles Tinguely's bric-a-brac machines, with no purpose other than the spectacle of their movement. That's why the imperative of mobility (soft mobility, if we may say so today) is the categorical imperative. Spatial mobility, of course, but also mobility in terms of functions: if you stay in one place too long, you get into a rut and become less useful to "society", and to force individuals into this mobility, they must always feel they're on an ejection seat. Anxiety is the feeling that every employee must feel first and foremost if they are to stay in their place. At a time when all we talk about is CO2 and saving the planet, airlines are placing orders for long- and medium-haul aircraft with a view to long-term growth in air traffic: the travelling employee is a social ideal, and anyone who doesn't want to "work abroad" (no matter which foreigner) is a stubborn slob. But the frameworks of change themselves must be constantly shifting: norms are overturned in a matter of years, and everyone has to worry about falling behind a norm. We play a kind of croquet game with the queen, like in *Alice in Wonderland*, where the hoops move unpredictably as soon as you hit the ball with a mallet. We take the circuit, but with no guarantee of where it will take us. The apparent rationality of the "traffic plan" and "master plans", now aided by "artificial intelligence", turns into chaos. It should be added that movement needs its opposite: the immobilization of bodies. Thanks to telecommuting, it's no longer necessary to go to work, and the family living room can become an annex to the office. There's no need to go shopping: home-delivered meals are here, and commercial platforms enable us to buy everything without having to go anywhere. Of course, this immobilization of some means that there are more and more delivery drivers, in vans or on bicycles.

Coding is the third of these perverse effects of modernity. Codes are almost as old as the civilization of the written word (see, for example, the Code of Hammurabi), but today we're talking about something quite different. As Chesneaux puts it:

> These systems of signs and simulacra have gradually replaced reality by isolating just one of its elements, just one of its functions. In the most diverse fields, they transmit injunctions, they filter exchanges, they provide access to equipment, they are the obligatory intermediaries of all personal and social activity.

We had to learn to "talk with machines", since one of the major preoccupations of computer scientists was and remains "man-machine dialogue". There's a fundamental difference between turning a key in a lock and entering an access code to open the building door or use your computer. Between the gesture and the thing is a sign. The advantage of the sign is that it "dematerializes" a certain number of operations: a sequence of characters is worth a key, but you can't lose the sequence of characters or have it stolen… Yet you can lose your memory, no longer remember the code, and have your access codes pirated. So we need increasingly complex codes, codes that are made by algorithms and are impossible to remember, and so we need new software "safes" containing the hundreds of different codes we now need. At first sight, it was easier to type A1984C on the electronic lock: we were freed from that annoying material thing, the key, but we soon fell back under the dependence of the machine, which produces its own codes, stores them and restores them in a totally opaque way.

If codes are everywhere, the computer is the master coder. It induces new attitudes, far beyond the circle of computer applications. Like this international language, reduced to a pure vehicle devoid of any substance, known as *travel English* or airport English, which is also business English. The IT world has completely subverted ordinary language, turning it into an insider's language (a la louchébem) and a kind of volapuk.

In traditional coding, it still took a human to "write code". That's something that's gradually disappearing. AI machines don't yet seem to be very good at writing imperishable works of literature, but when it comes to code, they've already reached a good level. It's not "optimized code", say computer scientists who want to reassure themselves… But soon, it will be optimized. Machines produce code for other machines. In the *Grundrisse*, Marx foresaw this situation, although of course he knew nothing of our modern automatic machines. He envisaged the abolition of "immediate labor" and the displacement of the worker to the side of the production process, ultimately becoming superfluous. Today's prodigious developments in information technology also promise the disappearance of "immediate labor".

It could be argued that a language is a code and that, consequently, modernity doesn't change anything fundamental. But a language is not a code. A code is finite (we have precise rules for forming all well-formed expressions (EBF) and each sign is univocal. A real language has no stable, finite rules for producing syntactically correct sentences, and the hallmark of a real language is its ambivalence, its plurivocity. Attempts to create a perfect language or, at the very least, to define its proper use, in the atmosphere of the Vienna Circle, have all failed. But if language is not a code, the place occupied by machines and man-machine dialogues in our world tends to reduce language to a code and speech to exchanges of duly codified signals. In *La parole humiliée* (1981), Jacques Ellul denounces the folly of reducing speech to algebra. But it is precisely this madness that we are engaged in.

The fourth perverse effect, according to Jean Chesneaux, is the multiplication of prostheses. We're not talking about the old-fashioned prostheses that simply tried to imitate nature when, due to age or accident, an individual was deprived of one of his or her faculties: a wooden leg, glasses, dentures or a hearing aid. Our modernity invents prostheses for healthy individuals, thus educating them to lose some of their faculties. The cell phone means I don't have to write letters or remember what I've learned. It has become so important that we wonder whether, one day, we won't be grafting it onto babies from birth... All these new prostheses are part of the system. To use a cell phone, you also need a whole network of relay antennas: "I don't have a network" is the despair of modern man. The device itself is an embodiment of globalization: designed in France, Finland or the United States, assembled in China by a Taiwanese manufacturer working for a Korean or Californian firm.

Cyborg is the dream of integrating prostheses directly into the human body to create an "augmented man". Exoskeletons are being built to carry a human body on board for heavy-duty work (e.g., movers) or warfare. Putting an end to the "privilege" accorded to organic matter over inorganic matter: this is the good moral cause that will give legitimacy to the enterprise. In fact, it's the human being who becomes a node in the network, an articulation of the machine. The machine is not an extension of man, since the opposite is true here. It used to be said that the tool is an extension of the hand. But with the exoskeleton, the hand extends the tool.

Ephemeral and instantaneous, capillary, above-ground, gigantic, violent, opaque—these are other perverse effects. For our purposes, the eleventh of these perverse effects, programming-guidance, is of particular interest. Time and space are subject to this strict programming. It accompanies the standardization of the world. Hotel chains, service stations and airports are now identical all over the planet, because they respond to the same constraints with the same solutions. Telecommuting makes it possible to program activities on a large scale, while freeing us from spatial constraints. The globalization of financial markets gave rise to the 24-hour stock market—finance is an empire on which the sun never sets. The "global reset" anticipated by the initiators of the Davos forum promises continuous work in every possible sector: a Japanese surgeon could operate on an English patient without leaving Japan, provided the English hospital has the appropriate equipment.

We are all, admittedly to varying degrees, parts of the gigantic global production machinery. It's no longer a question of Durkheim's methodological imperative, but of the actual transformation of men into things. "Do inanimate objects have a soul that attaches itself to our soul, and the strength to love?" asked Lamartine. The answer is well-known today: things have souls, but it's human beings who have lost them.

Making People the Way we Make Things

The transformation of humans into things cannot stop there. Reification has become total with the programmed production of humans through modern artifice. In his experience of Promethean shame (see above), Günther Anders evokes the shame humans feel at having been born by chance in the biological reproduction of living beings. Today, technoscience makes it possible to remedy this unfortunate state of affairs. We should even consider punishing parents (male and female) who procreate carelessly in the pleasure of an embrace, without having thought about the consequences of their "production".

The phrase "Hitler won the war" was coined by Pierre Legendre, denouncing the "butcher conception of humanity". We usually speak of "Nazi barbarism" as if it were a step backwards from the civilized age to the barbaric age. But the expression is misleading. In many ways, Nazism was ultramodern. The Nazis were enthusiasts of science, and some highly reputed scientists generously supported them—such as the great physicist Heisenberg. They were also adepts of biologism. The old conservatives want to return to an earlier state of society, to immemorial hierarchies. But that's not what the Nazis want at all. They want a profound improvement of the "human race" based on biology, which for them is the most fundamental science. That's why they set out to classify human beings and practice selection methods: negative selection by eliminating all those they considered to be degenerate forms of humanity (the Jews, the handicapped, the insane) and "positive" selection aimed at making good Aryans, in the *Lebensborn*, those human breeding farms. The means were detestable, we agree today, but *what about* the ends?

Biology as a technique for improving humanity is doing well. The discovery of DNA and its decoding have opened up the potential for manipulation (see above), leading to the prospect of standardized industrial production, with "zero-defect" humans. Initially, our societies saw in the possibility of having chosen children (those that parents decided to have and when they decided) a new freedom, and this was undeniably a freedom, even if we have not yet measured all the consequences of this freedom. But the next step is self-evident: it's not enough to choose whether or not to have children, we have to be able to choose which children to have. Sex selection, elimination of "defective products" such as Down's syndrome, we can hide behind our little finger, for the better (perhaps), but also for the worse (certainly), the eugenics project will unfold. And humans gradually become "projects" ("do you have a project for a child?"), meaning that they no longer really exist in their own right, but are reified *ab initio*.

It will be objected that some humans have always been "reified", i.e. treated as mere means to an end. Slaves are "chattel" and possess none of the attributes of human dignity. As we showed above, the worker, considered from the point of view of the capital production process, is merely a means (economists speak of the "labor factor" and employers speak of "human resources"). But this way of looking at certain human beings has always been problematic: slavery struggled to find its justification—see Aristotle's contortions on the subject—and while some argued that slaves were not strictly speaking human ("slaves by nature"), the Stoics, undoubtedly the first, stripped slavery of any legitimacy, and Christianity followed suit: There is no longer master or slave, says the apostle Paul, who nevertheless asks slaves to obey their masters, for true freedom is not of this world… What is completely new in our time is that it is man as such, man or woman, rich or poor, who is reduced to the state of a thing among things, the result of a procedure that the project must follow. For Kant, things have a price, and only man has a value. We have reached a point where the value of man is disappearing.

The World is a Machine

Günther Anders, in *The Machine Dream* (2022), argues that our world is dominated by machines, whose servants we are, and that human life has lost all value in the process. Individuals are mere cogs in the wheel. We shouldn't draw the conclusion that Günther Anders is some kind of science-fiction writer, like the *Matrix* scriptwriters who imagine that machines have seized power and that we now work for them. We're talking about something else, something far more serious! So what could be more serious? A lot, because science-fiction constructs are only fictions that are easy to disprove. And in the *Matrix-type* scenario, there's still room for resistance fighters waging a guerrilla war against the machines. Even if it's only for the sake of honor, at least honor can be saved. But we've gone down a road where honor can't be saved.

Marx, in the *Manuscripts of 1844*, writes:

> […] Instead of the medieval adage "no land without a lord", the modern proverb "money has no master" will appear, expressing the domination of inert matter over mankind.

The capitalist mode of production is thus a reversal of life, since its triumph is that of inert matter imposing itself on mankind. In fact, the world of life is increasingly structured by the technical productions of humans, and these are now making their mark on the inhabited regions of the Earth. Our traditional ecumene was made up of our immediate environment—the construction of dwellings, tools, technical devices essential to life, etc.—and, more broadly, the dense zones of human habitat, where we find electric wires, rails, transport networks, stacks of residential buildings, factories, offices and so on. This immediate environment of the vast majority of mankind was until recently surrounded by the countryside, i.e. nature cultivated with humans, in more or less scattered settlements, faced with the eternal task of extracting from nature what is necessary to feed mankind in general. The hedges are trimmed, but they grow of their own accord, the cows in the meadows are selected animals, but they remain natural beings and have an ontological status not very different from that of the fox that prowls near the henhouse or the kite that majestically flies over the countryside. And then beyond that, there's a "wilder" nature, right down to that part of nature impenetrable to man.

But this vision of our environment in concentric circles is completely obsolete. Wilderness only exists as a protected area (in nature parks, for example). It's only wild because we tolerate it! The countryside is less and less a union of nature and culture, of man and his artifices. It is increasingly structured not by the needs of animal husbandry or plant cultivation, but by networks. Freeways, high-speed train lines and new traffic zones, all identical, are enclaves and above-ground settlements that outline the figure of the countryside entirely framed by the imperatives of the division of labor as it functions in the age of absolute capitalism. Péguy wrote of his arrival in Chartres:

Star of the sea here is the heavy tablecloth
And the deep swell and the ocean of wheat
And the moving foam and our filled attics,
Here's how you look at this huge screed

The swell and ocean of wheat are now streaked with arrays of wind turbines; elsewhere, at the turn of a wood, shiny, metallic surfaces reflect the light: these are fields of photovoltaic panels. Thanks to the triumph of political ecology and the triumphal march of the "energy transition", the colonization of the countryside by the machine is advancing apace. Despite the claims of the crudest materialistic scientism, the difference between life and the inert products of human industry is obvious to anyone who still has eyes to see! Wherever we are, we are now as if imprisoned in the boxes that the tentacular extension of the productive machine concedes us before expelling us.

Marx posed the question of man's relationship with nature in terms of a dialectical relationship between the humanization of nature and the naturalization of man. But with the development of capitalism today, we are witnessing something quite different: the transformation of nature into elements of the machine. Nature is so imperfect, so unpredictable, so ill-suited to the demands of technical standards, that it's imperative that we put things right! To restore order! In *The Eye of the State* (1998), James C. Scott clearly shows how states—whatever their political stripe—have played a decisive role in these attempts to normalize nature, for example by planting trees in straight lines, all at regular intervals and of the same species, like soldiers in a Prussian army parade. We could also mention the way in which the concept of race was introduced into breeding, as a principle of standardization and submission to the order of industrial production. The submission of nature to the mechanical order is one of the most striking features of capitalism.

However, since we must pretend to maintain a link between human society and nature, we've invented new ways of living: mini-gardens are planted at the top of buildings, and a kind of urban market gardening is gradually taking its place in the sales brochures of new "ecological" and "responsible" neighborhoods. There are AI-controlled market gardening laboratories: the above-ground plant is connected to sensors that measure its condition, its "water stress", its nutrient requirements, etc., and the AI controls the injection of the water or nutrients requested. Promoters of these trials point to water savings, for example, and perfectly predictable product quality. It's the whole natural process that comes under the control of the machines.

The advantages of this type of innovation are twofold: on the one hand, it's good for advertising (look how green I am!) and on the other, it's good for ideology: it's a way of getting the idea into the heads of people who are still recalcitrant, that the only nature possible is a squared-off nature, entirely subject to the industrial order, an entirely artificial nature after all. At the same time, soil-less industrial market gardening is practiced in factories producing so-called vegetables calibrated for mass consumption. In China, pigs are bred in skyscraper piggeries set up in the heart of cities: in Ezhou, near Wuhan, there is room for 650,000 pigs on 26 floors. The vegan craze is fuelling a whole series of *start-ups* that are raising a lot of money to build laboratories producing entirely artificial food from bacteria duly fed with chemical ingredients. Behind this ideology for retarded children lies an entire industry enabling a complete break with nature—just as the great French chemist Marcellin Berthelot predicted long ago in a speech at the Maison de la Chimie in 1894, announcing the wonders that chemistry promises us for the year 2000. On this subject, see *Steak barbare* (2020), an investigation by Gilles Luneau that should have been better known.

Under the guise of fighting world hunger—the road to hell is paved with good intentions—"charitable foundations", the most important of which is that of Bill and Melinda Gates, working in conjunction with chemical "bigwigs" such as Bayer-Monsanto, are busy developing GMO plants that can replace traditional crops, integrating farmers in poor countries into the great mechanics of value creation and capital accumulation.

Perhaps worst of all, the so-called defenders of nature and the environment often play a particularly harmful role in this artificialization of nature, which is gradually being stripped of all its natural, spontaneous and living elements. In the past, polluters swallowed their own pollution: coal was the bane of blackening cities, whose air was overloaded with combustion particles. Today, city dwellers who heat their homes with electricity live "healthier" lives, since the pollution they generate has been transported elsewhere. We cover our fields with wind turbines and solar panels: we use nature "in the same way as the trades of our craftsmen" (cf. Descartes), i.e. as simple inert matter that goes into the composition and installation of our machines. Great advocates of "renewable energies", ecologists actively campaign for wind turbines and solar panels (but not in their own backyards, NIMBY demands).

It's sometimes hard to make out this gigantic global machinery, of which we know only one part, seemingly isolated from the others. But we must try to put the pieces of the puzzle together, to get an idea of its contours and its global character. There is still, of course, a "wilderness", but it is excluded from the human world, just as part of nature cultivated by "old-fashioned" farmers is doomed to progressive desertification.

Sade a Brilliant Precursor (if you will)

In many respects, the Marquis de Sade is a brilliant precursor who theorized the modern world. The theses expounded in *Philosophy in the Boudoir* (1795) constitute the most radical atheism: all impulses, including those that seem the worst to us, are natural and as such must be satisfied. Pasolini clearly saw how *The 120 Days of Sodom* (1785) was the very essence of the Nazi spirit. Desiring machines are given free rein in the Sadian universe. But it's another aspect that interests us here: in a preface to the French reprint *of Philosophie dans le boudoir ou* les *Instituteurs immoraux*, Yvon Belaval, philosopher and Leibniz specialist, shows what the Sadian mechanics of body interlocking are all about.

In *Philosophy in the Boudoir*, for example, we witness various scenes of sexual gymnastics that are nothing more than mechanical combinatorics, moving from one scene to the next by changing the individuals and their means of connection. Every possible combination has to be tried. In the words of Mme de Saint-Ange, LGBTQ muse avant la lettre, "I'm an amphibious animal; I like everything, I enjoy all genres". Faced with Dolmancé, "a sodomite on principle", she wants, "bizarrely fanciful", to be his Ganymede. The Chevalier (Mme de Saint-Ange's brother) recounts his love-making with Dolmancé: 1) the Chevalier sodomizes Dolmancé; 2) Dolmancé sodomizes the Marquis. And so begins a farandole in which every position and combination is tested. Body parts are machine parts: speaking of Dolmancé's testicles, Mme de Saint-Ange says "the technical word is *balls*". Pleasure alone is sought, pleasure without the slightest sentiment—nature doesn't make sentiment, the various protagonists assure us. In the various scenes, our "immoral teachers" teach different mechanisms. The male sex is a contraption, a common enough term in erotic and pornographic literature, and Sade offers lessons in how to handle the contraption, which, as its etymology suggests, presupposes a certain ingenuity.

Sade was a man of his time. He was almost contemporary with the publication of Diderot and d'Alembert's *Encyclopédie*, which was accompanied by plates detailing trades and machines. Sade proposes a methodical encyclopedia of the art of cumming. The pornographic cinema develops all this in animated plates. In its early days, pornographic cinema, quickly classified as "X", more or less told stories. There were scripts that allowed us to string together scenes that were either erotic or pornographic (as we know, the difference is purely technical: a pornographic film is one in which sex is not simulated). But very quickly, after the cassette, the porn platforms offer something quite different: videos classified by type of connection and according to the objects connected. All that's left is mechanics. Nothing to do with *Histoire d'O* or *Lady Chatterley's Lover*. It's because of the same developments that we see films more and more systematically interspersed with sex scenes that, more often than not, have no interest whatsoever in the narrative.

Sade is therefore a precursor. The erotic genre was relatively widespread in the 18th century, but it is much older—in some respects, as old as human culture. Sade innovates: he heralds the transformation of this literary genre according to the criteria of mechanics. So we can take the analysis a step further. Why are we so fascinated by machines that we organize the machinization of life? Sade hints at the answer: in the machine, there is jouissance. The enjoyment of power is the most immediately visible. A construction machine is a machine! Gears have something sexual about them. The power of machines that work alone and never seem to run out makes us envious. Everything that is fallible in human beings seems infallible in machines. Machines are animate like the living, but inanimate like the dead. Marx spoke of capital as "the living dead", and machines are indeed part of this world of the living dead, uniting the two impulses that intertwine and tear each other apart within us.

It's not surprising, then, that we find in the megamachine a kind of fulfillment and suppression of humanity. In this way, we place the forces of life at the service of death. In his dialectical spirit, Anders even sees the creation of the megamachine as proof of the obsolescence of the machine:

Machines become a single machine. This reification does not occur only occasionally and at a single level. The principle of reiteration […] applies to all machines. This means that individual machines "fall apart"—that is, if they become parts of larger machines—the same thing happens with these larger machines, which also begin to "fall apart", becoming mere machine parts, elements of larger complexes, and so on.

Obsolescence de l'homme, II, "L'obsolescence des machines", 1980

Machine obsolescence thus goes far beyond the debatable "programmed obsolescence" that justifies the renewal of machines and thus accelerates the turnover of capital. In the background of current developments in the capitalist mode of production, there is a death-bringing phenomenon that affects all the products of human industry, a phenomenon that Byung-Chul Han analyzes with his usual finesse in *La fin des choses. Bouleversement du monde de la vie* (Actes Sud, 2022):

As information hunters, we become blind to things that are mute, lacklustre, and even to ordinary, incidental or common things that lack excitement, but anchor us in Being.

The loss of nature extends into the loss of things. Our being-in-the-world vanishes.

Human Expulsion

Some authors consider that the evolution of the megamachine is purely preparing the expulsion of humans. Human obsolescence should not be understood as a metaphor, but as an ongoing process. Bill Joy (b. 1954) is a well-known computer scientist—he is the co-founder of Sun *Microsystems*, a major software production company. He is also the designer of a whole series of well-known software programs still in use thirty or forty years after their invention. Starting with a meeting with Ray Kurweil, an engineer who produced the first handwriting recognition software and became an idol of transhumanism in the United States, Joy developed a whole line of questioning recounted in a text that circulated widely on the Internet: *"Why The Future Doesn't Need Us"*, first published in *Wired Magazine* (2000). For him, robotics (and artificial intelligence), genetic engineering and nanotechnologies could constitute "weapons of mass destruction" that will lead to the extinction of humanity. Evoking the dystopias foreshadowed by new technologies, Joy writes:

> Why hadn't I worried about this kind of robotic dystopia before? And why didn't others worry more about these nightmarish scenarios?
>
> The answer to this question undoubtedly lies in our attitude to the new, i.e. in our tendency towards immediate familiarity and unconditional acceptance. While technological advances may seem to us to be nothing more than routine events, we're going to have to face the fact that the most unavoidable technologies of the 21st century—robotics, genetic engineering and nanotechnology—represent a different threat to earlier technologies. In concrete terms, robots, genetically modified organisms and "nanorobots" all have one factor in common: their ability to self-replicate. A bomb only explodes once; a robot, on the other hand, can proliferate and rapidly get out of control.
>
> Bill Joy, *Why Future Doesn't Need Us*

Éric Sadin, more recently (see *La vie spectrale*, 2023), makes assumptions similar to those of Bill Joy. Applications of so-called "generative AI" can mechanically process astronomical quantities of information stored on the global network, quantities of information that no human, no human team, will ever be able to process, and, through "lifelong learning" guided by teams who know the "specifications", AI produces sensible and even argumentative texts based on texts already stored. All of a sudden, millions of jobs, often held by highly qualified humans, are on the chopping block and doomed to disappear—writers of newspaper articles, legal memos, courses, screenplays, novels, etc.—while advances in image recognition mean that over-trained machines are becoming far better than oncologists at detecting cancerous tumors. In the not-too-distant future, we could well envisage all medical imaging professions being replaced by automated machines, possibly with the assistance of a human operator to ensure that the patient is properly groomed.

Let's face it, there's an element of science fiction in all this. But we know how many science-fiction scenarios have come true: after all, we're not far from Aldous Huxley's *Brave New World* (1932), and we've had occasion to point out the similarities between our world and that of *Unbearable Happiness*. We can reasonably exclude the possibility of machines taking over, as in the *Matrix* scenario! However, the machinization of human life in a totally hierarchical society is something that is taking place before our very eyes, with the prospect not of an orderly society, but rather of the disintegration of human civilization as a whole.

The machinization of the world is potentially catastrophic, and this is what rules out the hypothesis that this process will continue to its end, whatever term we imagine. In *Matrix,* machines have taken over because man is the worst predator the planet has ever known. But the worst predator is the machine as an extension of man, and as an instrument for subjugating the majority to the small ruling caste. Machines have no life, even if they absorb life. They don't reproduce, and produce nothing but piles of junk unfit for anything else. The world of machines implies the limitless exploitation of the planet's resources, the extraction of minerals, thousands of tons of which have to be crushed to extract the few kilos needed to run the precious machines. Ultimately, the triumph of the machine implies, in the strictest sense, the destruction of life on Earth.

Chapter VI: Resisting the Destruction of the World

Freud writes in *Malaise in Civilization* (1930) that man cannot be turned into a termite, and that he will always fight to defend his individual freedom (see above). The same Freud who so insisted that "the Ego is not the master in its own house", this eminent scholar and philosopher who watches the rise of perils with concern, seems to believe in man's inexhaustible capacity to defend his freedom. Is he too optimistic? I don't think so, provided we approach things from the right angle.

Life Drive and Death Drive

Capital is the strongest manifestation of the dominance of the death drive in our time. However, the death drive only exists in tandem with the life drive: it is because he wants to create, to build complex structures, to extend the power of humanity, starting with his own, that man works. It's only when it's disintegrated that the death drive is transformed into mass destructiveness, the destructiveness that manifests itself in wars and the devastation of entire countries. But capital is forced to rely on the life drive: without living labor to convert into dead labor, capitalism is doomed to disappear. And living labor is that of the living individual, the individual who converts his or her life drive—or *conatus*, to use Spinoza's term—into productive activity.

The strength of capital lies in the fact that it is first and foremost a vehicle for the liberation of mankind—liberation from tradition, liberation from a burdensome obscurantism, liberation for human initiative and power to unfold. As Descartes said, "Make ourselves masters and possessors of nature", this was not a call for unlimited domination, and even less for the private appropriation of the Earth and the living beings that populate it, but rather the project of a humanity that ceases to suffer, of an Earth that is no longer a valley of tears. Progressivism, with all its illusions and perversions, was first and foremost this aspiration, a reconciliation of man with his own life. The last part of Spinoza's *Ethics* is entitled *On the Power of the Intellect or Human Freedom*. This impulse to deploy human power cannot be extinguished. We are well aware of its drifts, its dangers, and even its deadly character when it is completely unbridled. But so is the power of life. Giambattista Vico (see *La science nouvelle*, 1725) imagined that the first ancestors of the human species (with the exception of Noah and his descendants) were left to their own devices, deprived of laws and language, and thus became giants incapable of curbing their appetites—a fact well known to anyone who has read a little Greek mythology or contemplated Giulio Romano's extraordinary fresco of the fall of the giants in Mantua's Palazzo Tè. But, still following Vico, these big brutes, the *bestioni*, learned to civilize themselves, because they were terrorized by the forces of nature. When it comes down to it, we're not much further ahead than the *bestioni* of the great Neapolitan philosopher. Our fantasies of mastery come up against the harsh reality already enunciated by Spinoza: the power of nature infinitely surpasses the power of man. But the *bestioni* don't want to believe it. Their unbridled appetites push them ever further. In the *Ethics*, Spinoza teaches a lesson:

Bliss is not the reward of virtue, but virtue itself, and it is not because we thwart lustful appetites that we enjoy it; but on the contrary, it is because we enjoy it that we can thwart lustful appetites.

Let's not confine ourselves to lustful appetites, and let's not interpret this passage as an ascetic claim that many other passages in the *Ethics* belie. Let's just say that if we're always longing to possess new things, to accumulate material goods, to want to "enjoy without hindrance", to quote a famous 1968 watchword, it's because we're not happy, because we lack the company of others, that community of free men of which Spinoza speaks. And we lack it because our relations with others are mediated by things. The triumph of machinism in all of life has brought us back to the state of the *bestioni*.

To continue living, we have to relearn our limits and stop thinking like machines, stop believing that there's a technological answer to all our anxieties, and admit that there's nowhere else to live but on Earth. Even if billionaires and transhumanists dream of "getting laid", of moving civilization elsewhere that we can no longer even call human, the silence of infinite space cannot be our dwelling place. The "demachinization" of the world doesn't mean that we have to go back even before *homo sapiens*, even before the mastery of fire, because that's really where it all began. It just means rediscovering the meaning of man's embrace with nature, his metabolism, to use Marx's phrase.

Our Native Soil

We should return to what is most archaic in man, archaic in the Greek sense of *arkhè*, meaning both origin and foundation. "In the beginning was the Word", says John's Gospel. But it's not that beginning we're talking about here, but the point of origin of human reason and intellect, and that point of origin is affectivity. We are affected, and we experience these affects as our affects. This is where the sense of self begins. I feel hunger as my hunger, pain as my pain, pleasure as my pleasure. But I can never feel your pain as my pain. As Wittgenstein points out, the sentence "I hurt your teeth", while not nonsensical, doesn't say what it means. As has already been said over and over again, the starting point is subjectivity, the self-affectation of life, as Michel Henry would put it. It can also be called sensitivity. It manifests itself both in the search for pleasure and the avoidance of pain, but also in the aesthetic sense, and therefore in a certain type of relationship with nature.

The first characteristic of our machine-transformed world is its profound ugliness. Without doubt, this ugliness is the result of the rational calculations that guide political and economic decisions. The multiplication of freeways and airports is indispensable to the functioning of the globalized megamachine, if the law is the categorical imperative of capital growth. Some contemporary art has understood this new imperative well, promoting a veritable "aesthetic of ugliness": recycling waste, seeking out the grotesque at all costs, hymning the machine—everything points in the same direction: beauty is the enemy. In *La barbarie* (1987), Michel Henry gives some telling examples.

But beauty is not just about the fine arts, as Hegel thought, it's also about the world we inhabit. We've already mentioned the artificialization of nature, which is at the same time its ugliness. But cities, especially their outskirts, have become totally ugly, with overflowing shopping areas, occupied or abandoned warehouses and industrial wastelands. Pretty, often lifeless town centers are desperately trying to maintain the memory of the "world before".

Our relationship with nature, with the Earth as our "archè", to borrow from Husserl, is essential. The whole modern vision, born of Galilean physics, consists in extracting man from the world. Objectivity is a point of view from nowhere. But we can only exist, perceive and order our perceptions from this immobile Earth on which we stand.

Whether the Earth is a planet that moves in the great waltz of the planets—in *2001 A Space Odyssey* (1968), the spaceship's journey is accompanied by the music of Strauss's waltz, "The Blue Danube"—we don't really care, since humanity has lived most of its history without knowing it. What matters is the stability of the ground on which we live, the immobility of the Earth that supports our bodies and serves as a reference point for everything we observe and do. Every little thing we do every day is based on the Earth's immobility. When Husserl, in a text from 1934, maintains that "The Earth does not move", he is not supporting an absurd theory of "geostatism", for it is not a question of physical theory at all, but of questioning the basis of any physical or astronomical theory. For us, it's about understanding that the Earth is first and foremost what we stand on and rise from. The Earth is inhabited by human beings, it is the ecumene (to use Augustin Berque's terminology). This essential relationship is made possible because the Earth is also a biosphere—the origins of life can be traced back over 3 billion years—and human beings have only been able to appear and develop through this biosphere, whose variations have so conditioned human history. But within this biosphere, mankind has built a whole technical and symbolic universe. The balance between all these dimensions of human life is anything but stable, and no one can fix this ideal point of equilibrium. But we can be certain that there is no other place where human life can be sheltered. We can imagine a few colonies on inhospitable planets not too far away, but the technical feat would be matched only by its utter uselessness. There's a fundamental reason for this: Earth alone is home to life on a horizon accessible to man. That a planet a few light-years away harbours some form of life is useful for our curiosity, but no human will ever be able to go there, since we can't conceive of spaceships whose speed would be on the order of the speed of light. Only in Philip K. Dick's novels do humans send humanoid robots to conquer the "Alphanian Moons".

Whatever we do, we're riveted to this planet, and when it disappears, humans themselves will have disappeared long ago. Some scientists and, above all, science-fiction enthusiasts imagine the ways we might find to enable humanity to survive off the Earth, but there's one old way, all certain, and that's belief in the immortality of the soul, no more and no less serious than these fantasies.

What exists is what can be posited by a consciousness as an ex-sistent object, standing outside consciousness, facing the consciousness of the subject. If we take Spinoza's definition, "by eternity I mean existence itself", it follows that life, i.e. our life as conscious subjects, is, in certain respects, eternal, and that we belong to this eternal life, which is that of life in our "ecumene". Do we need any more certainties? Absolutely not. The search for other certainties exceeds the capacity of our understanding.

Rooting

Here, we are referred back to that rootedness to which Simone Weil devoted her last reflections, a theme that could already be found in Barrès. For Simone Weil, rootedness appears in the context of reflections prior to a declaration of obligations towards man, since, for her, obligations precede rights (since no right is worth anything unless it is guaranteed by an obligation).

Rootedness is perhaps the most important and most misunderstood need of the human soul. It is one of the most difficult to define. A human being is rooted by his real, active and natural participation in the existence of a community that keeps alive certain treasures of the past and certain presentiments of the future. Natural participation, in other words, automatically brought about by place, birth, profession and environment. Every human being needs multiple roots. He needs to receive almost all of his moral, intellectual and spiritual life from the environments of which he is a natural part.

Rooting, 1949

This is precisely why, in the megamachine, where man is torn from the world of man, man is deprived of his roots, not accidentally, but essentially, since man is expelled from nature to be reintegrated only as a body-machine, part of the global machine. In her plan to re-root workers, Simone Weil proposed abolishing large factories and replacing them with small workshops scattered across the countryside. This was the state of industry in a country like France in the 19th century, and the dispersal of large factories has been partly achieved in our time, when production units are scattered all over the world. The worker is no longer uprooted from the countryside to the big city, but uprooted from his craft, and his work is uprooted to be included in the global division of labor. Re-rooting is not possible without a process of "de-globalization" at all levels.

The pages Simone Weil devotes to the uprooting of peasants, which she considers even more scandalous than the uprooting of workers, could find many illustrations today that she could never have imagined. Unfortunately, when she talks about uprooting, she confines herself almost exclusively to the history of the homeland, and her comments don't do us much good in this respect. Nevertheless, the notion of uprootedness remains operative. The uprooting of workers was organized as a radical break between the modern worker and the old trades, organized into guilds. The triumph of the machine was the destruction of the craft, of the pride that went with it, but also of the sense of freedom that comes from *homo faber*'s feeling of being lord and master, and not of being reduced to the role of *animal laborans*, a beast of burden. Re-rootedness would require the rehabilitation of trade and craft.

269

We know that in our societies, the craftsman is becoming rare—
the search for the plumber is proverbial—but we also know that,
if we want a more frugal society, one that consumes fewer natural
resources, we'll have to break with the "throw-away" mentality
and design repairable objects for use, in every field. We also need
to relearn how to cook at home, not just for the *happy few* who
see cooking as a mark of distinction, but for the working classes
who are often the first consumers of junk food. In short, we need
to relearn how to "cultivate our garden", to follow the precept of
Voltaire's Candide.

All Connected

For the whole world to function like a machine, all players
must be connected. The imperative of connection is categorical,
and no one can escape it. Rapid means of communication are the
first element in the great forward march of the capitalist mode
of production. Trains, steamships and telegraphs began weaving
a web around the world in the second half of the 19th century.
The first transatlantic cable was laid in 1858 between Ireland and
Newfoundland, linking the two continents by telegraph. The
Internet is simply a further development of what began to take
shape at that time.

The capitalist mode of production naturally tends towards a
global division of labor—something Marx spotted early on, and
"globalization" is its most appropriate mode of existence. Where
once a car was built in a single factory or a small group of factories, today a car is an assembly of parts manufactured all over the
world. If machinery gives factories their unity, today's machinery
is global. But people need to be globalized. Connecting the whole
of humanity to the Internet—a connection that has been most
fully developed by the smartphone—radically transforms the

human condition. Distances seem abolished, and time is the "real time" of machines, i.e. the time it takes for signals to circulate in a computer.

Being plugged in is exactly what happens in hospital when you're in a very advanced state of trauma or illness: perfusion, artificial respirator and other electronic monitoring devices. It's a perfect illustration of the social ideal to which we should submit: to become incapable of the slightest autonomy, to be under permanent infusion of information. In many science-fiction films, we see humanoids, "droids" as in *Star Wars*, with a plug in the back of their necks to recharge their batteries or upgrade their software. The smartphone replaces the neck plug, but the result is the same.

Being "*no-plug*" is the most deplorable state to which ultra-modern man can be subjected. It's not simply that he's out of fashion, as in that song from the "yéyé" era, "t'es plus dans l'coup, papa", it's that he's de facto excluded from "real" human society, i.e. from the fake society that's being manufactured to replace real society. Today, we know that what's good is what's inclusive, and what's bad is what's exclusive. Society has to be totally inclusive, and so everyone has to be hooked up to the devices that make this inclusivity possible. The rebel himself has no place unless he's an included rebel, a strange rebel we'll admit. Transgression must be inclusive, and in fact it has become part of the overall functioning of society. Homosexuals are no longer people who transgress the law, but archetypes of that law, manifested for all to see in those grotesque pride fairs. The true rebel, the *no-plug*, is just a poor unplugged, disconnected guy who eventually needs to be taken care of and put back on the right track with medication and adapted cognitive behavioral therapies—the absolute horror of the "benevolent" world is depicted in a remarkable way, let's quote this book again, in Ira Levin's *Unbearable Happiness*. The rebel, simply the one who doesn't walk straight, is a misfit, a sick person, who must be cared for and rewired "with benevolence".

General connectivity is also a prerequisite for the operation of the global megamachine. The "knowledge" of all the AIs connected to the network (and not just the chatGPT) depends on the human producers of knowledge: the AI has no eyes, ears, hands, nose, desires or hatreds. We have to feed the machine with our desires, sensations and actions. If I'm driving under the control of an AI like *Waze* or *Coyotte*, I have to tell my favorite AI that there's a new speed camera or that there's been an accident at a certain point along my route. For factories to manufacture this or that product, customers must have expressed their wishes in an order, and if they have consulted a travel agency in the near future, looked for a train or chatted with a machine, these are all pieces of information that the AI can mix and match. Everything works according to the matrix model from the Wachowskis' famous film: human activity is used to supply the machine with energy, but to do this, these larval humans need to be intellectually stimulated.

In his illuminating book *En attendant les robots. Enquête sur le travail du clic* (2019), Antonio Casilli analyzes the workings of the platforms that today play a major role in the global governance of the capitalist mode of production. Casalli begins by questioning the grand narrative of automation, which his heralds claim will lead to the end of work. "Rather than the programmed disappearance of work, we are witnessing its displacement or concealment outside the field of vision of citizens, but also of analysts and political decision-makers, quick to adhere to the *storytelling* of platform capitalists." In an almost provocative way, he shows that humans not only put themselves at the service of robots, but are even called upon to replace them—here he returns to Marx's analysis in Book I of *Capital*, which shows that capitalists have no obsession with automation as long as the "cost of labor" is low enough. On the contrary, in some respects, they prefer "human automata", which ultimately cost much less. What's more, machines don't learn by themselves; they need humans to teach them how to think.

Workers (paid by the slingshot) and users (working free of charge) provide the machines with the elements they need to operate "*machine learning*". Casilli points out that "machines cannot exist without humans willing to teach them how to think." So

> the artificiality of artificial intelligence lies precisely in the fact that, while these tasks do not require any discernment, they nevertheless produce, like an emergent property, a semblance of intelligence.

The examples are numerous: character recognition based on clicks on reCAPTCHA, validation of so-called automatic translations, validation of image recognition, and so on:

> The scientific program of artificial intelligence thus becomes inseparable from a certain cybernetics, i.e. the art of controlling human beings and disciplining the execution of their activities.

So there is no "great replacement":

> The figures, in fact, run counter to the thesis defended by proponents of the "great automatic replacement". This paradox is particularly apparent in the robotics sector. A survey of seventeen countries between 1993 and 2007 found no significant effect of multifunctional industrial robots on overall employment in terms of total hours worked.

Of course, you have to take into account the resistance… of the material!

> A comparative study by the Organisation for Economic Co-operation and Development (OECD) of twenty-one countries in 2016 demonstrates the overestimation of the automatability of today's professions.

If there's a "great replacement", it's that of employees by users:

Above all, it's the users, the consumers, the customers who take responsibility for making the machines work. From now on, it is they, not the tellers, who identify themselves; it is they, not the tellers, who carry out the transactions; it is they, not the tellers, who count the money. The same applies to other technologies that facilitate self-service, such as self-registration kiosks or automatic checkouts in supermarkets.

The connection, then, is not the elimination of humans to make way for a great machinery that would operate in a closed circuit, but the inclusion of humans as elements of this global megamachine which, like the good old machinery analyzed by Marx in Book I of *Capital,* lives only by sucking the blood of the living.

Of course, we must be wary of mistaking metaphors for concepts. In the megamachine, people are divided up, as they were "in the old days". Some command and profit handsomely from the system, while the vast majority are reduced to a mutilated exis- tence. Although it dictates its law to humanity, the megamachine remains human, at the service of certain humans in particular. Conflicts between peoples, classes and nations remain, and no arti- ficial intelligence seems to dictate these conflicts or be capable of resolving them. Optimization algorithms do not lead to the same conclusions in Beijing as they do in Washington… The dominant ideology would have us believe that decisions taken by machines are more rational than decisions taken by humans, who are subject to all sorts of "cognitive biases", to use the fashionable expression, but machines learn nothing other than what humans are willing to teach them, since they are the real interfaces available to machines. And if we assume that humans have the same basic affects and desires, and that they want to "optimize their utility", then they will necessarily find themselves hostile to each other. It's not very reasonable, therefore, to rely on the emotional "neutrality" of AIs to move towards a more peaceful world.

The fact remains that there is a deep affinity between machines and capitalist man. The machine is designed for maximum efficiency and utility, not for other human qualities. Capitalist man sees efficiency and utility as the two cardinal virtues, one might even say the theological virtues, of the celestial empire of money. Every capitalist is compelled to strive for maximum efficiency and utility, or risk being swallowed up by the competition. And because they must face up to competition, to the categorical imperative of "value valorization", they all follow more or less the same paths and, overall, their behavior becomes almost as predictable as the behavior of machines. As for the capitalist mode of production as a whole, it functions like an automaton (see chapter one). So it's only natural that the world itself should become a kind of global machine, including the machinization of the whole of nature, which is bound to happen, unless the great catastrophe puts an end to the unbridled ambitions of the advocates of growth, however sustainable.

Defending Nature: Rousseau

Even so, one might say, there are defenders of nature, there is an ecological will to preserve nature from the destruction wrought upon it by human industry. Since the beginning of the industrial era, there has been both intellectual and popular protest against the artificialization and mechanization of the world. It was perhaps Jean-Jacques Rousseau, one of the greatest philosophers of the Enlightenment, who launched the first systematic theoretical attack on the "progress" of the "sciences and arts". Rousseau was well aware (even then!) that challenging the progress and benefits of the "sciences and arts" was bound to get him into trouble: "How dare he blame the Sciences before one of the most learned Companies in Europe, praise ignorance in a famous Academy, and

reconcile contempt for study with respect for the true Savants?"
The sciences and the arts, i.e. precisely what developed in the
"Age of Enlightenment", industry, technology and with them the
considerable enrichment of a good part of society, are not sources
of progress, since they do not make men better, more virtuous, but
meaner and more vicious, and produce luxury instead of things
useful to life. Awarded a prize by the Dijon Academy, Rousseau's
text earned him hatred and ridicule right up to the present day.
Proponents of growth at all costs are quick to accuse their opponents of wanting to return to the Stone Age, just as Voltaire
claimed that reading Rousseau made people want to crawl on all
fours… Whatever the case, Rousseau is at the origin of a tradition,
to be found in Romanticism, which sees nature as the mother
from whom we must not separate ourselves, and which must be
defended against the fury of industrialists. He could well remain
one of our sources of inspiration.

Metabolism

Nature, says Marx, is "the non-organic body of man". This
formula, which might seem rather enigmatic, seems to be a trans-
position of the Spinozist thesis, which distinguishes in a composed
body between parts that are the body's own parts and external parts.
Let's take an example: the human body is a body made up of a great
many bodies, which are themselves very composed, says Spinoza.
But this body contains within itself a great many bodies that are not
directly part of it, but live within it: billions of bacteria of all kinds
live their bacterial lives within each of us. On our skin, we'll also
find billions of bacteria that perform certain vital functions for us,
and whose destruction, through excessive hygiene for example, will
cause us serious problems. But the air in which we always bathe and
the water in which we (sometimes) swim are also in some way part

of our body; they are our external parts, although not organically linked to our body, since we can change air and never bathe in the same river twice! Man can only live in a certain environment, and it is impossible to separate him from his environment, except through thought, which always proceeds by abstraction.

Marx conceived of this link between man and his natural environment as metabolism. Work is the metabolism of man and nature," says Marx. It's not the only one, of course, but it's the most visible, the most tangible form of this metabolism, and it's even the one that's specific to human beings, and for which there's practically no equivalent in animals. Marx explains this human specificity in a famous passage from *Capital* (book I, ch. V), comparing the bee and the architect. Let's recall this passage:

> A spider performs operations akin to those of a weaver, and a bee relies on many a human architect in the construction of its cells. But what immediately distinguishes the worst architect from the best bee is that he built the cell in his head before constructing it in wax. The result of the work process was already in the worker's imagination at the outset, and thus already existed as an idea. Not that he is simply modifying the form of natural reality: at the same time, he is realizing his own goal, which he knows, which determines the modality of his action like a law, and to which he must subordinate his will.

What makes man is consciousness as self-consciousness: Marx says nothing else here. But if we retain the definition of nature as man's non-organic body, we can say, conversely, that man is nature becoming conscious of itself. From this follows something essential: man's relationship with nature is also a relationship with himself, and cannot therefore be a merely technical one. While we can know the elements that make up nature "in the same way that we know the trades of our craftsmen", our fundamental relationship is not one of simple utility. A river is not a flowing road or a

277

fishpond. A mountain is nothing like the building that supports a ski slope in a Dubai shopping mall.

Posing the question of man's relationship with nature in this way runs counter to philosophies that, from Thoreau to Aldo Leopold, make wilderness the model from which to measure the degradation of nature for which man is responsible. This prioritization of wilderness is linked to the idea that only wilderness is free. But to speak of the freedom of wild animals, for example, is an expression that makes no sense. Wild animals are determined to act by virtue of their nature. Lions don't pity gazelles or give up eating them. Man can certainly be worse than wild beasts, but he can also be much better.

If ecology is the science of the habitation of living beings in their environment, ecology is not the science of human habitation. Rather, we should speak of an "ecumenology", i.e., a science of the habitation of the Earth by humans, a science which, in contrast to deep ecology, would be situated from a resolutely humanist point of view. The humanist, in fact, is not one who wants to be "master and possessor of nature", but one who seeks to harmonize the best possible space for human freedom within nature. The paradigm of the engineer and mechanic must be replaced by the paradigm of the farmer, gardener or physician. Although today's farmers are often referred to as wheat or meat producers, they don't produce anything in the sense that to produce is to manufacture. No one produces meat: cows and oxen are perfectly capable of growing on their own. The farmer has to keep an eye on them, supply them with hay, look after them when they're sick and even help them give birth. Basically, for the whole life of these animals, it's the breeder who's at their service. Even if the animal ends up in the slaughterhouse. Everyone has to make a living. And neither does the gardener produce potatoes. Potatoes are not produced like nails, needles (dear to Adam Smith) or 4x4s for urbanites in search of domination. Potatoes have to be planted, watered and ridged, in the hope that pests will spare them, that the Colorado beetle will stay at home and that mildew won't devour the leaves! To eat French fries or mashed potatoes, Mother Nature has to be willing to follow our instructions, but we can only hope to do so if we follow her laws—don't plant early, respect the seasons, don't plant too deep or too high…

The gardener and the farmer are merely paradigms here. We have the "right" to exploit the planet's resources, since only humans (and God, if he exists!) can create law. The "right of nature" is an empty phrase. But we have a duty, first and foremost to ourselves, to respect life and the possibility of a sufficiently satisfactory living environment for all humans.

***

We're caught between the increasing artificialization of our world and "resistance" movements, which are far from being limited to "labelled" ecology movements: associations for the protection of nature, attempts to return to the land, "organic" consumption, with all its ambiguities… We could also ask ourselves what might become of this relationship with nature, provided we are capable of halting the march towards catastrophe—which is possible, but not at all certain. Here, we could bring in that "sociology of our relationship with the world" that Hartmunt Rosa proposes under the name of "resonance", taking the word resonance in its physical sense of a system's capacity to oscillate when subjected to excitations, until it reaches a maximum amplitude:

> Modernity needs nature not just as a resource or an underground world, but also as a sphere of resonance, as something that maintains a kind of relationship with us.

Let's accelerate the resonance!
For education in the Anthropocene, 2022

CONCLUSION

Man's becoming a machine is the signature of a very particular historical epoch, that which stretches from the beginnings of "modern times", i.e. the beginnings of the capitalist mode of production, to the present day. In the past, certain categories of men had been treated as oxen, as beasts of war, as less than men, but it is the modern age which, while proclaiming man's entry into the age of majority, "dares to know" says Kant, undertakes the systematic transformation of the whole of life into machines, then into machines of machines, and finally into a global system governed by the laws of machines.

Behind this movement, as we have shown, lies a formidable paradox. Machines were supposed to liberate man from work, but it is man who finds himself chained and enslaved to machines. The new science was supposed to usher in a new age for mankind, and while it held out tremendous promise, it has gradually been transformed into a one-dimensional, purely operative way of thinking, whose ultimate purpose is to format human brains so that they can take their place in the great global network-system. This involution, already analyzed by Husserl in *La crise de l'humanité européenne et la philosophie* (1950), now appears to be fully complete.

We have witnessed an inversion of values linked to modernity and progress. Here's what's happening. Modernity is based on the opposition of the party of movement and the party of order, progress versus reaction, freedom versus fatalism, equality—even if it's reduced to equality of opportunity—versus natural or supposedly natural hierarchies. But today, the party of the established order is the party of permanent movement, the party that breaks all natural and moral laws to advance the domination of capital. The refusal of progress at all costs has become a demand of those who oppose the established order. This situation explains the muddle in which traditional political cleavages find themselves, cleavages that date back to the era of triumphant modernity and are now completely obsolete.

The involution of the power of the human spirit, as expressed in man's "becoming a machine", in the triumph of the mechanical over the living, in the unleashed death drive, as a drive to return to the inert state, which has seized our world, can only be understood and combated by the weapons of reason. It's not a question of opposing the irrational, the magical or the imaginary to a world from which the spirit has been driven out, but of rebuilding a philosophy of life, a philosophy that sees nature not as a dead and mortifying order, but as a vital principle. If we are dying, there is still time to return to life, since reason cannot be contrary to life.

BIBLIOGRAPHY

ANDERS G., *L'obsolescence de l'homme*, Éditions de l'Encyclopédie des Nuisances-Ivrea, translated from German by Christophe David, 2005.

ANDERS G., *L'obsolescence de l'homme, tome II: sur la destruction de la vie à l'époque de la troisième révolution industrielle*, éditions Fario, 2011.

ARISTOTLE, *The Parts of Animals*, Flammarion, "GF" collection, 2011.

BENNETT M. R. & HACKER PMS, *Philosophical Foundation of Neuroscience*, Wiley Blackwell, second edition, 2021.

BERGSON H., *L'évolution créatrice*, Félix Alcan, 1907, PUF reprint.

BERGSON H., *La pensée et le mouvant*, Félix Alcan, 1934, PUF reprint.

BIHOUIX P., *L'âge des low tech*, Seuil, 2021.

CASILLI A., *Waiting for the robots. Enquête sur le travail du clic*, Seuil, collection "La Couleur des idées", 2019.

CHANGEUX J.-P., *L'homme neuronal*, Fayard, 1983.

CHANGEUX J.-P. & RICŒUR P., *Ce qui nous fait penser. La Nature et la Règle*, ODILE Jacob, 1998.

CHESNEAUX J., *De la modernité*, La Découverte, 1983.

DEHAENE S., *Vers une science de la vie mentale*, inaugural lecture at the Collège de France, 2006.

DESCARTES, *Discours de la méthode*, Adam & Tannery edition, VI, 1902.

DESCARTES, *Méditations métaphysiques* et *Objections*, Adam & Tannery edition, IX, 1904.

DUBOIS M.J.F., *Le vivant et l'indéterminé*, 2 volumes, éditions universitaires européennes, 2014.

FODOR J., *L'esprit, ça ne marche pas comme ça*, Odile Jacob, 2003.

HENRY M., *La barbarie*, Grasset & Fasquelle, 1987.

HENRY M., *Marx*, 2 volumes, *1. Une philosophie de la réalité*, and *2. Une philosophie de l'économie*, Gallimard, 1976, reprinted in the "Tel" collection.

HUSSERL E., *La crise des sciences européennes et la phénoménologie transcendantale,* translated and prefaced by Gérard Granel, Gallimard, 1976, reprinted in the "Tel" collection.

KANT E., *Œuvres en 3 volumes*, Pléiade edition, Gallimard, 1980, 1985, 1986.

LEVIN I., *Un bonheur insoutenable*, French translation by Press Pocket, 1970.

LUKÁCS G., *Histoire et conscience de classe,* 1923, éditions de Minuit, 1960.

MARCUSE H., *Éros et civilisation*, 1963, éditions de Minuit, French translation by Jean-Guy Nény and Boris Frankael, republished by Seuil, "Points" collection, 1971.

MARCUSE H., *L'homme unidimensionnel*, 1968, éditions de Minuit, French translation by Monique Wittig, republished by Seuil, "Points" collection, 1969.

MARX K., *Capital*, Book I, translation by J.-P. Lefebvre, PUF, "Quadrige" collection, 1993.

MARX K., *Manuscripts 1857-1858 ("Grundrisse")*, Éditions Sociales, translation edited by J.-P. Lefebvre, 1980.

MARX K., Œuvres en 4 volumes, éditions de la Pléiade edited by Maximilien Rubel, 1963, 1968, 1982, 1994.

MERLEAU-PONTY M., *Phénoménologie de la perception*, Gallimard, 1945, reprinted in the "Tel" collection.

NAESS A., *Vers l'écologie profonde*, interviews with David Rothenberg, Wildproject editions, 2023.

PUTNAM H., *Definitions. Pourquoi ne peut pas "naturaliser" la raison*, interview with Christian Bouchindhomme, ed. de l'Éclat, 1993.

SADIN É., *La vie spectrale. Penser l'ère du métavers et des IA génératives*, Grasset, 2023.

SEARLE J. R., *La Redécouverte de l'esprit* (trans. Claudine Tiercelin), Gallimard, 1995.

SEARLE J. R., *The Mystery of Consciousness*, Odile Jacob, 2000.

SPINOZA, *Éthique* in Œuvres complètes, collection La Pléiade, edited by Bernard Pautrat, Gallimard, 2022.

THAGARD P., *The Cognitive Science of Science: Explanation, Discovery, and Conceptual Change*, MIT Press, 2012.

THAGARD P., *Brain-Mind: From Neurons to Consciousness and Creativity (Treatise on Mind and Society)*, Oxford Series on Cognitive Models and Architectures, Oxford University Press, 2019.

WEIL S., *L'enracinement*, Gallimard, 1949.

WITTGENSTEIN L., *Le cahier bleu et le cahier brun*, Gallimard, coll. "Tel", 2004.

Table of Contents